TKO STUDIOS

SALVATORE SIMEONE - CEO & PUBLISHER

TZE CHUN - PRESIDENT & PUBLISHER

JATIN THAKKER - CHIEF OPERATIONS OFFICER

SEBASTIAN GIRNER - EDITOR-IN-CHIEF

REDFORK #1-6.

Published by TKO Studios, LLC.
Office of Publication: 450 7th Ave., Suite 2107. New York, NY 10123.
 Printed in the USA.
ISBN: 978-1-952203-09-1

TKOPRESENTS.COM

TKO PRESENTS A WORLD BY:

ALEX PAKNADEL
WRITER

NIL VENDRELL
ART

GIULIA BRUSCO
COLOR ART

RYAN FERRIER
LETTERER

SEBASTIAN GIRNER
EDITOR

MARIAM FAYEZ
EDITORIAL ASSISTANT

NIL VENDRELL
COVER ART

JARED K FLETCHER
TITLE & COVER DESIGN

JEFF POWELL
BOOK DESIGN

REDFORK

CHAPTER 1

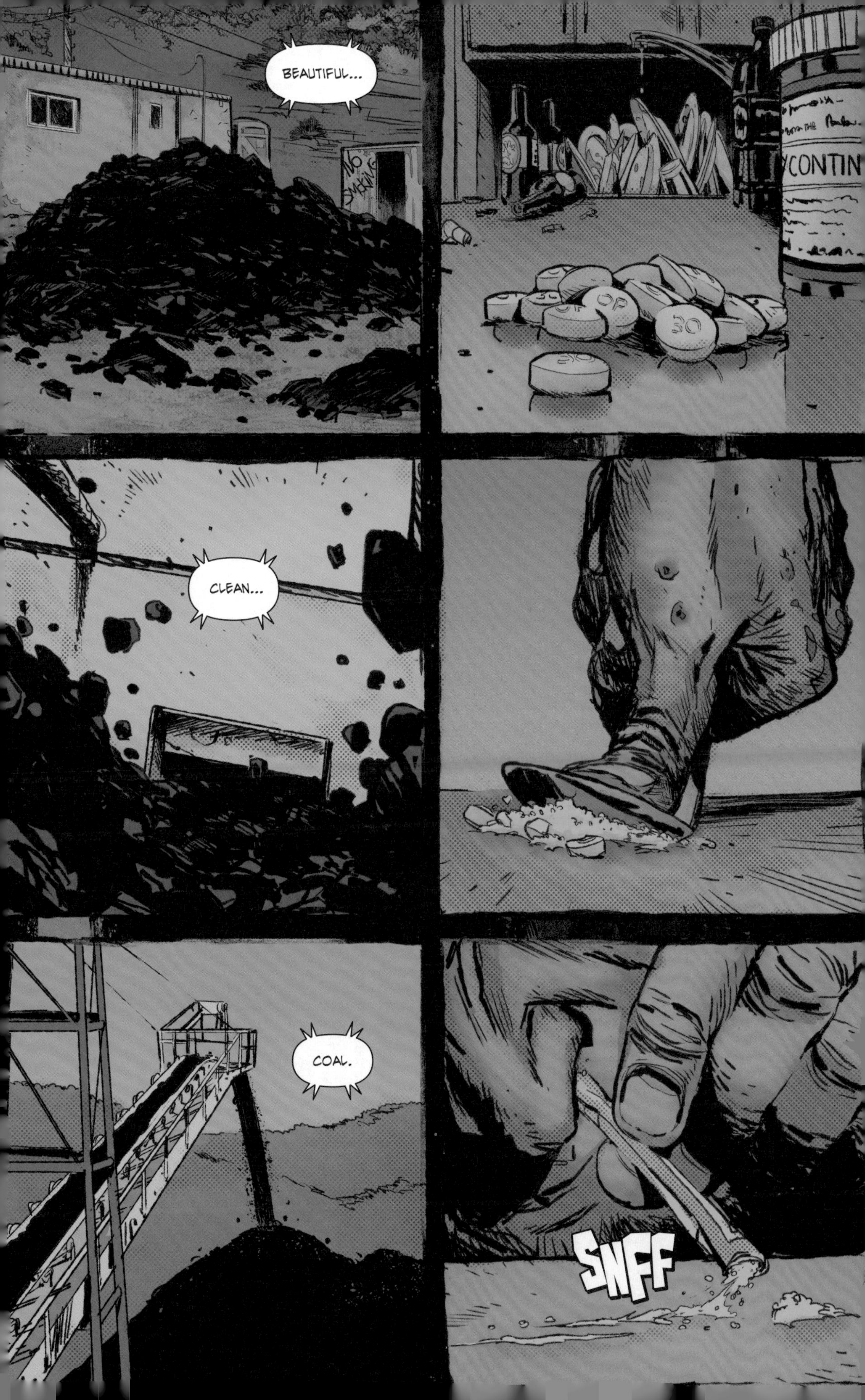
BEAUTIFUL...
NO SMOKING
CONTIN
OP
30
CLEAN...
COAL.
SNFF

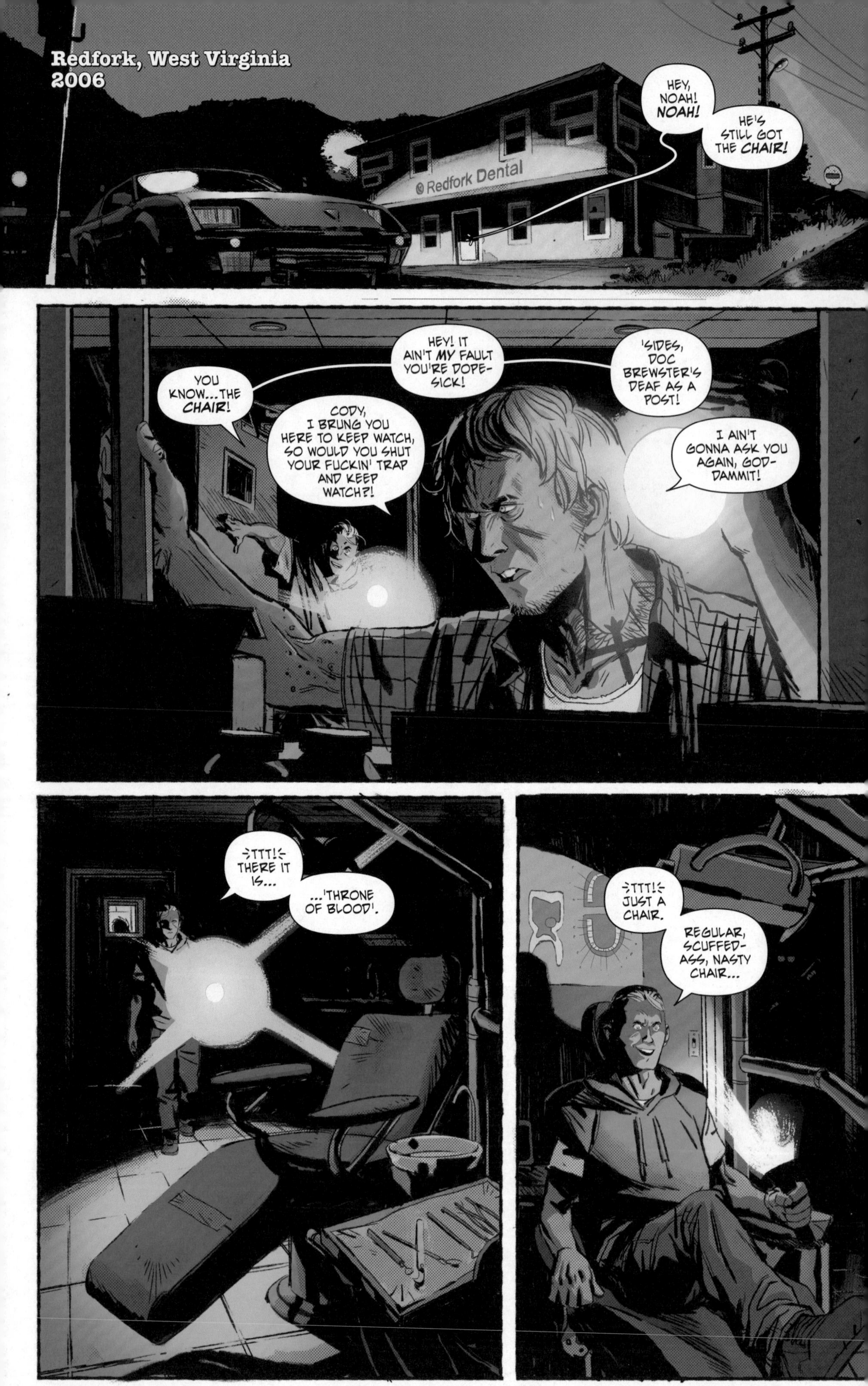
Redfork, West Virginia
2006
Redfork Dental
HEY, NOAH! NOAH!
HE'S STILL GOT THE CHAIR!
YOU KNOW... THE CHAIR!
CODY, I BRUNG YOU HERE TO KEEP WATCH, SO WOULD YOU SHUT YOUR FUCKIN' TRAP AND KEEP WATCH?!
HEY! IT AIN'T MY FAULT YOU'RE DOPE-SICK!
'SIDES, DOC BREWSTER'S DEAF AS A POST!
I AIN'T GONNA ASK YOU AGAIN, GOD-DAMMIT!
TTT! THERE IT IS...
...'THRONE OF BLOOD'.
TTT! JUST A CHAIR.
REGULAR, SCUFFED-ASS, NASTY CHAIR...

WELL, DON'T THAT JUST BEAT ALL...

...YOU CAN ONLY SIT IN THE ASS GROOVE IF YOU CLENCH.

≳SIGH≲ FUCKIN' IDIOT.

NOW C'MON, WHERE ARE YOU?

WARMER.

BENZAMYCIN
TOPICAL JEL

TTT! FREEZING.

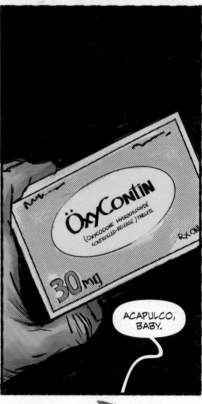

ÖxyContin
(OXYCODONE HYDROCHLORYDE CONTROLLED-RELEASE) TABLETS

RX ON

30mg

ACAPULCO, BABY.

KRUM!!!

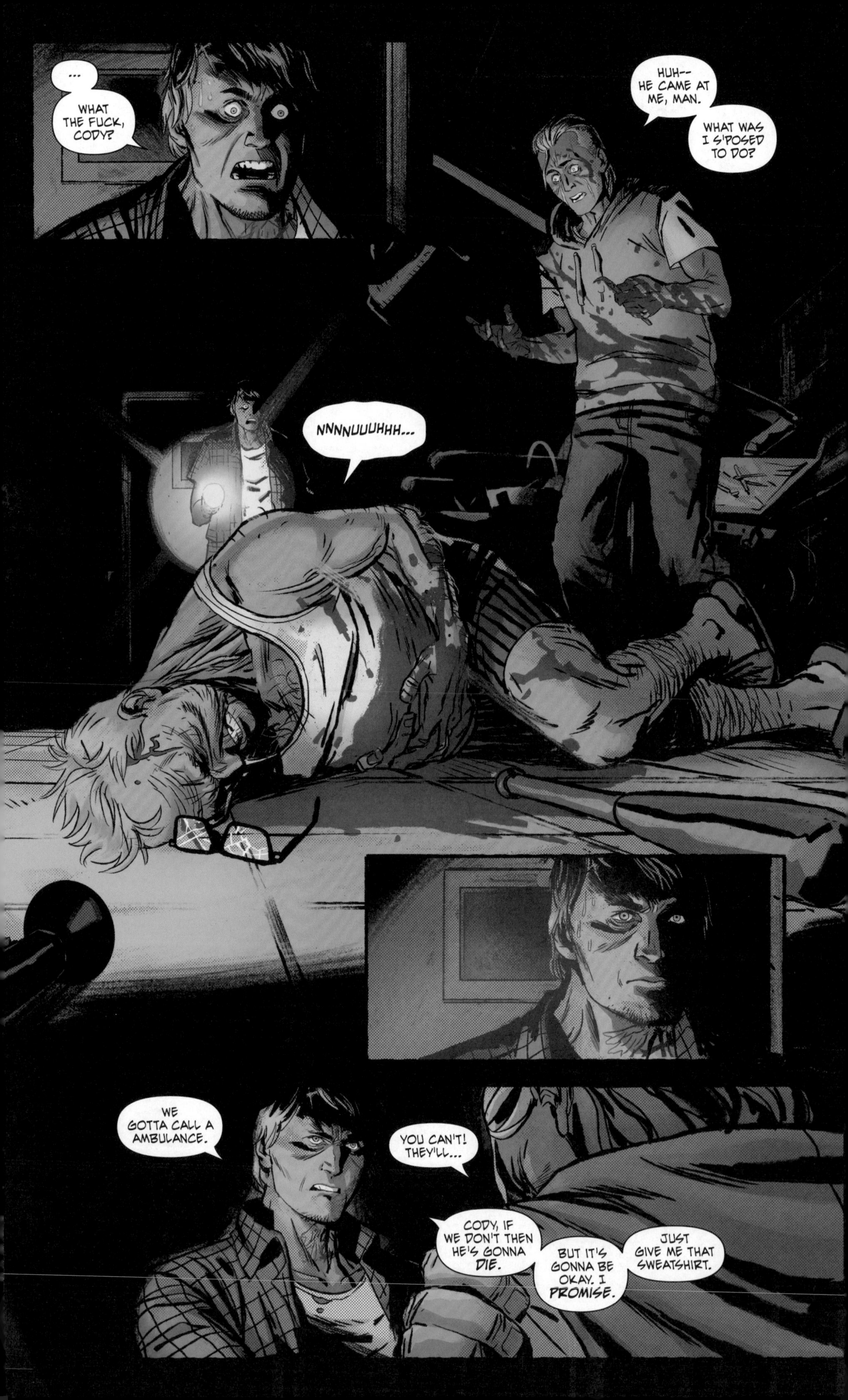
...
WHAT THE FUCK, CODY?
HUH-- HE CAME AT ME, MAN.
WHAT WAS I S'POSED TO DO?
NNNNUUUHHH...
WE GOTTA CALL A AMBULANCE.
YOU CAN'T! THEY'LL...
CODY, IF WE DON'T THEN HE'S GONNA DIE.
BUT IT'S GONNA BE OKAY. I PROMISE.
JUST GIVE ME THAT SWEATSHIRT.

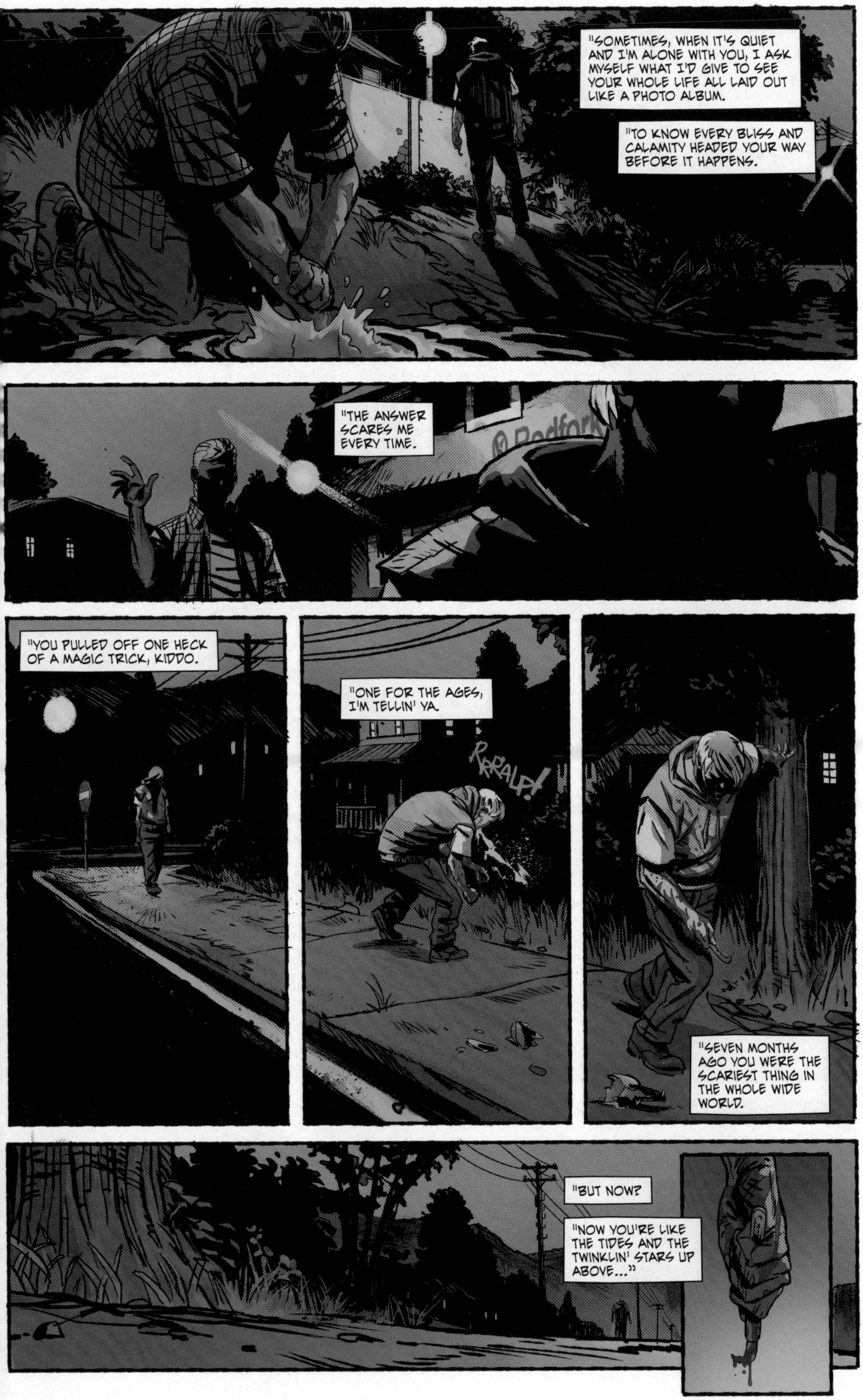
"SOMETIMES, WHEN IT'S QUIET AND I'M ALONE WITH YOU, I ASK MYSELF WHAT I'D GIVE TO SEE YOUR WHOLE LIFE ALL LAID OUT LIKE A PHOTO ALBUM.
"TO KNOW EVERY BLISS AND CALAMITY HEADED YOUR WAY BEFORE IT HAPPENS.
"THE ANSWER SCARES ME EVERY TIME.
"YOU PULLED OFF ONE HECK OF A MAGIC TRICK, KIDDO.
"ONE FOR THE AGES, I'M TELLIN' YA.
RRRALP!
"SEVEN MONTHS AGO YOU WERE THE SCARIEST THING IN THE WHOLE WIDE WORLD.
"BUT NOW?
"NOW YOU'RE LIKE THE TIDES AND THE TWINKLIN' STARS UP ABOVE..."

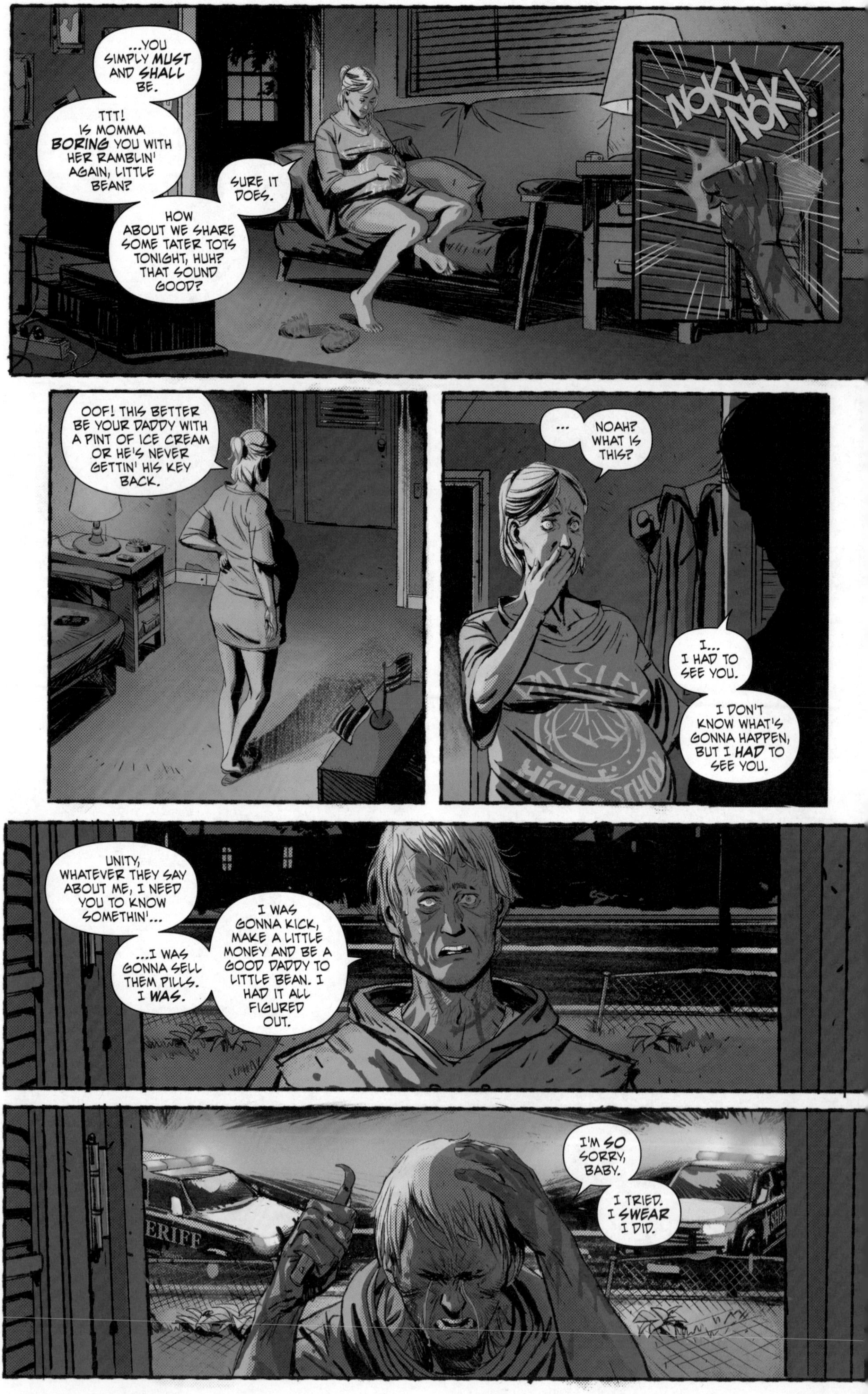

...YOU SIMPLY MUST AND SHALL BE.
TTT! IS MOMMA BORING YOU WITH HER RAMBLIN' AGAIN, LITTLE BEAN?
SURE IT DOES.
HOW ABOUT WE SHARE SOME TATER TOTS TONIGHT, HUH? THAT SOUND GOOD?
NOK! NOK!
OOF! THIS BETTER BE YOUR DADDY WITH A PINT OF ICE CREAM OR HE'S NEVER GETTIN' HIS KEY BACK.
...
NOAH? WHAT IS THIS?
I... I HAD TO SEE YOU.
I DON'T KNOW WHAT'S GONNA HAPPEN, BUT I HAD TO SEE YOU.
UNITY, WHATEVER THEY SAY ABOUT ME, I NEED YOU TO KNOW SOMETHIN'...
...I WAS GONNA SELL THEM PILLS. I WAS.
I WAS GONNA KICK, MAKE A LITTLE MONEY AND BE A GOOD DADDY TO LITTLE BEAN. I HAD IT ALL FIGURED OUT.
I'M SO SORRY, BABY.
I TRIED. I SWEAR I DID.

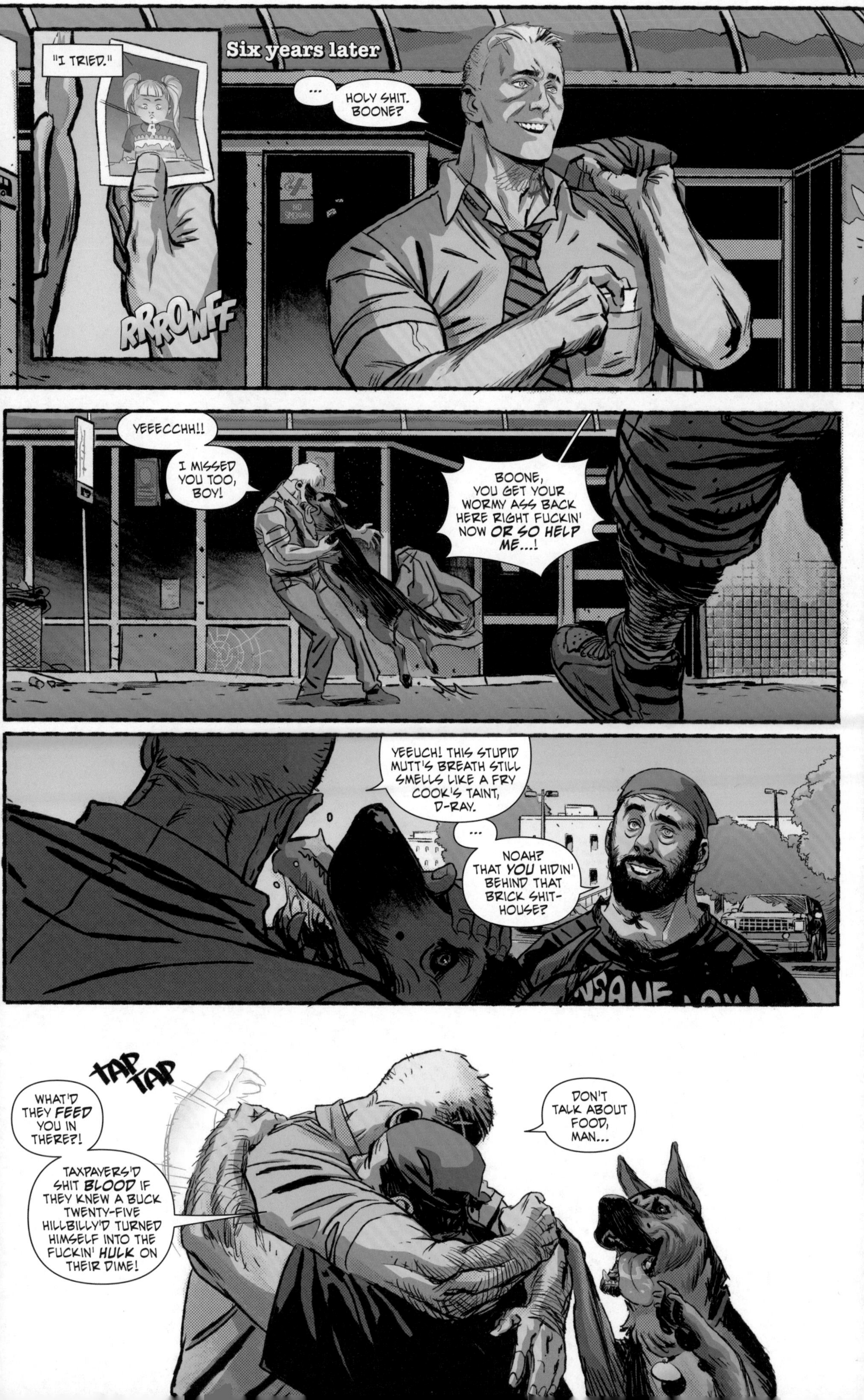
"I TRIED."
Six years later
RRROWFF
...
HOLY SHIT. BOONE?
YEEECCHH!!
I MISSED YOU TOO, BOY!
BOONE, YOU GET YOUR WORMY ASS BACK HERE RIGHT FUCKIN' NOW OR SO HELP ME...!
YEEUCH! THIS STUPID MUTT'S BREATH STILL SMELLS LIKE A FRY COOK'S TAINT, D-RAY.
...
NOAH? THAT YOU HIDIN' BEHIND THAT BRICK SHIT-HOUSE?
TAP TAP
WHAT'D THEY FEED YOU IN THERE?!
TAXPAYERS'D SHIT BLOOD IF THEY KNEW A BUCK TWENTY-FIVE HILLBILLY'D TURNED HIMSELF INTO THE FUCKIN' HULK ON THEIR DIME!
DON'T TALK ABOUT FOOD, MAN...

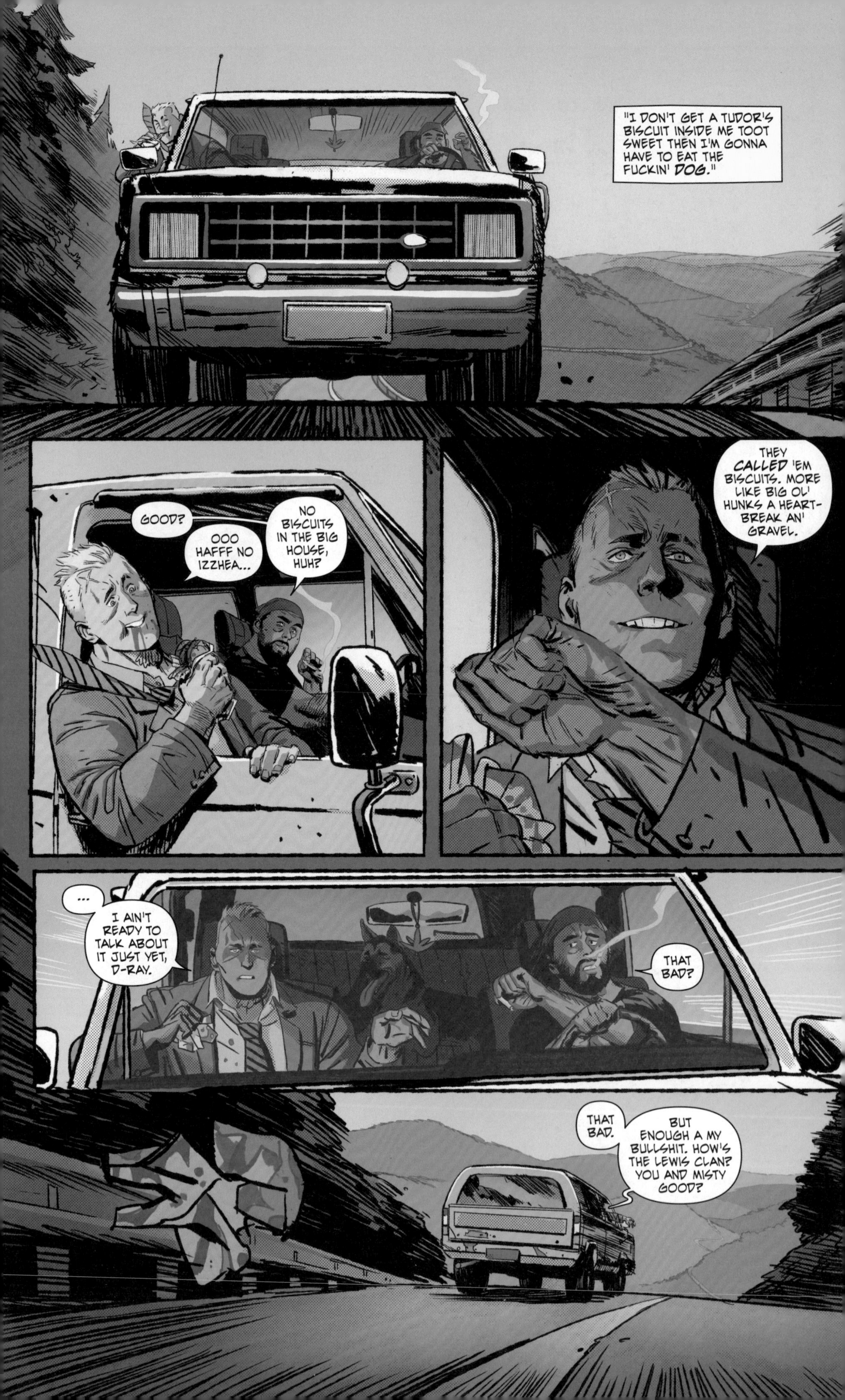
"I DON'T GET A TUDOR'S BISCUIT INSIDE ME TOOT SWEET THEN I'M GONNA HAVE TO EAT THE FUCKIN' DOG."
GOOD?
OOO HAFFF NO IZZHEA...
NO BISCUITS IN THE BIG HOUSE, HUH?
THEY CALLED 'EM BISCUITS. MORE LIKE BIG OL' HUNKS A HEART-BREAK AN' GRAVEL.
...
I AIN'T READY TO TALK ABOUT IT JUST YET, D-RAY.
THAT BAD?
THAT BAD.
BUT ENOUGH A MY BULLSHIT. HOW'S THE LEWIS CLAN? YOU AND MISTY GOOD?

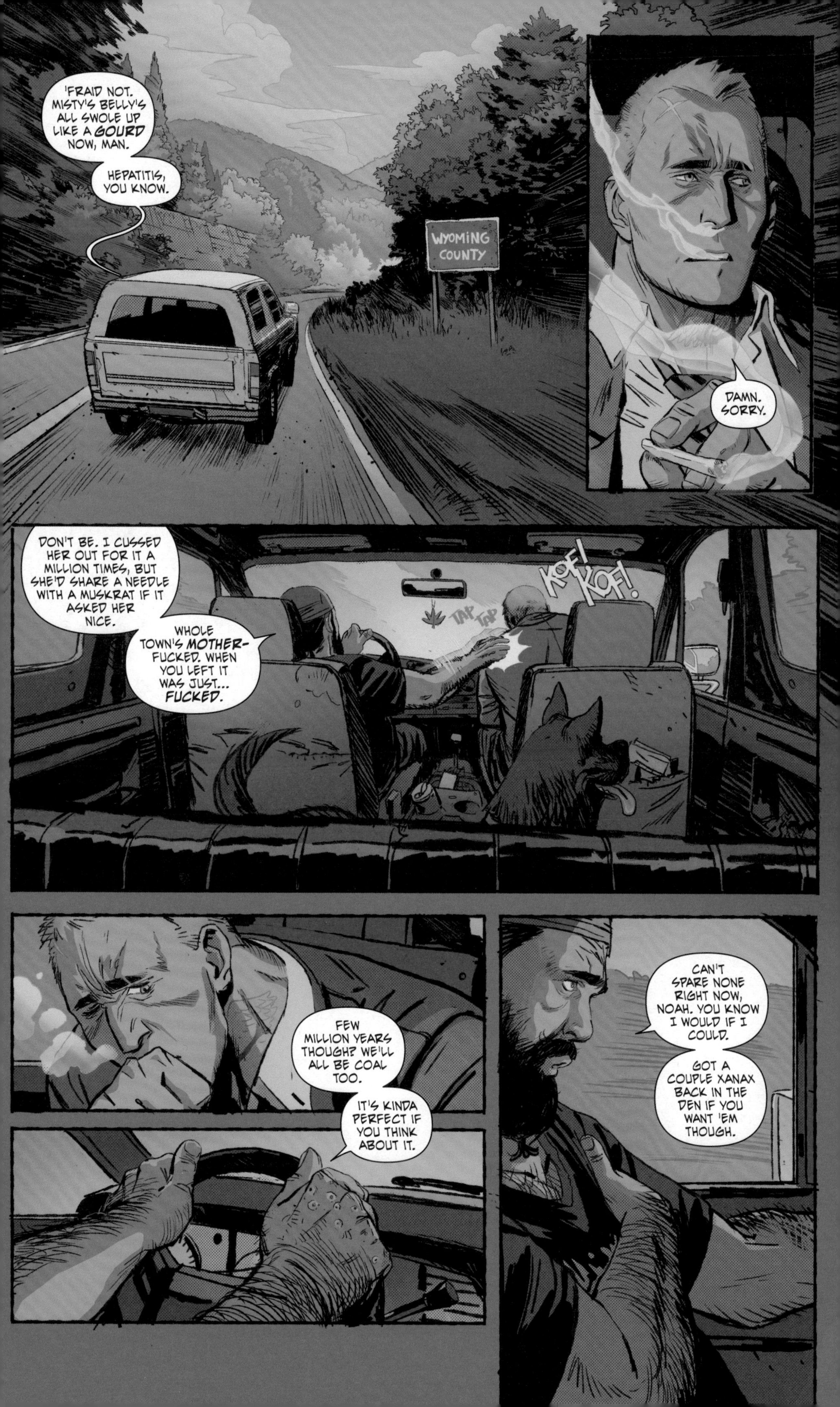
'FRAID NOT. MISTY'S BELLY'S ALL SWOLE UP LIKE A GOURD NOW, MAN.
HEPATITIS, YOU KNOW.
WYOMING COUNTY
DAMN. SORRY.
DON'T BE. I CUSSED HER OUT FOR IT A MILLION TIMES, BUT SHE'D SHARE A NEEDLE WITH A MUSKRAT IF IT ASKED HER NICE.
WHOLE TOWN'S MOTHER-FUCKED. WHEN YOU LEFT IT WAS JUST... FUCKED.
TAP TAP
KOF! KOF!
FEW MILLION YEARS THOUGH? WE'LL ALL BE COAL TOO.
IT'S KINDA PERFECT IF YOU THINK ABOUT IT.
CAN'T SPARE NONE RIGHT NOW, NOAH. YOU KNOW I WOULD IF I COULD.
GOT A COUPLE XANAX BACK IN THE DEN IF YOU WANT 'EM THOUGH.

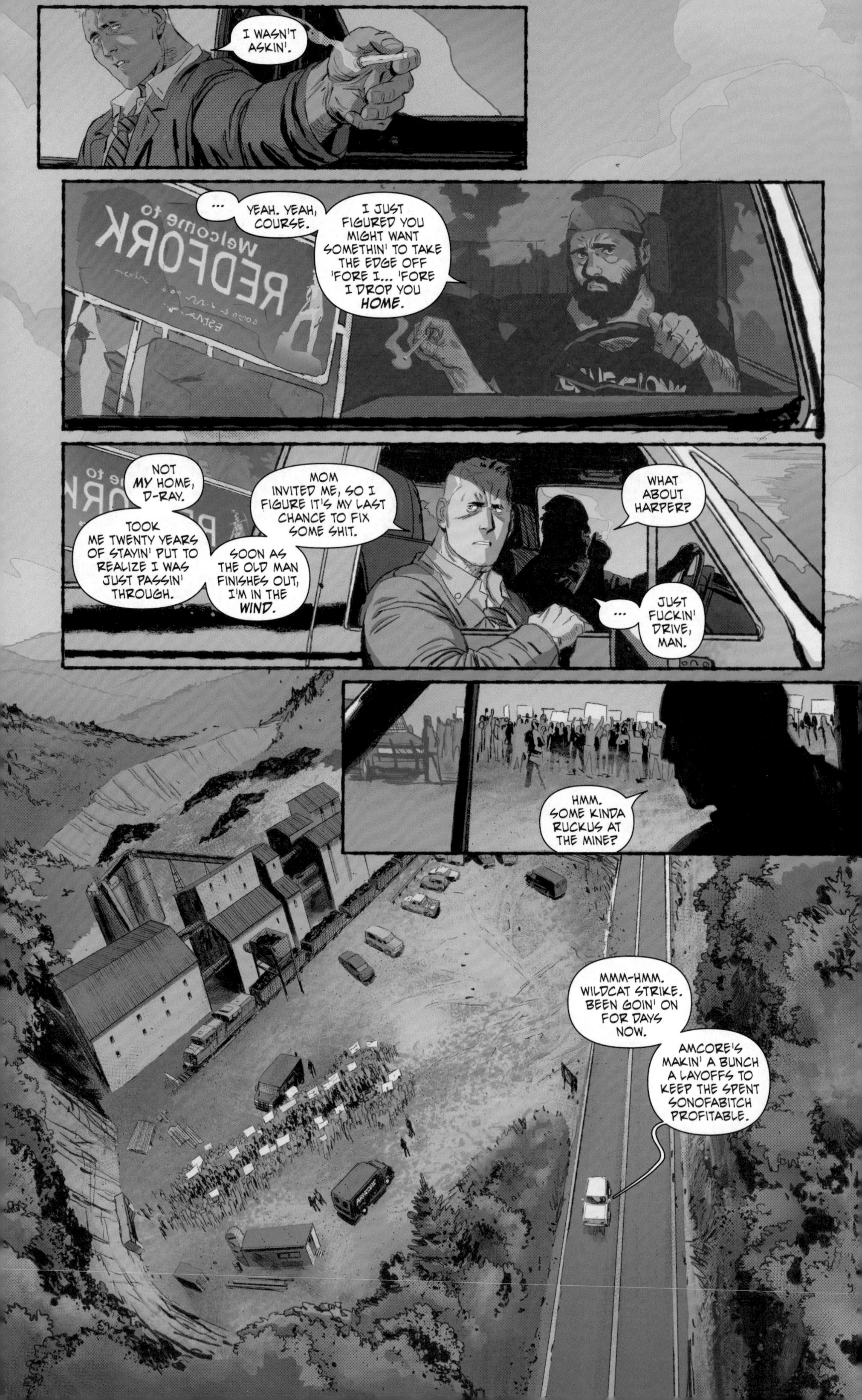
I WASN'T ASKIN'.
...
YEAH. YEAH, COURSE.
I JUST FIGURED YOU MIGHT WANT SOMETHIN' TO TAKE THE EDGE OFF 'FORE I... 'FORE I DROP YOU HOME.
Welcome to REDFORK
NOT MY HOME, D-RAY.
TOOK ME TWENTY YEARS OF STAYIN' PUT TO REALIZE I WAS JUST PASSIN' THROUGH.
MOM INVITED ME, SO I FIGURE IT'S MY LAST CHANCE TO FIX SOME SHIT.
SOON AS THE OLD MAN FINISHES OUT, I'M IN THE WIND.
WHAT ABOUT HARPER?
...
JUST FUCKIN' DRIVE, MAN.
HMM. SOME KINDA RUCKUS AT THE MINE?
MMM-HMM. WILDCAT STRIKE. BEEN GOIN' ON FOR DAYS NOW.
AMCORE'S MAKIN' A BUNCH A LAYOFFS TO KEEP THE SPENT SONOFABITCH PROFITABLE.

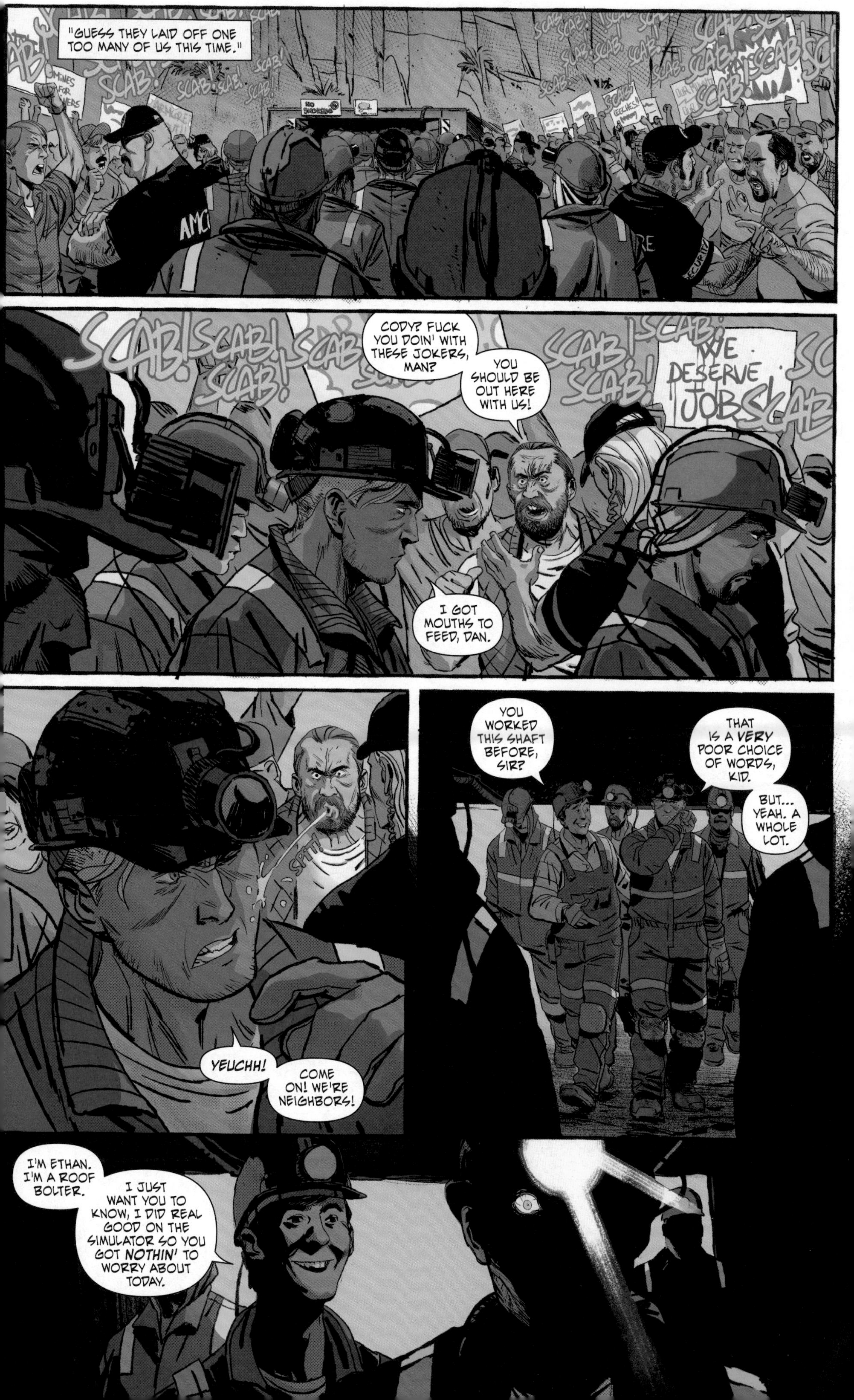
"GUESS THEY LAID OFF ONE TOO MANY OF US THIS TIME."
SCAB! SCAB! SCAB!
CODY? FUCK YOU DOIN' WITH THESE JOKERS, MAN?
YOU SHOULD BE OUT HERE WITH US!
WE DESERVE JOBS
SCAB! SCAB! SCAB!
I GOT MOUTHS TO FEED, DAN.
SPIT!
YEUCHH!
COME ON! WE'RE NEIGHBORS!
YOU WORKED THIS SHAFT BEFORE, SIR?
THAT IS A VERY POOR CHOICE OF WORDS, KID.
BUT... YEAH. A WHOLE LOT.
I'M ETHAN. I'M A ROOF BOLTER.
I JUST WANT YOU TO KNOW, I DID REAL GOOD ON THE SIMULATOR SO YOU GOT NOTHIN' TO WORRY ABOUT TODAY.

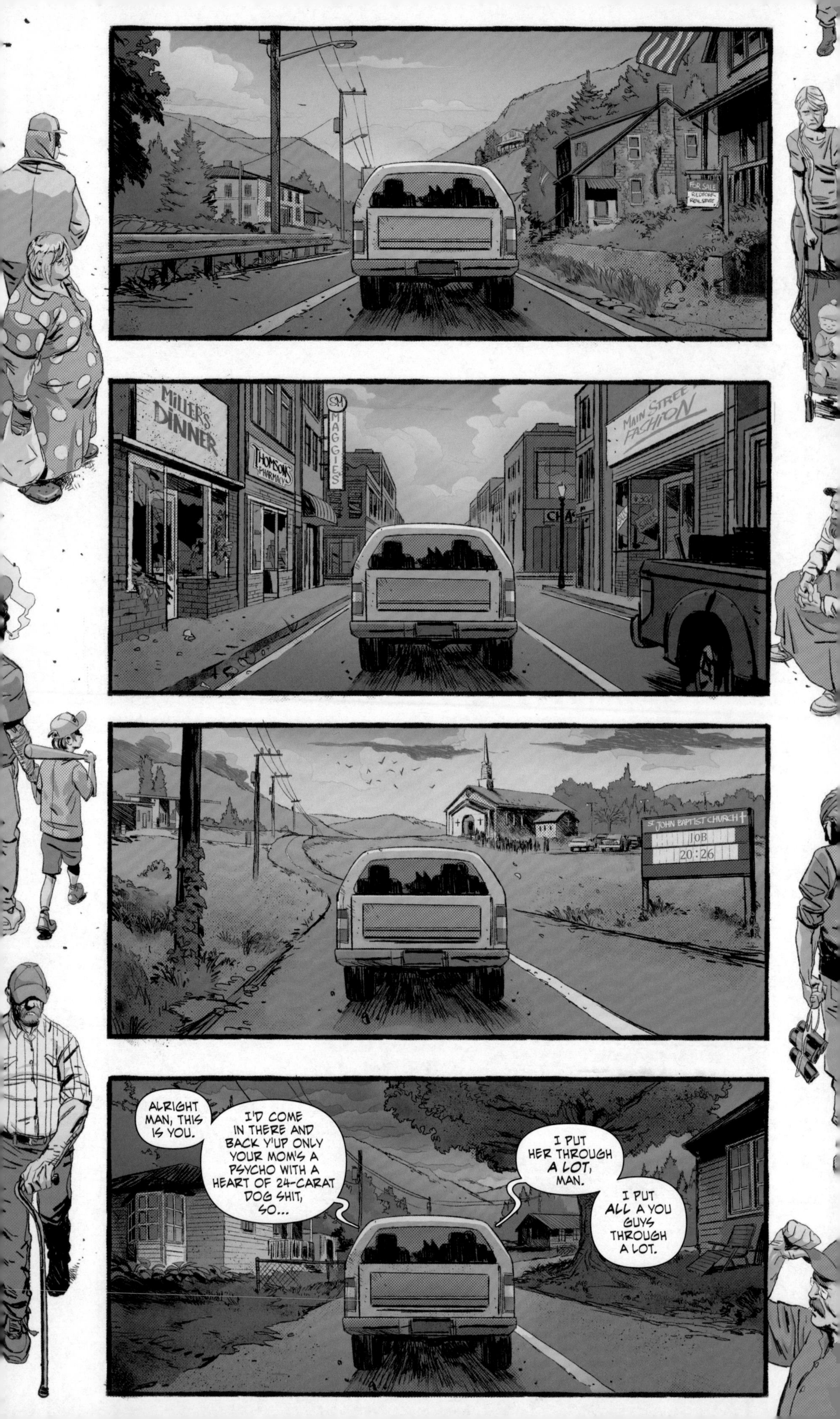
FOR SALE
MILLER'S DINNER
THOMSON'S PHARMACY
SM MAGGIES
MAIN STREET FASHION
ST JOHN BAPTIST CHURCH
JOB 20:26
ALRIGHT MAN, THIS IS YOU.
I'D COME IN THERE AND BACK Y'UP ONLY YOUR MOM'S A PSYCHO WITH A HEART OF 24-CARAT DOG SHIT, SO...
I PUT HER THROUGH A LOT, MAN.
I PUT ALL A YOU GUYS THROUGH A LOT.

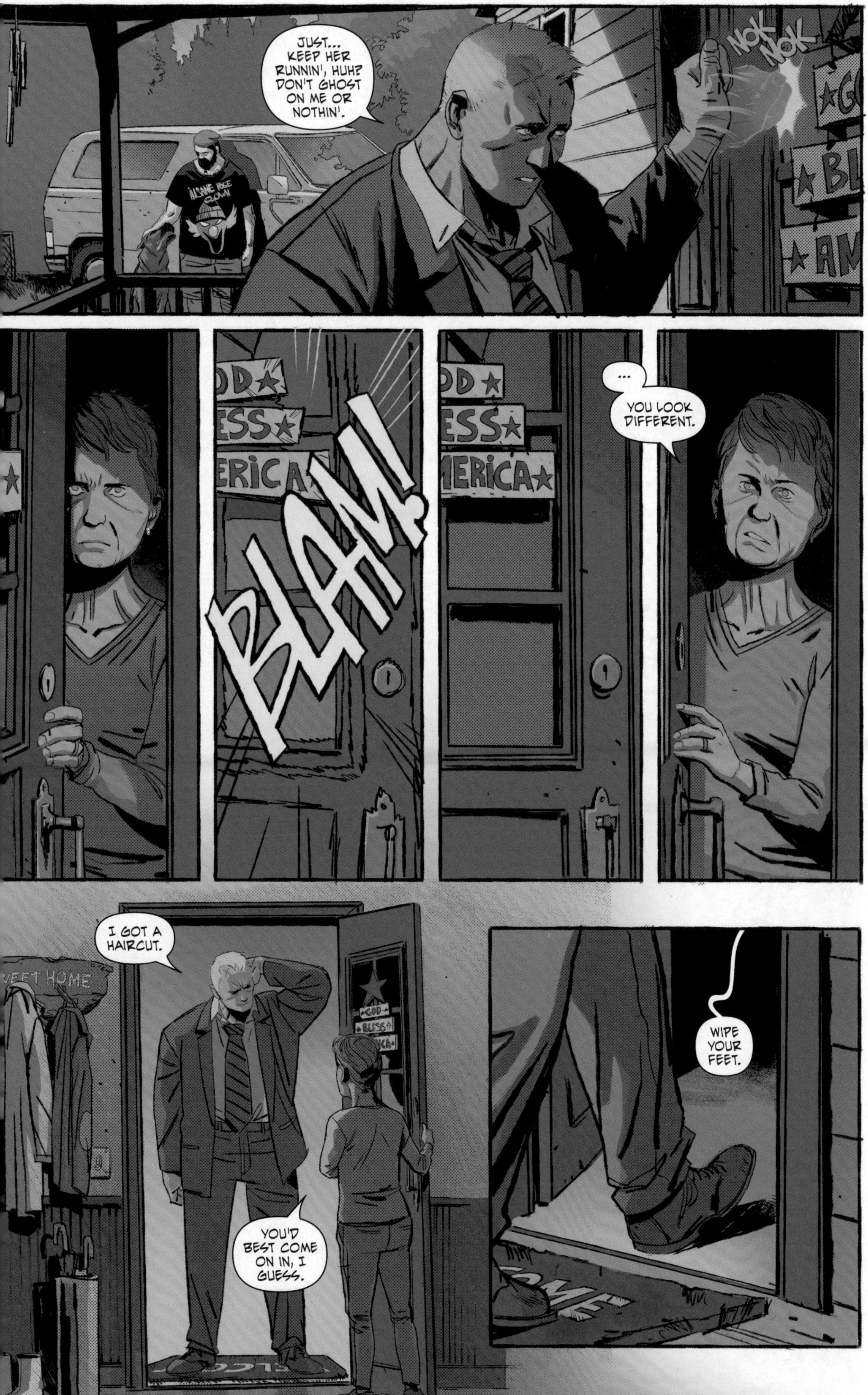
JUST... KEEP HER RUNNIN', HUH? DON'T GHOST ON ME OR NOTHIN'.
NOK NOK
INSANE POSSE CLOWN
BLAM!
... YOU LOOK DIFFERENT.
I GOT A HAIRCUT.
YOU'D BEST COME ON IN, I GUESS.
WIPE YOUR FEET.

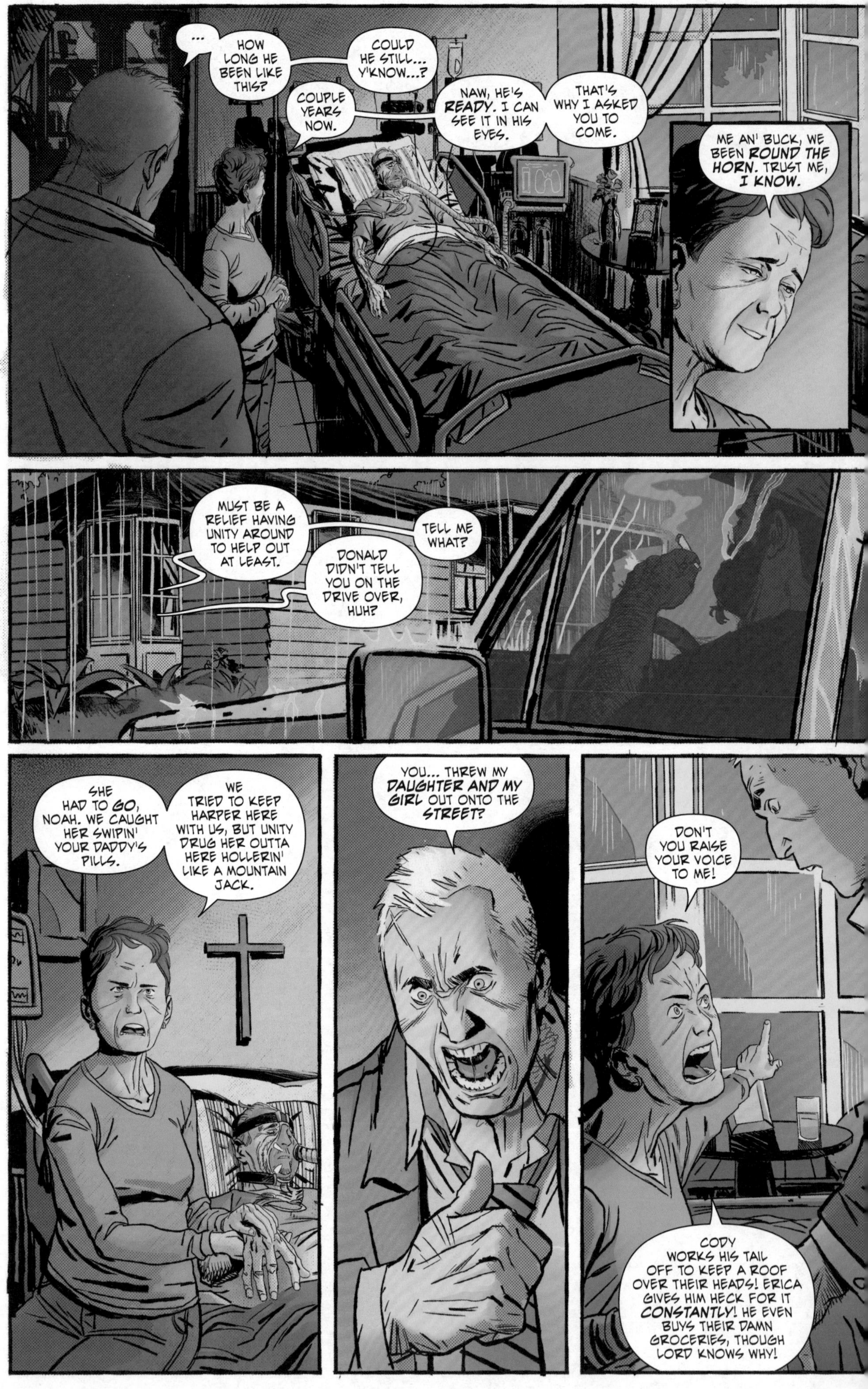
...
HOW LONG HE BEEN LIKE THIS?
COUPLE YEARS NOW.
COULD HE STILL... Y'KNOW...?
NAW, HE'S READY. I CAN SEE IT IN HIS EYES.
THAT'S WHY I ASKED YOU TO COME.
ME AN' BUCK, WE BEEN ROUND THE HORN. TRUST ME, I KNOW.
MUST BE A RELIEF HAVING UNITY AROUND TO HELP OUT AT LEAST.
TELL ME WHAT?
DONALD DIDN'T TELL YOU ON THE DRIVE OVER, HUH?
SHE HAD TO GO, NOAH. WE CAUGHT HER SWIPIN' YOUR DADDY'S PILLS.
WE TRIED TO KEEP HARPER HERE WITH US, BUT UNITY DRUG HER OUTTA HERE HOLLERIN' LIKE A MOUNTAIN JACK.
YOU... THREW MY DAUGHTER AND MY GIRL OUT ONTO THE STREET?
DON'T YOU RAISE YOUR VOICE TO ME!
CODY WORKS HIS TAIL OFF TO KEEP A ROOF OVER THEIR HEADS! ERICA GIVES HIM HECK FOR IT CONSTANTLY! HE EVEN BUYS THEIR DAMN GROCERIES, THOUGH LORD KNOWS WHY!

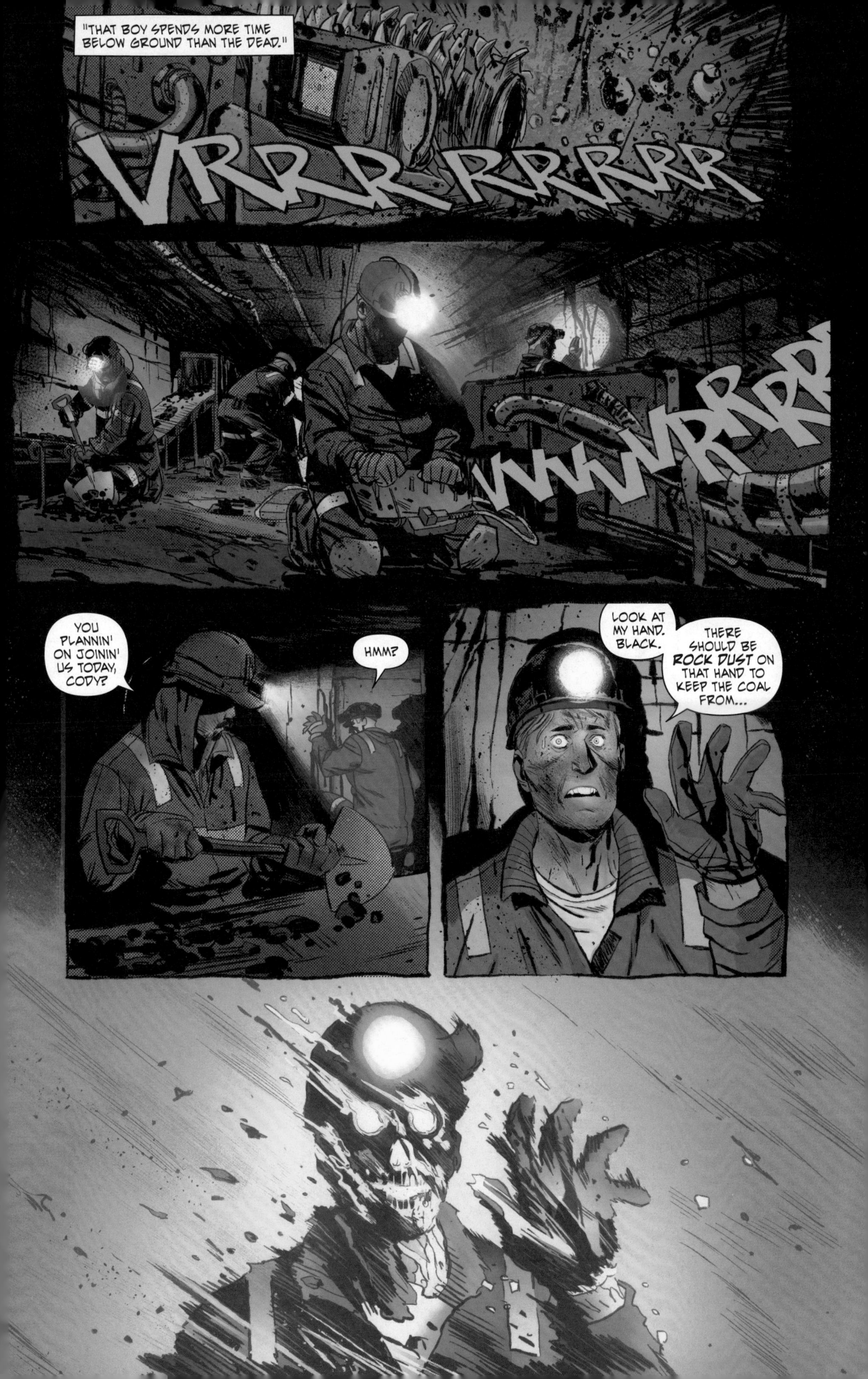
"THAT BOY SPENDS MORE TIME BELOW GROUND THAN THE DEAD."
VRRRRRRRRR
VVVVVRRRR
YOU PLANNIN' ON JOININ' US TODAY, CODY?
HMM?
LOOK AT MY HAND. BLACK.
THERE SHOULD BE ROCK DUST ON THAT HAND TO KEEP THE COAL FROM...

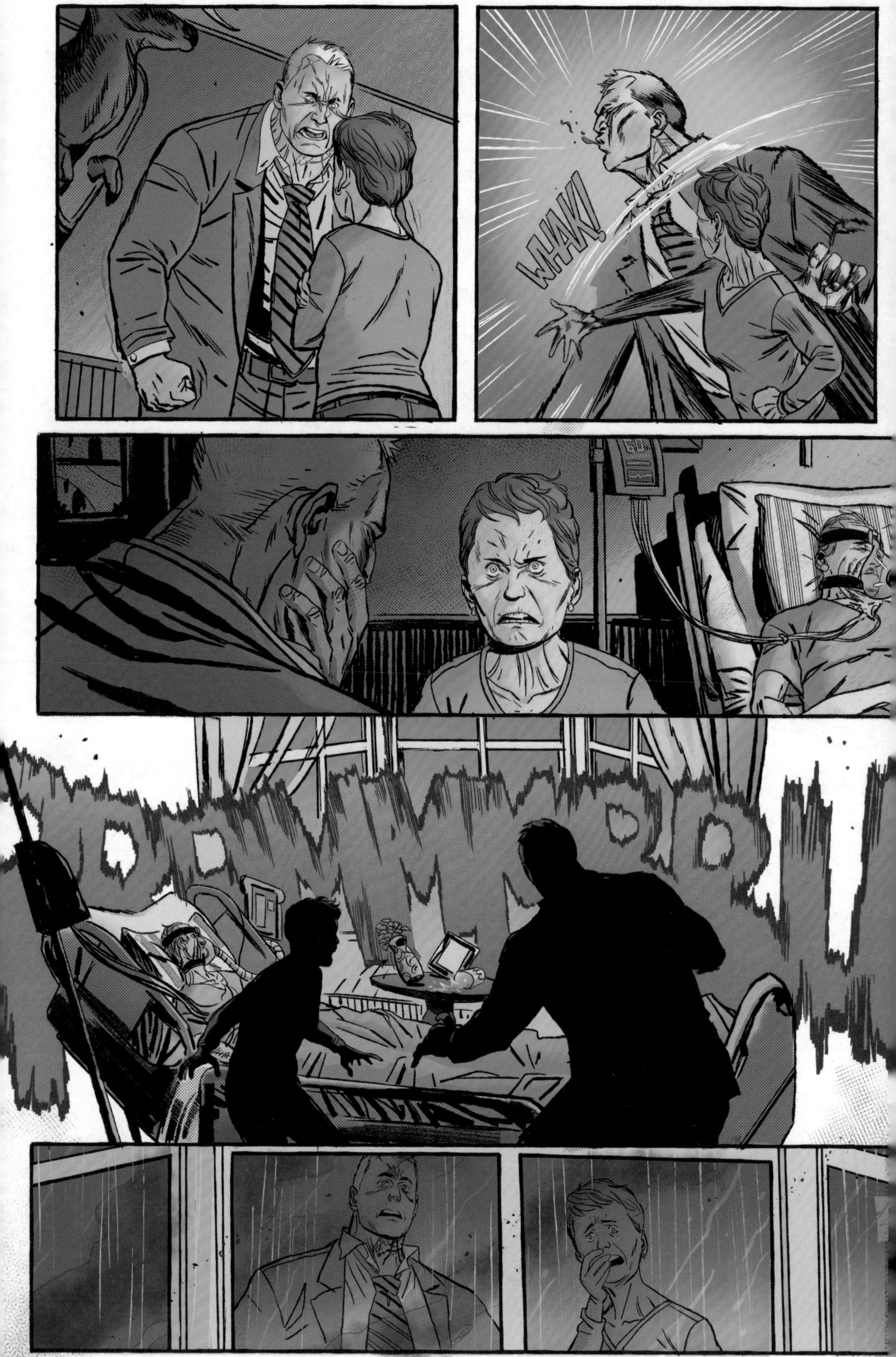
WHAK!

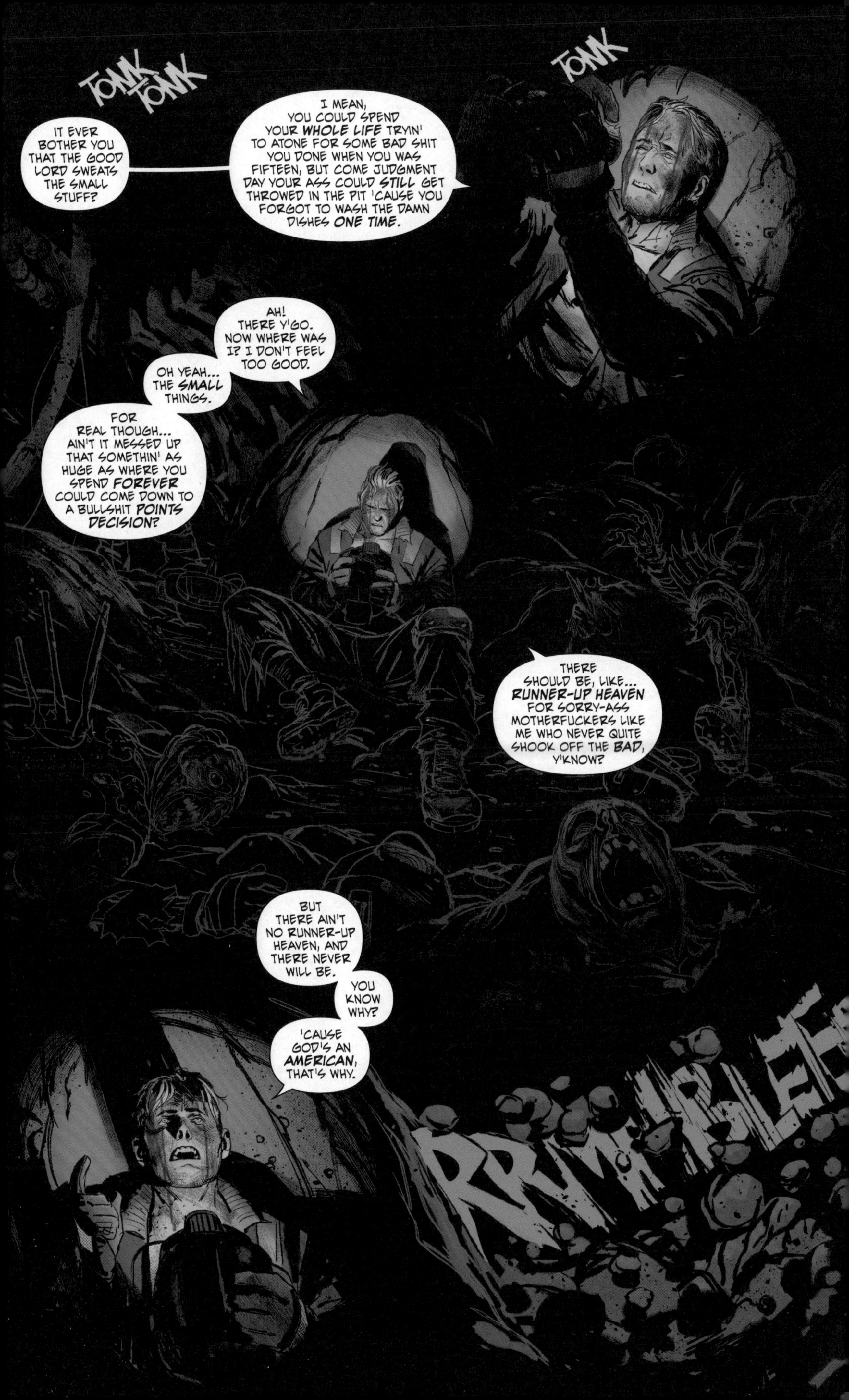
TONK TONK
IT EVER BOTHER YOU THAT THE GOOD LORD SWEATS THE SMALL STUFF?
I MEAN, YOU COULD SPEND YOUR WHOLE LIFE TRYIN' TO ATONE FOR SOME BAD SHIT YOU DONE WHEN YOU WAS FIFTEEN, BUT COME JUDGMENT DAY YOUR ASS COULD STILL GET THROWED IN THE PIT 'CAUSE YOU FORGOT TO WASH THE DAMN DISHES ONE TIME.
TONK
AH! THERE Y'GO. NOW WHERE WAS I? I DON'T FEEL TOO GOOD.
OH YEAH... THE SMALL THINGS.
FOR REAL THOUGH... AIN'T IT MESSED UP THAT SOMETHIN' AS HUGE AS WHERE YOU SPEND FOREVER COULD COME DOWN TO A BULLSHIT POINTS DECISION?
THERE SHOULD BE, LIKE... RUNNER-UP HEAVEN FOR SORRY-ASS MOTHERFUCKERS LIKE ME WHO NEVER QUITE SHOOK OFF THE BAD, Y'KNOW?
BUT THERE AIN'T NO RUNNER-UP HEAVEN, AND THERE NEVER WILL BE.
YOU KNOW WHY?
'CAUSE GOD'S AN AMERICAN, THAT'S WHY.

ANYONE BREATHING IN THERE?!
WHU... YEAH! YEAH! RIGHT HERE, MAN!
A-ARE YOU REAL?
STAND BACK NOW!
KRRRNNCH
MY THINKIN'S ALL FUCKED UP, BROTHER!
PLEASE BE REAL!
WHAT HAPPENED HERE?
Y-YOU DON'T KNOW? YOU'RE NOT WITH AMCORE?
I'M WITH THE FREEHOLDER. NAME'S GALLOWGLASS.
NOW, ARE YOU GOING TO TELL ME WHAT HAPPENED HERE OR NOT?

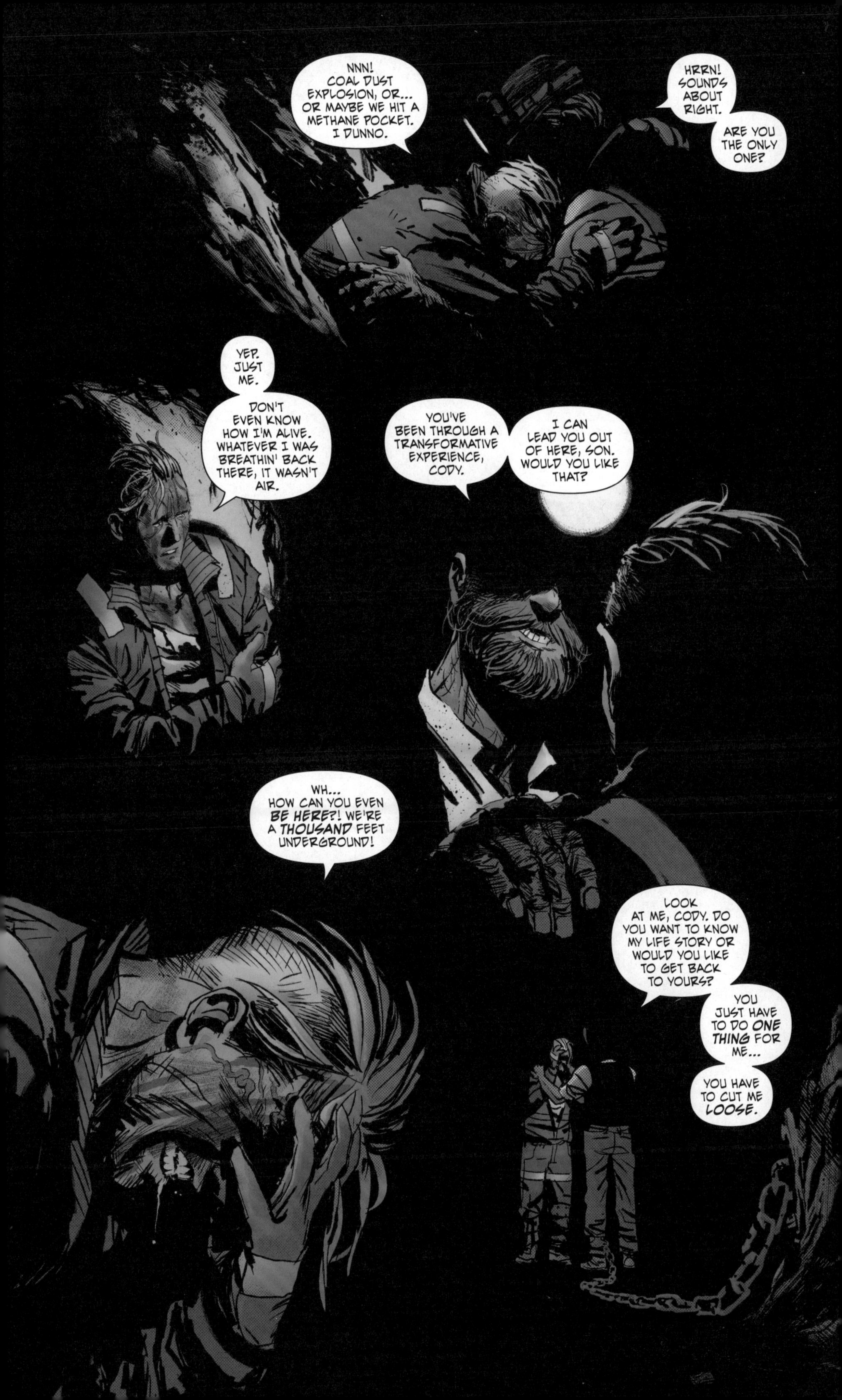

NNN! COAL DUST EXPLOSION, OR... OR MAYBE WE HIT A METHANE POCKET. I DUNNO.
HRRN! SOUNDS ABOUT RIGHT.
ARE YOU THE ONLY ONE?
YEP. JUST ME.
DON'T EVEN KNOW HOW I'M ALIVE. WHATEVER I WAS BREATHIN' BACK THERE, IT WASN'T AIR.
YOU'VE BEEN THROUGH A TRANSFORMATIVE EXPERIENCE, CODY.
I CAN LEAD YOU OUT OF HERE, SON. WOULD YOU LIKE THAT?
WH... HOW CAN YOU EVEN BE HERE?! WE'RE A THOUSAND FEET UNDERGROUND!
LOOK AT ME, CODY. DO YOU WANT TO KNOW MY LIFE STORY OR WOULD YOU LIKE TO GET BACK TO YOURS?
YOU JUST HAVE TO DO ONE THING FOR ME...
YOU HAVE TO CUT ME LOOSE.

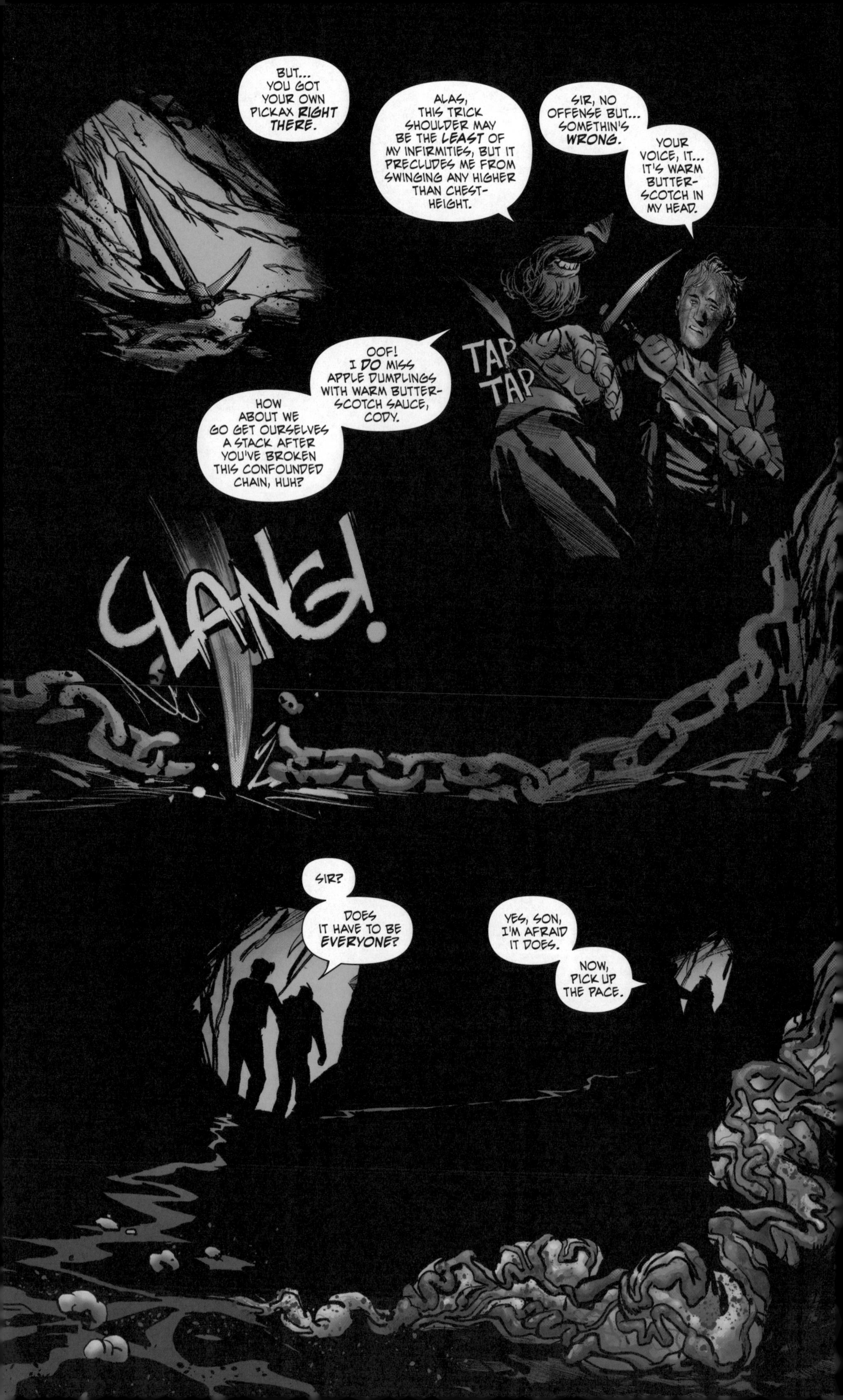
BUT... YOU GOT YOUR OWN PICKAX RIGHT THERE.
ALAS, THIS TRICK SHOULDER MAY BE THE LEAST OF MY INFIRMITIES, BUT IT PRECLUDES ME FROM SWINGING ANY HIGHER THAN CHEST-HEIGHT.
SIR, NO OFFENSE BUT... SOMETHIN'S WRONG.
YOUR VOICE, IT... IT'S WARM BUTTER-SCOTCH IN MY HEAD.
TAP TAP
OOF! I DO MISS APPLE DUMPLINGS WITH WARM BUTTER-SCOTCH SAUCE, CODY.
HOW ABOUT WE GO GET OURSELVES A STACK AFTER YOU'VE BROKEN THIS CONFOUNDED CHAIN, HUH?
CLANG!
SIR?
DOES IT HAVE TO BE EVERYONE?
YES, SON, I'M AFRAID IT DOES.
NOW, PICK UP THE PACE.

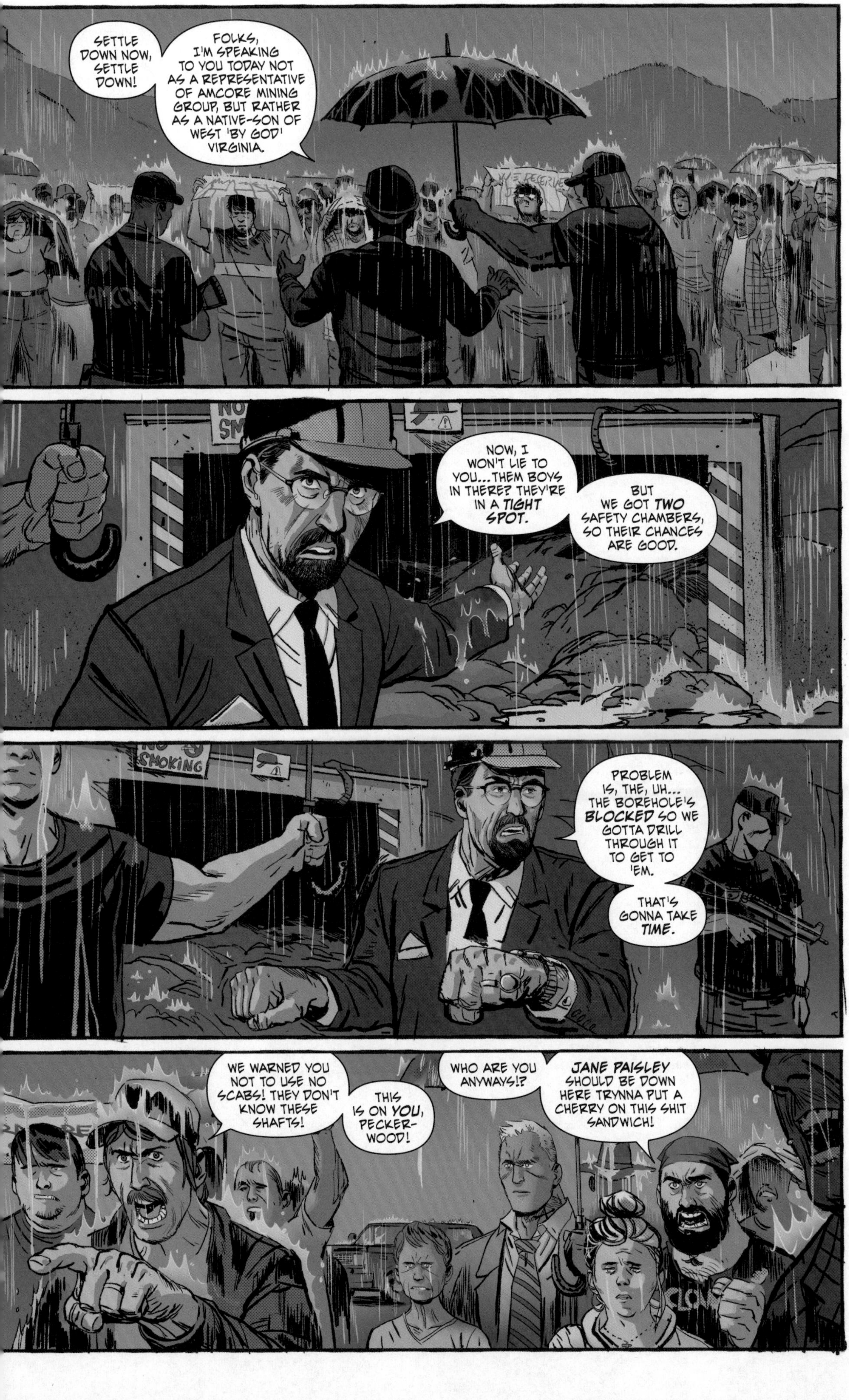
SETTLE DOWN NOW, SETTLE DOWN!
FOLKS, I'M SPEAKING TO YOU TODAY NOT AS A REPRESENTATIVE OF AMCORE MINING GROUP, BUT RATHER AS A NATIVE-SON OF WEST 'BY GOD' VIRGINIA.
NOW, I WON'T LIE TO YOU... THEM BOYS IN THERE? THEY'RE IN A TIGHT SPOT.
BUT WE GOT TWO SAFETY CHAMBERS, SO THEIR CHANCES ARE GOOD.
SMOKING
PROBLEM IS, THE, UH... THE BOREHOLE'S BLOCKED SO WE GOTTA DRILL THROUGH IT TO GET TO 'EM.
THAT'S GONNA TAKE TIME.
WE WARNED YOU NOT TO USE NO SCABS! THEY DON'T KNOW THESE SHAFTS!
THIS IS ON YOU, PECKER-WOOD!
WHO ARE YOU ANYWAYS!?
JANE PAISLEY SHOULD BE DOWN HERE TRYNNA PUT A CHERRY ON THIS SHIT SANDWICH!

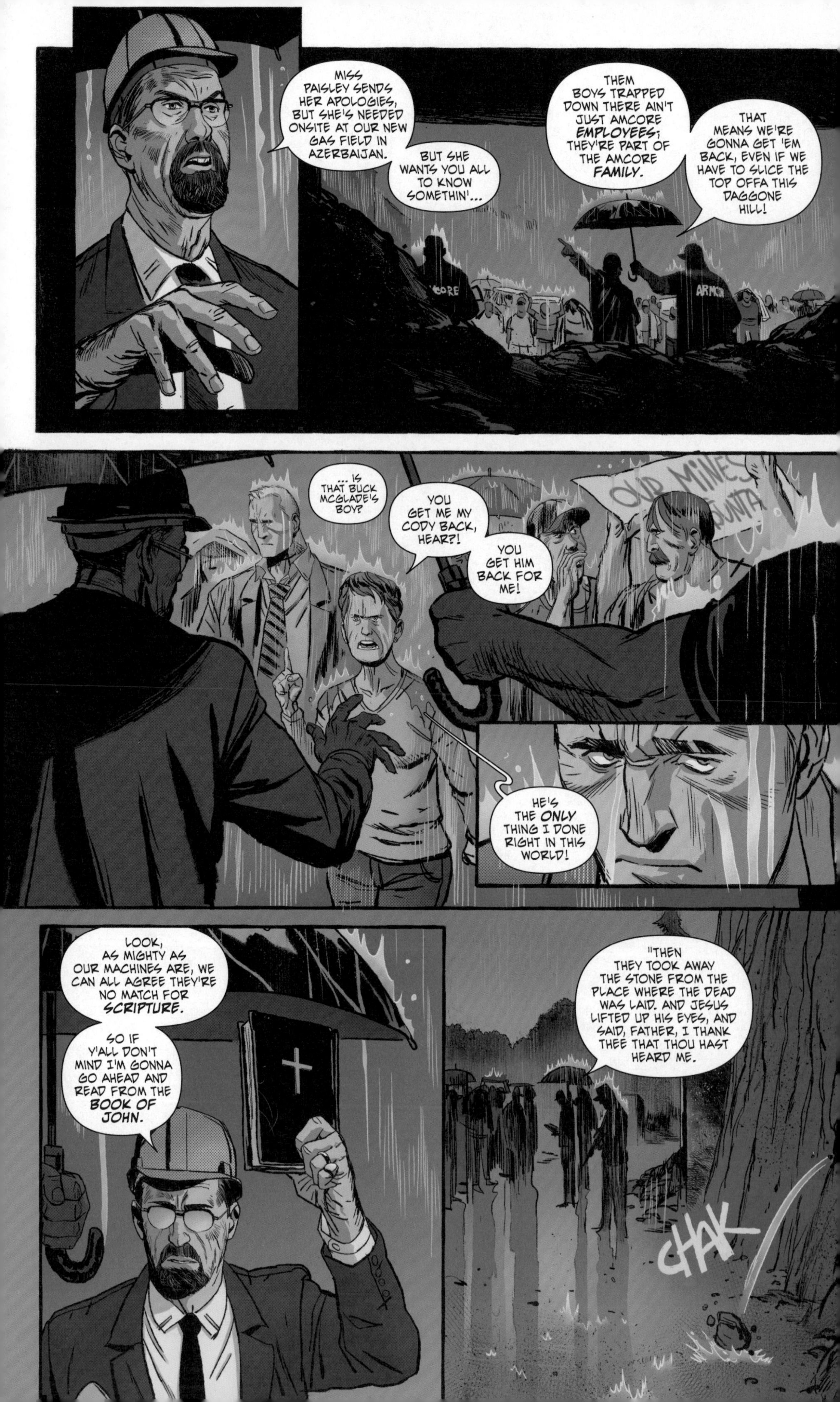

MISS PAISLEY SENDS HER APOLOGIES, BUT SHE'S NEEDED ONSITE AT OUR NEW GAS FIELD IN AZERBAIJAN.
BUT SHE WANTS YOU ALL TO KNOW SOMETHIN'...
THEM BOYS TRAPPED DOWN THERE AIN'T JUST AMCORE **EMPLOYEES**; THEY'RE PART OF THE AMCORE **FAMILY**.
THAT MEANS WE'RE GONNA GET 'EM BACK, EVEN IF WE HAVE TO SLICE THE TOP OFFA THIS DAGGONE HILL!
...IS THAT BUCK MCGLADE'S BOY?
YOU GET ME MY CODY BACK, HEAR?!
YOU GET HIM BACK FOR ME!
HE'S THE **ONLY** THING I DONE RIGHT IN THIS WORLD!
LOOK, AS MIGHTY AS OUR MACHINES ARE, WE CAN ALL AGREE THEY'RE NO MATCH FOR **SCRIPTURE**.
SO IF Y'ALL DON'T MIND I'M GONNA GO AHEAD AND READ FROM THE **BOOK OF JOHN**.
"THEN THEY TOOK AWAY THE STONE FROM THE PLACE WHERE THE DEAD WAS LAID. AND JESUS LIFTED UP HIS EYES, AND SAID, FATHER, I THANK THEE THAT THOU HAST HEARD ME.
CHAK

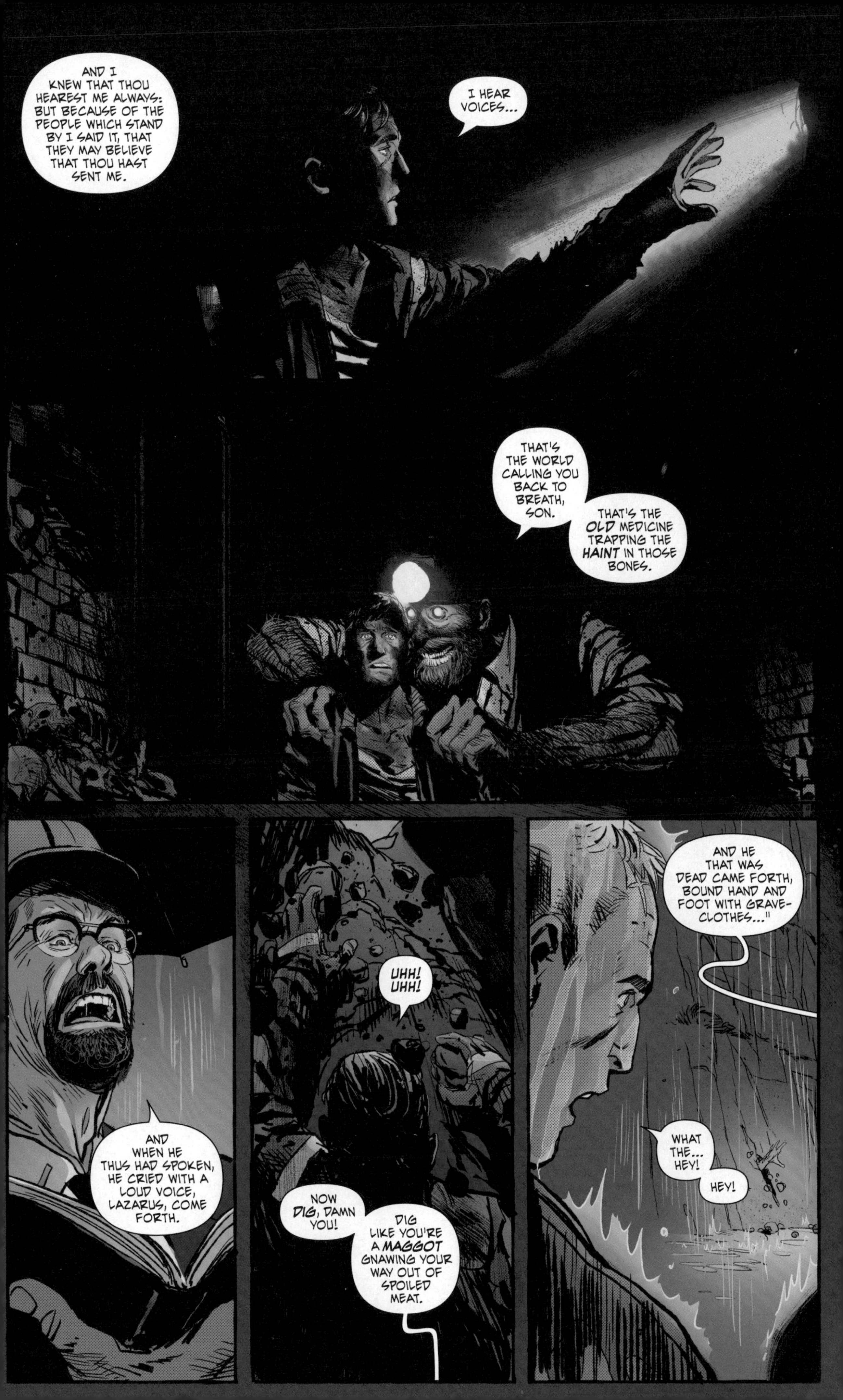
AND I KNEW THAT THOU HEAREST ME ALWAYS: BUT BECAUSE OF THE PEOPLE WHICH STAND BY I SAID IT, THAT THEY MAY BELIEVE THAT THOU HAST SENT ME.
I HEAR VOICES...
THAT'S THE WORLD CALLING YOU BACK TO BREATH, SON.
THAT'S THE OLD MEDICINE TRAPPING THE HAINT IN THOSE BONES.
AND WHEN HE THUS HAD SPOKEN, HE CRIED WITH A LOUD VOICE, LAZARUS, COME FORTH.
UHH! UHH!
NOW DIG, DAMN YOU!
DIG LIKE YOU'RE A MAGGOT GNAWING YOUR WAY OUT OF SPOILED MEAT.
AND HE THAT WAS DEAD CAME FORTH, BOUND HAND AND FOOT WITH GRAVE-CLOTHES..."
WHAT THE... HEY!
HEY!

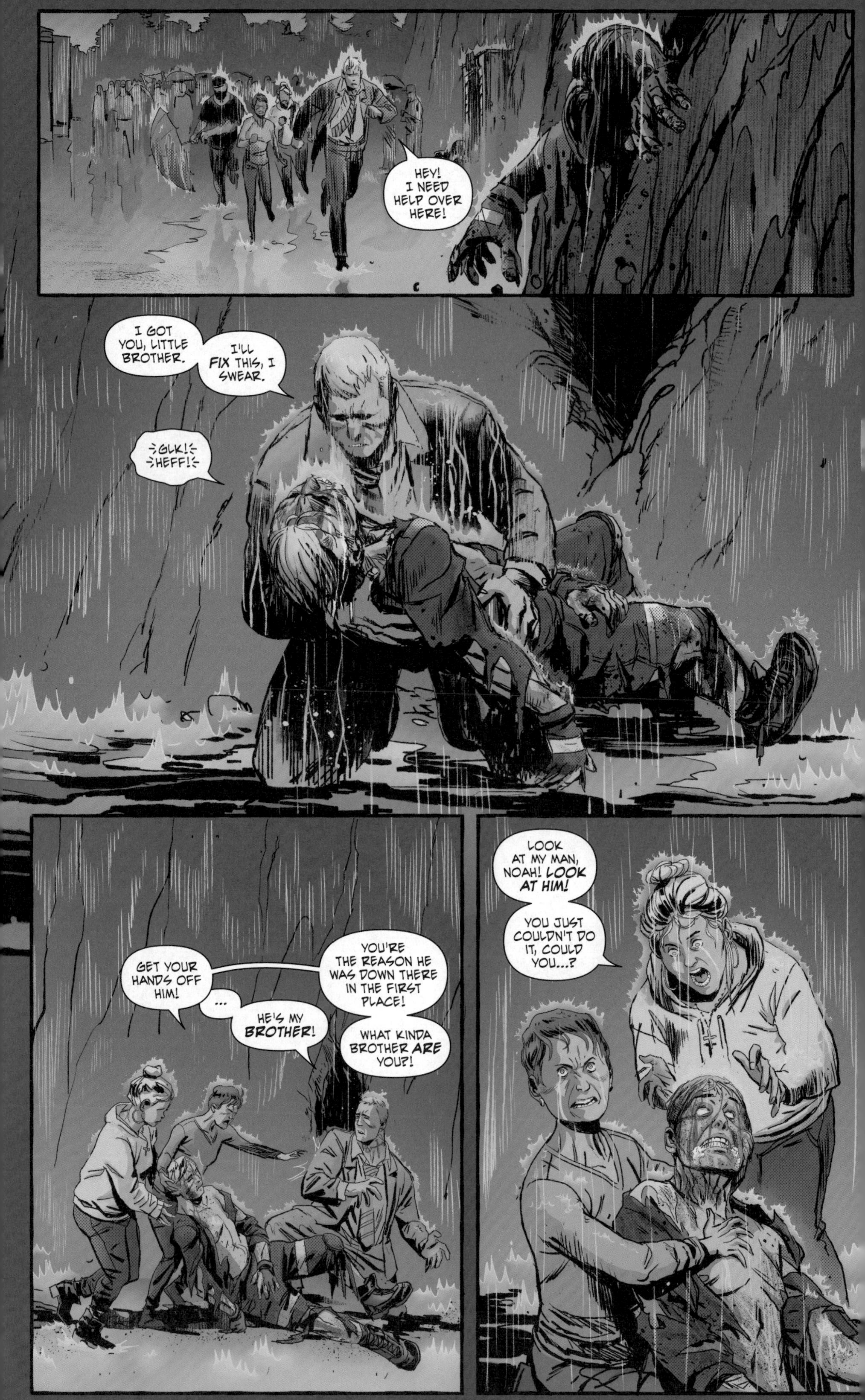
HEY! I NEED HELP OVER HERE!
I GOT YOU, LITTLE BROTHER.
I'LL FIX THIS, I SWEAR.
GLK! HEFF!
GET YOUR HANDS OFF HIM!
YOU'RE THE REASON HE WAS DOWN THERE IN THE FIRST PLACE!
...
HE'S MY BROTHER!
WHAT KINDA BROTHER ARE YOU?!
LOOK AT MY MAN, NOAH! LOOK AT HIM!
YOU JUST COULDN'T DO IT, COULD YOU...?

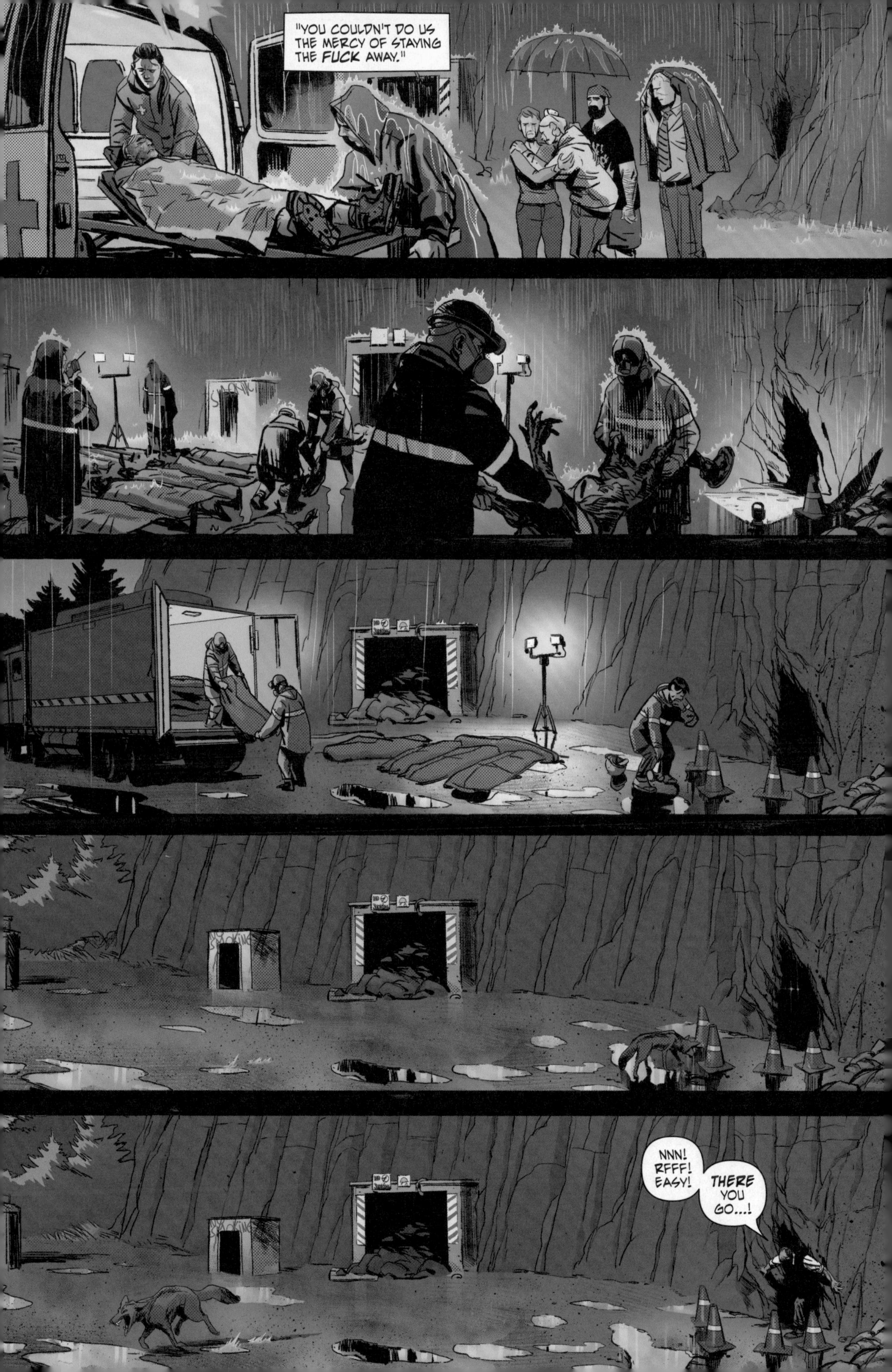
"YOU COULDN'T DO US THE MERCY OF STAYING THE **FUCK** AWAY."
NNN! RFFF! EASY!
THERE YOU GO...!

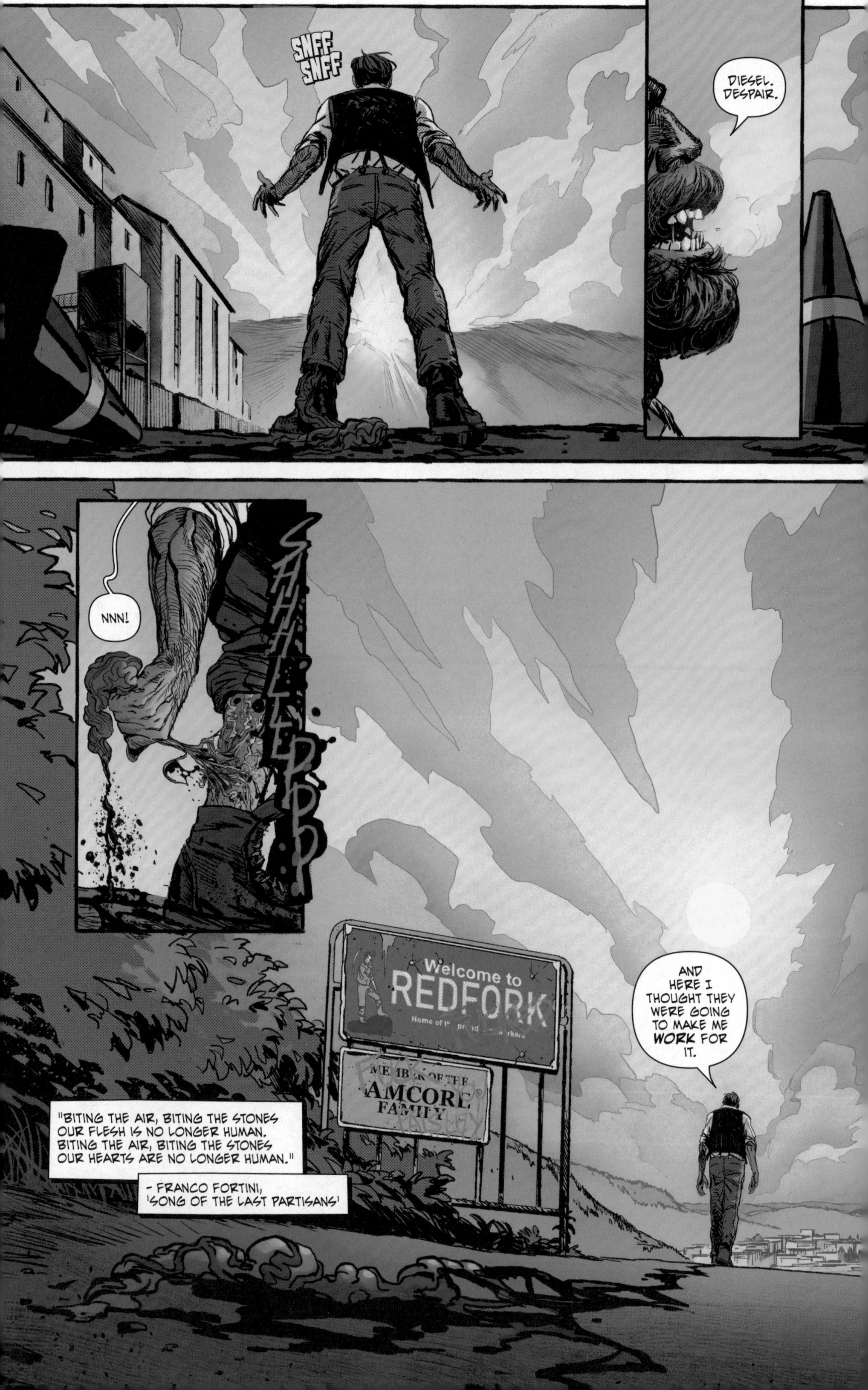
SNFF SNFF
DIESEL. DESPAIR.
NNN!
Welcome to REDFORK
AMCORE FAMILY
AND HERE I THOUGHT THEY WERE GOING TO MAKE ME **WORK** FOR IT.
"BITING THE AIR, BITING THE STONES OUR FLESH IS NO LONGER HUMAN. BITING THE AIR, BITING THE STONES OUR HEARTS ARE NO LONGER HUMAN."
- FRANCO FORTINI, 'SONG OF THE LAST PARTISANS'

CHAPTER 2

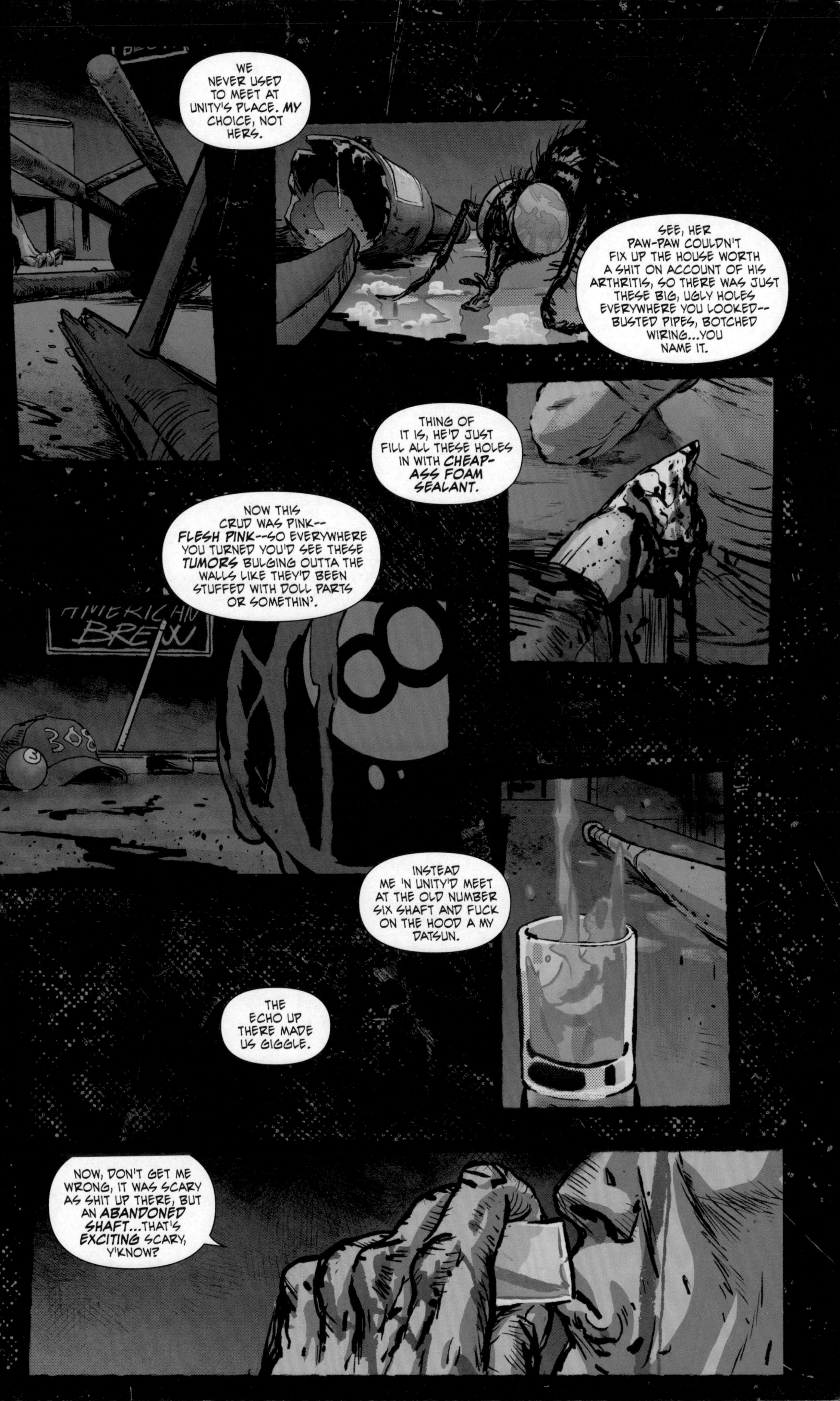
WE NEVER USED TO MEET AT UNITY'S PLACE. MY CHOICE, NOT HERS.
SEE, HER PAW-PAW COULDN'T FIX UP THE HOUSE WORTH A SHIT ON ACCOUNT OF HIS ARTHRITIS, SO THERE WAS JUST THESE BIG, UGLY HOLES EVERYWHERE YOU LOOKED--BUSTED PIPES, BOTCHED WIRING...YOU NAME IT.
THING OF IT IS, HE'D JUST FILL ALL THESE HOLES IN WITH CHEAP-ASS FOAM SEALANT.
NOW THIS CRUD WAS PINK--FLESH PINK--SO EVERYWHERE YOU TURNED YOU'D SEE THESE TUMORS BULGING OUTTA THE WALLS LIKE THEY'D BEEN STUFFED WITH DOLL PARTS OR SOMETHIN'.
BREW
308
INSTEAD ME 'N UNITY'D MEET AT THE OLD NUMBER SIX SHAFT AND FUCK ON THE HOOD A MY DATSUN.
THE ECHO UP THERE MADE US GIGGLE.
NOW, DON'T GET ME WRONG, IT WAS SCARY AS SHIT UP THERE, BUT AN ABANDONED SHAFT...THAT'S EXCITING SCARY, Y'KNOW?

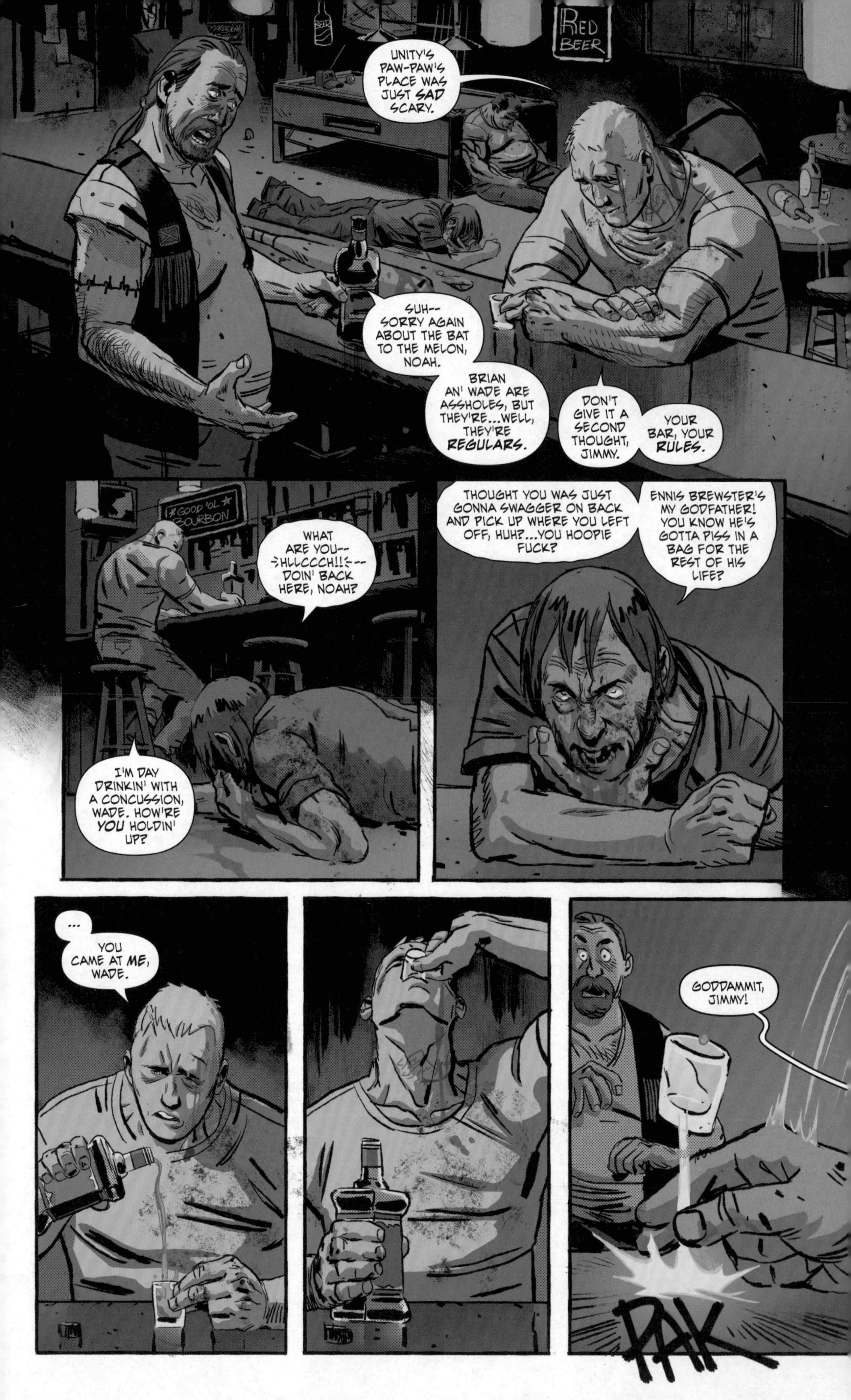

RED BEER
UNITY'S PAW-PAW'S PLACE WAS JUST SAD SCARY.
SUH-- SORRY AGAIN ABOUT THE BAT TO THE MELON, NOAH.
BRIAN AN' WADE ARE ASSHOLES, BUT THEY'RE...WELL, THEY'RE REGULARS.
DON'T GIVE IT A SECOND THOUGHT, JIMMY.
YOUR BAR, YOUR RULES.
GOOD 'OL BOURBON
WHAT ARE YOU-- HLLCCCH!!-- DOIN' BACK HERE, NOAH?
I'M DAY DRINKIN' WITH A CONCUSSION, WADE. HOW'RE YOU HOLDIN' UP?
THOUGHT YOU WAS JUST GONNA SWAGGER ON BACK AND PICK UP WHERE YOU LEFT OFF, HUH?...YOU HOOPIE FUCK?
ENNIS BREWSTER'S MY GODFATHER! YOU KNOW HE'S GOTTA PISS IN A BAG FOR THE REST OF HIS LIFE?
... YOU CAME AT ME, WADE.
GODDAMMIT, JIMMY!
PAK

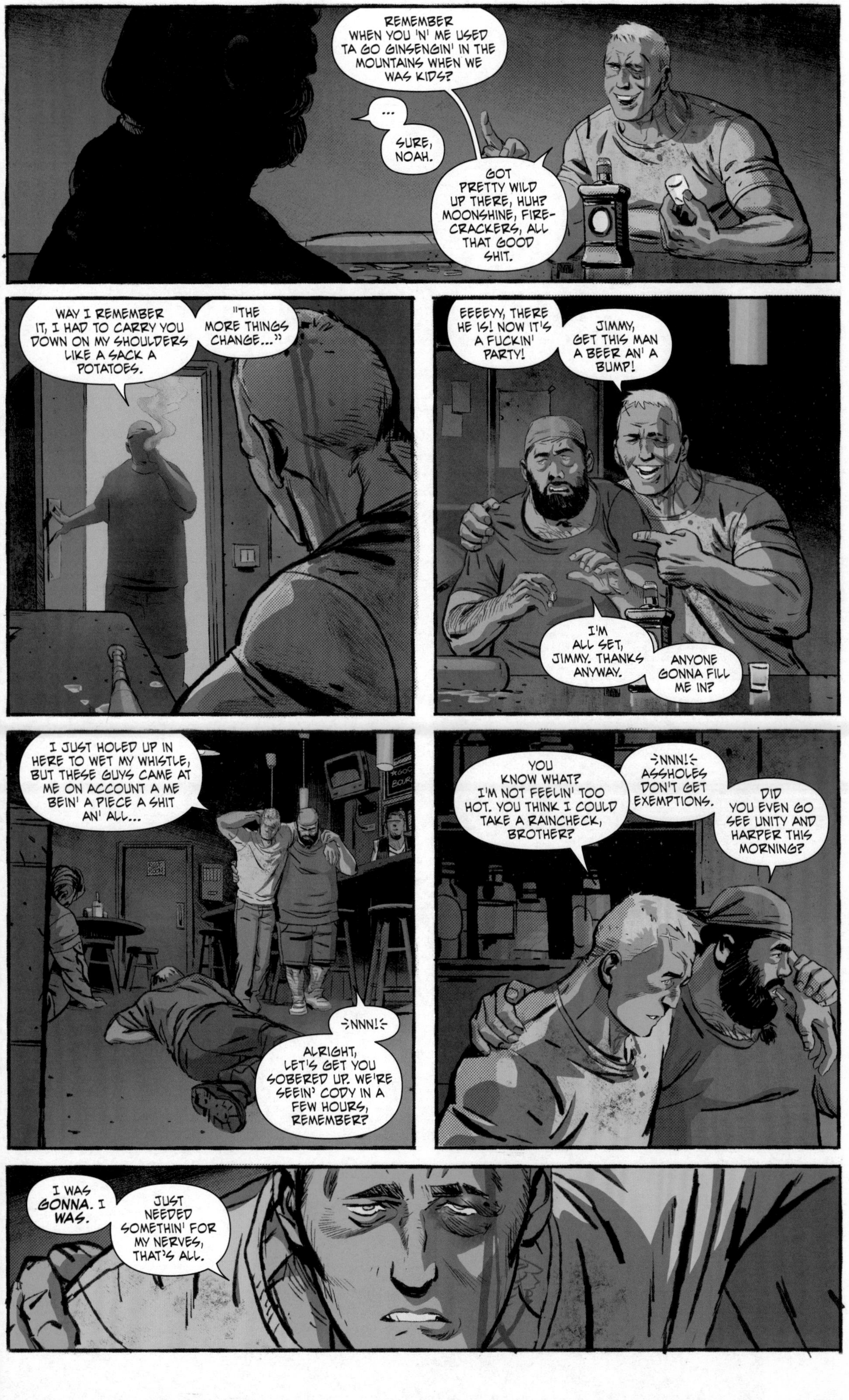
REMEMBER WHEN YOU 'N' ME USED TA GO GINSENGIN' IN THE MOUNTAINS WHEN WE WAS KIDS?
...
SURE, NOAH.
GOT PRETTY WILD UP THERE, HUH? MOONSHINE, FIRE-CRACKERS, ALL THAT GOOD SHIT.
WAY I REMEMBER IT, I HAD TO CARRY YOU DOWN ON MY SHOULDERS LIKE A SACK A POTATOES.
"THE MORE THINGS CHANGE..."
EEEEYY, THERE HE IS! NOW IT'S A FUCKIN' PARTY!
JIMMY, GET THIS MAN A BEER AN' A BUMP!
I'M ALL SET, JIMMY. THANKS ANYWAY.
ANYONE GONNA FILL ME IN?
I JUST HOLED UP IN HERE TO WET MY WHISTLE, BUT THESE GUYS CAME AT ME ON ACCOUNT A ME BEIN' A PIECE A SHIT AN' ALL...
NNN!
ALRIGHT, LET'S GET YOU SOBERED UP. WE'RE SEEIN' CODY IN A FEW HOURS, REMEMBER?
YOU KNOW WHAT? I'M NOT FEELIN' TOO HOT. YOU THINK I COULD TAKE A RAINCHECK, BROTHER?
NNN! ASSHOLES DON'T GET EXEMPTIONS.
DID YOU EVEN GO SEE UNITY AND HARPER THIS MORNING?
I WAS GONNA. I WAS.
JUST NEEDED SOMETHIN' FOR MY NERVES, THAT'S ALL.

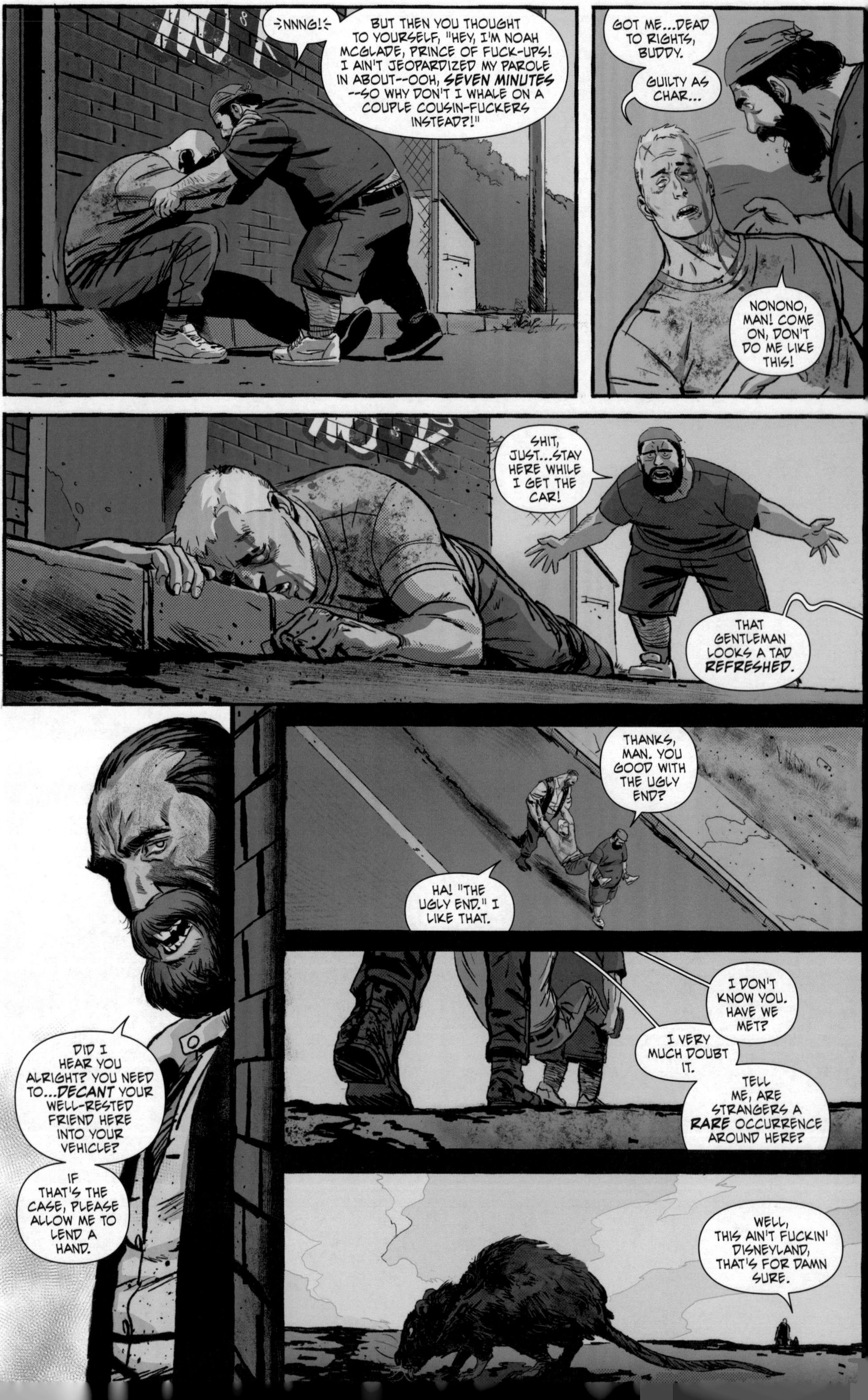

≈NNNG!≈
BUT THEN YOU THOUGHT TO YOURSELF, "HEY, I'M NOAH MCGLADE, PRINCE OF FUCK-UPS! I AIN'T JEOPARDIZED MY PAROLE IN ABOUT--OOH, SEVEN MINUTES --SO WHY DON'T I WHALE ON A COUPLE COUSIN-FUCKERS INSTEAD?!"
GOT ME...DEAD TO RIGHTS, BUDDY.
GUILTY AS CHAR...
NONONO, MAN! COME ON, DON'T DO ME LIKE THIS!
SHIT, JUST...STAY HERE WHILE I GET THE CAR!
THAT GENTLEMAN LOOKS A TAD REFRESHED.
DID I HEAR YOU ALRIGHT? YOU NEED TO...DECANT YOUR WELL-RESTED FRIEND HERE INTO YOUR VEHICLE?
IF THAT'S THE CASE, PLEASE ALLOW ME TO LEND A HAND.
THANKS, MAN. YOU GOOD WITH THE UGLY END?
HA! "THE UGLY END." I LIKE THAT.
I DON'T KNOW YOU. HAVE WE MET?
I VERY MUCH DOUBT IT.
TELL ME, ARE STRANGERS A RARE OCCURRENCE AROUND HERE?
WELL, THIS AIN'T FUCKIN' DISNEYLAND, THAT'S FOR DAMN SURE.

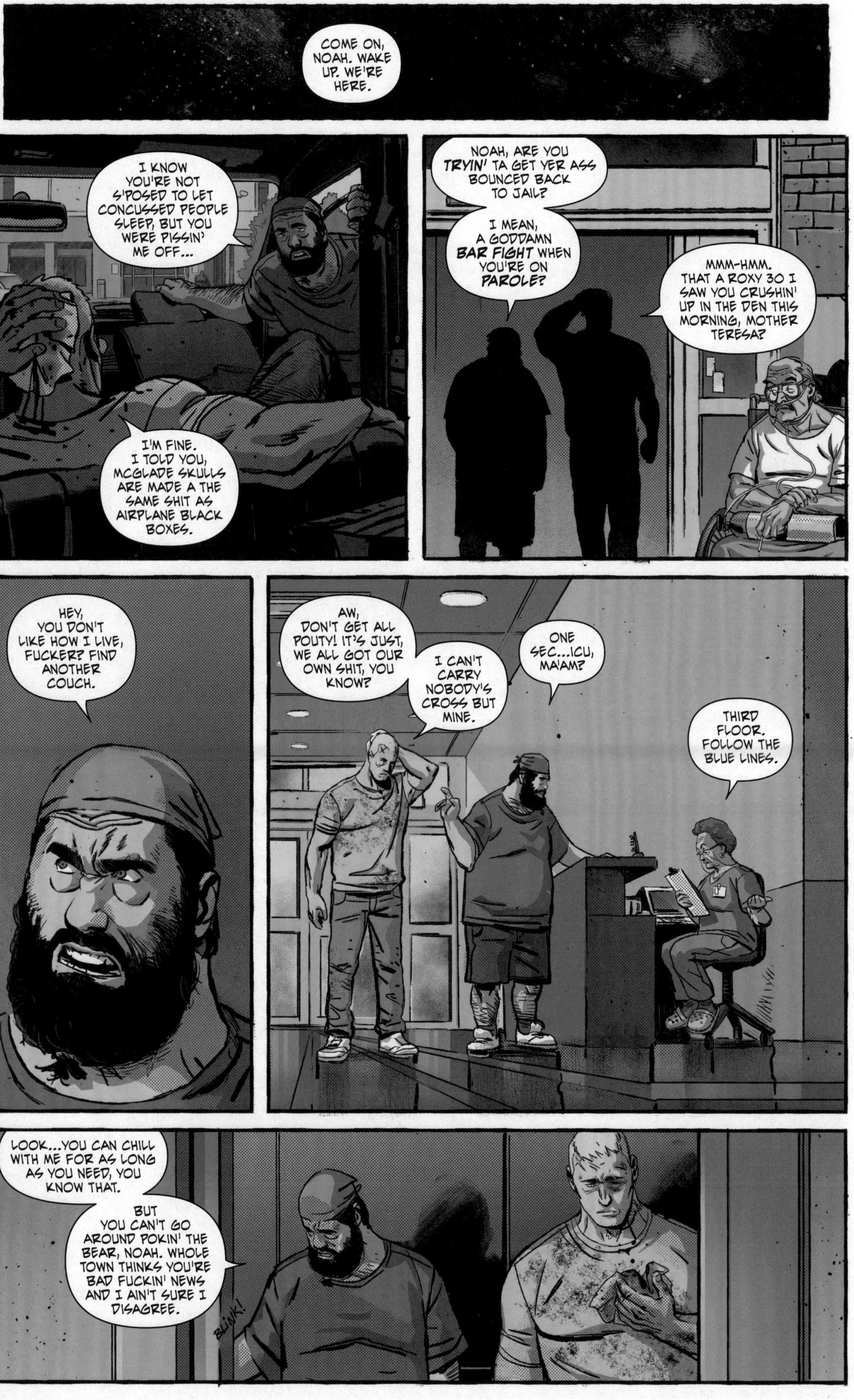
COME ON, NOAH. WAKE UP. WE'RE HERE.
I KNOW YOU'RE NOT S'POSED TO LET CONCUSSED PEOPLE SLEEP, BUT YOU WERE PISSIN' ME OFF...
I'M FINE. I TOLD YOU, MCGLADE SKULLS ARE MADE A THE SAME SHIT AS AIRPLANE BLACK BOXES.
NOAH, ARE YOU TRYIN' TA GET YER ASS BOUNCED BACK TO JAIL?
I MEAN, A GODDAMN BAR FIGHT WHEN YOU'RE ON PAROLE?
MMM-HMM. THAT A ROXY 30 I SAW YOU CRUSHIN' UP IN THE DEN THIS MORNING, MOTHER TERESA?
HEY, YOU DON'T LIKE HOW I LIVE, FUCKER? FIND ANOTHER COUCH.
AW, DON'T GET ALL POUTY! IT'S JUST, WE ALL GOT OUR OWN SHIT, YOU KNOW?
I CAN'T CARRY NOBODY'S CROSS BUT MINE.
ONE SEC...ICU, MA'AM?
THIRD FLOOR. FOLLOW THE BLUE LINES.
LOOK...YOU CAN CHILL WITH ME FOR AS LONG AS YOU NEED, YOU KNOW THAT.
BUT YOU CAN'T GO AROUND POKIN' THE BEAR, NOAH. WHOLE TOWN THINKS YOU'RE BAD FUCKIN' NEWS AND I AIN'T SURE I DISAGREE.
BLINK!

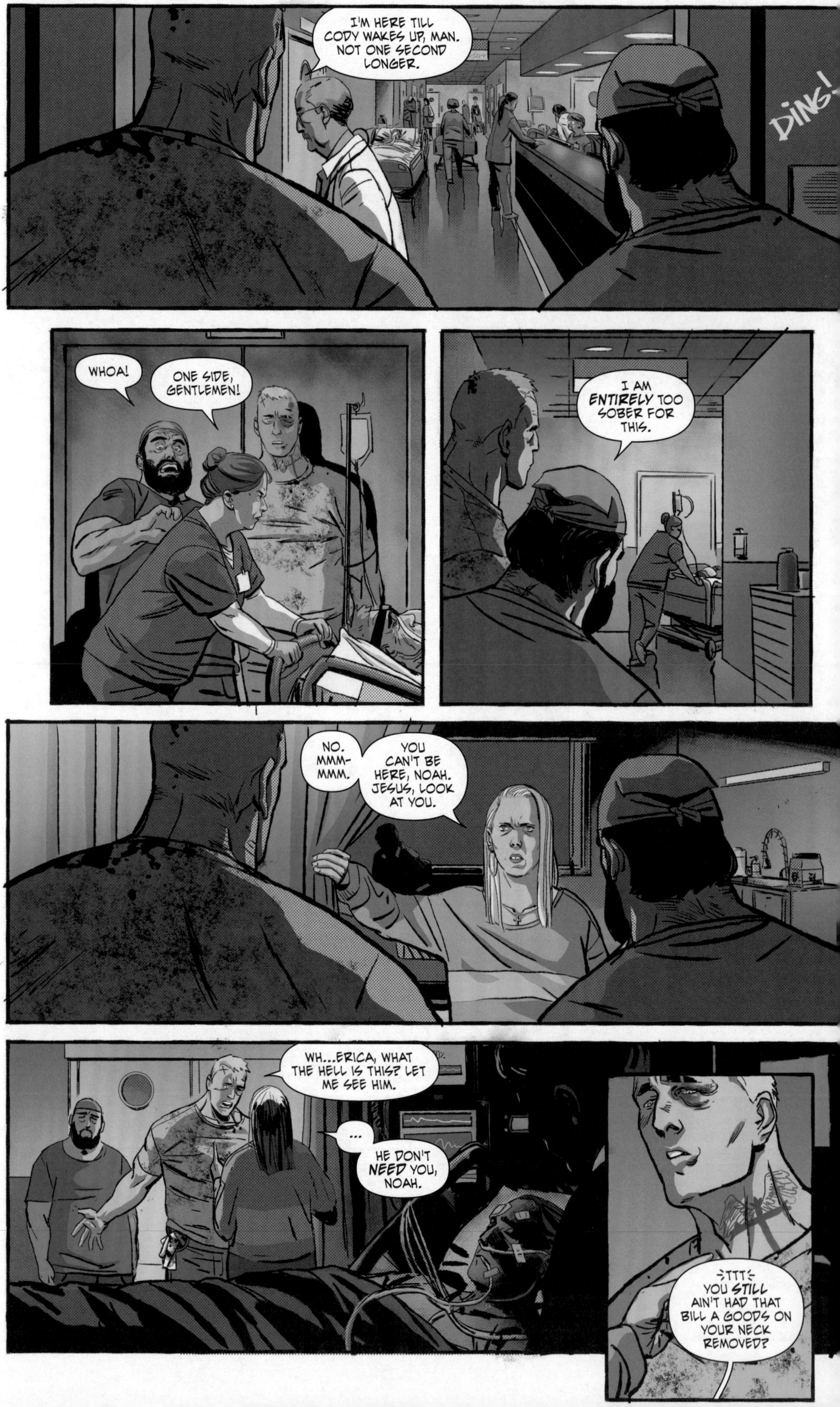
I'M HERE TILL CODY WAKES UP, MAN. NOT ONE SECOND LONGER.
DING!
WHOA!
ONE SIDE, GENTLEMEN!
I AM ENTIRELY TOO SOBER FOR THIS.
NO. MMM-MMM.
YOU CAN'T BE HERE, NOAH. JESUS, LOOK AT YOU.
WH...ERICA, WHAT THE HELL IS THIS? LET ME SEE HIM.
...
HE DON'T NEED YOU, NOAH.
TTT
YOU STILL AIN'T HAD THAT BILL A GOODS ON YOUR NECK REMOVED?

HOW LONG WERE YOU BACK BEFORE A GODDAMN *MOUNTAIN* FELL ON MY FIANCÉ'S HEAD?

A MINUTE? TWO?

EVERYTHIN' ALWAYS FALLS TO SHIT THE MOMENT YOU SLITHER ON BACK, AND YOU NEVER ASK YOURSELF WHY.

AND WHO ALWAYS CLEANS UP AFTER YOU, HMM?

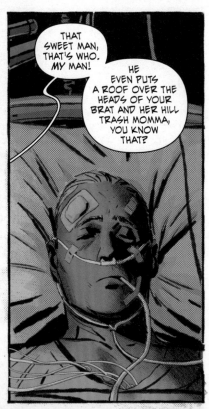

THAT SWEET MAN, THAT'S WHO. *MY MAN!*

HE EVEN PUTS A ROOF OVER THE HEADS OF YOUR BRAT AND HER HILL TRASH MOMMA, YOU KNOW THAT?

WE WERE GONNA MOVE TO COLUMBUS!

HEY! LET'S EVERYBODY JUST TAKE A BREATH HERE, HUH?

YOU'RE A CURSE ON TWO LEGS! JUST GO!

PAM! PAM!

HE STAYS.

THEY'RE *MY* BOYS. I SAY NOAH STAYS WHILE WE WAIT FOR CODY TO COME BACK TO HIMSELF.

THAT'S WHAT CODY DID FOR HIM, SO THAT'S WHAT HE'S GONNA DO FOR CODY.

IF IT TAKES 30 SECONDS OR 30 *YEARS,* NOAH STAYS, AND HE WAITS WITH US... *RIGHT HERE IN PURGATORY.*

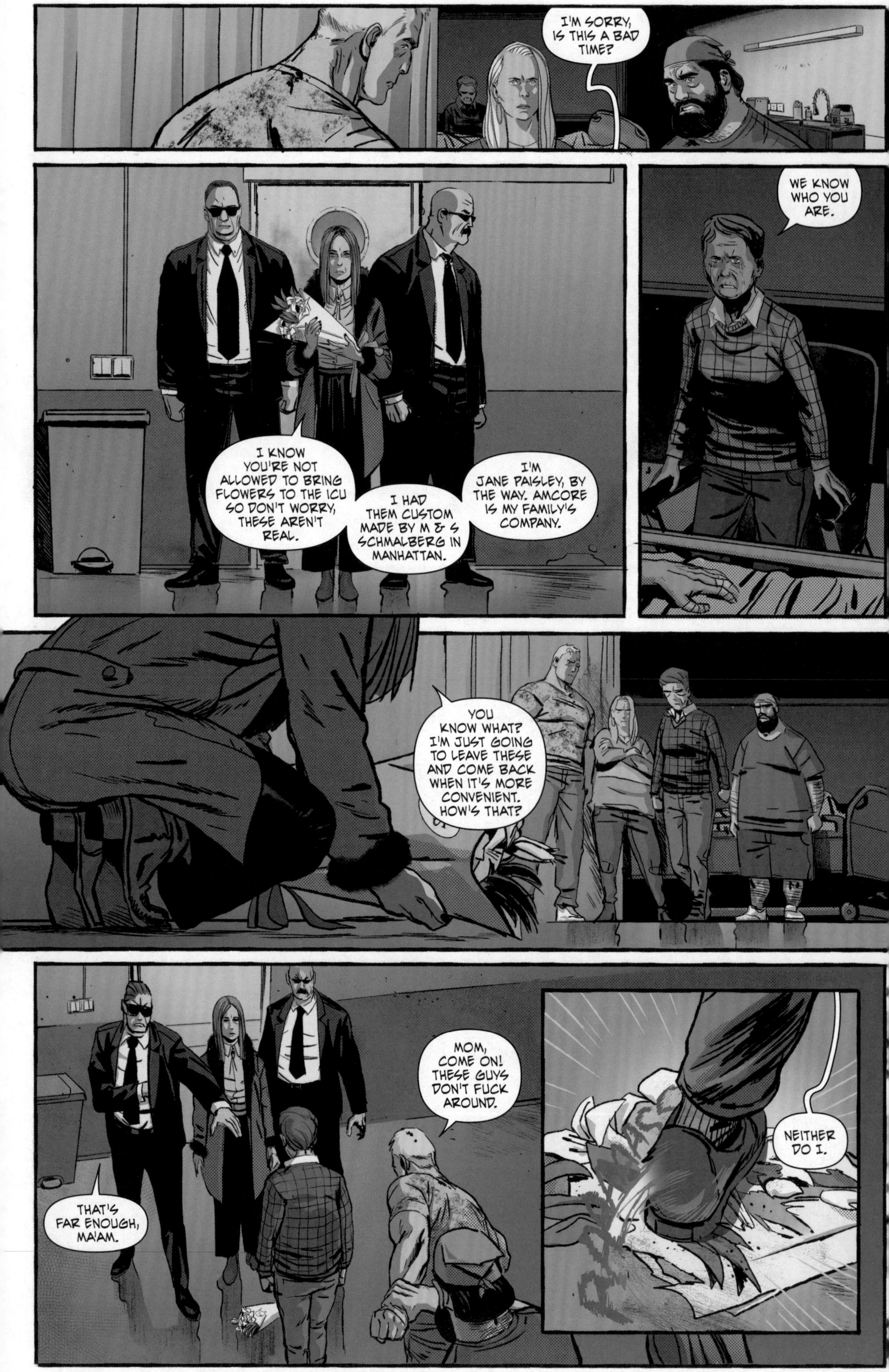
I'M SORRY, IS THIS A BAD TIME?
I KNOW YOU'RE NOT ALLOWED TO BRING FLOWERS TO THE ICU SO DON'T WORRY, THESE AREN'T REAL.
I HAD THEM CUSTOM MADE BY M & S SCHMALBERG IN MANHATTAN.
I'M JANE PAISLEY, BY THE WAY. AMCORE IS MY FAMILY'S COMPANY.
WE KNOW WHO YOU ARE.
YOU KNOW WHAT? I'M JUST GOING TO LEAVE THESE AND COME BACK WHEN IT'S MORE CONVENIENT. HOW'S THAT?
MOM, COME ON! THESE GUYS DON'T FUCK AROUND.
THAT'S FAR ENOUGH, MA'AM.
NEITHER DO I.

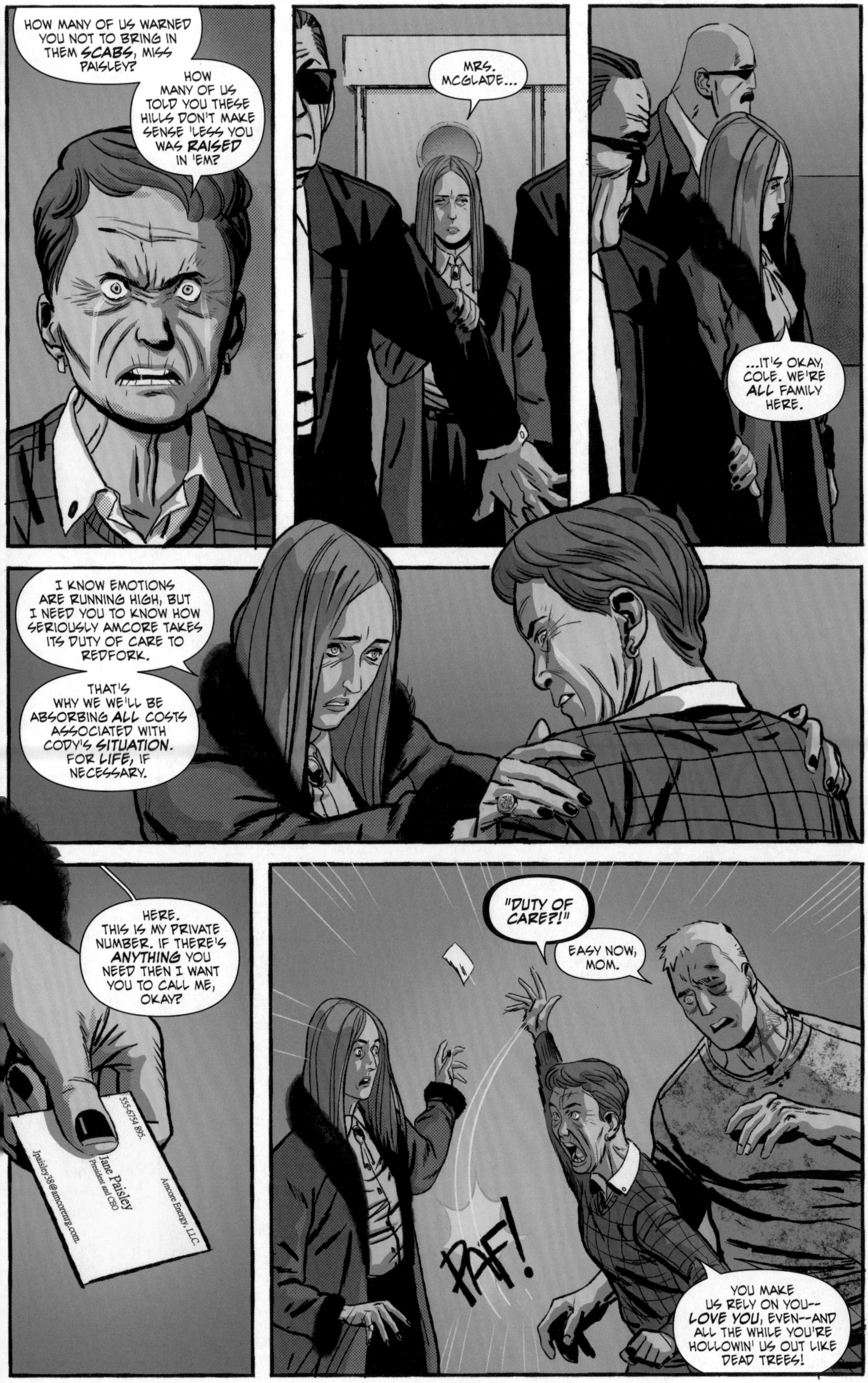
HOW MANY OF US WARNED YOU NOT TO BRING IN THEM SCABS, MISS PAISLEY?
HOW MANY OF US TOLD YOU THESE HILLS DON'T MAKE SENSE 'LESS YOU WAS RAISED IN 'EM?
MRS. MCGLADE...
...IT'S OKAY, COLE. WE'RE ALL FAMILY HERE.
I KNOW EMOTIONS ARE RUNNING HIGH, BUT I NEED YOU TO KNOW HOW SERIOUSLY AMCORE TAKES ITS DUTY OF CARE TO REDFORK.
THAT'S WHY WE WE'LL BE ABSORBING ALL COSTS ASSOCIATED WITH CODY'S SITUATION. FOR LIFE, IF NECESSARY.
HERE. THIS IS MY PRIVATE NUMBER. IF THERE'S ANYTHING YOU NEED THEN I WANT YOU TO CALL ME, OKAY?
555-6754 805.
Amcore Energy, LLC.
Jane Paisley
President and CEO
Jpaisley38@amcoreng.com.
"DUTY OF CARE?!"
EASY NOW, MOM.
PAF!
YOU MAKE US RELY ON YOU--LOVE YOU, EVEN--AND ALL THE WHILE YOU'RE HOLLOWIN' US OUT LIKE DEAD TREES!

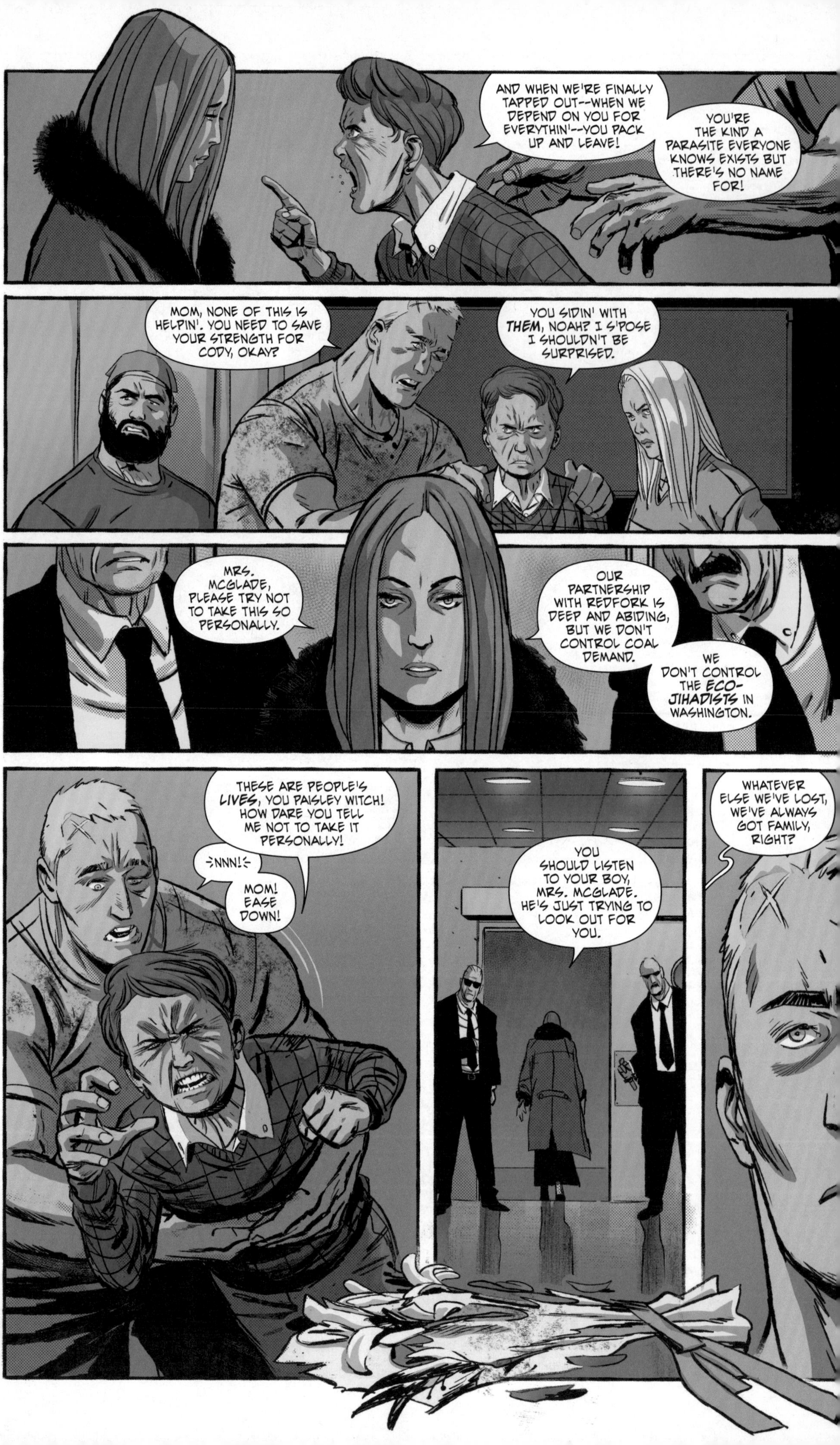
AND WHEN WE'RE FINALLY TAPPED OUT--WHEN WE DEPEND ON YOU FOR EVERYTHIN'--YOU PACK UP AND LEAVE!
YOU'RE THE KIND A PARASITE EVERYONE KNOWS EXISTS BUT THERE'S NO NAME FOR!
MOM, NONE OF THIS IS HELPIN'. YOU NEED TO SAVE YOUR STRENGTH FOR CODY, OKAY?
YOU SIDIN' WITH THEM, NOAH? I S'POSE I SHOULDN'T BE SURPRISED.
MRS. MCGLADE, PLEASE TRY NOT TO TAKE THIS SO PERSONALLY.
OUR PARTNERSHIP WITH REDFORK IS DEEP AND ABIDING, BUT WE DON'T CONTROL COAL DEMAND.
WE DON'T CONTROL THE ECO-JIHADISTS IN WASHINGTON.
THESE ARE PEOPLE'S LIVES, YOU PAISLEY WITCH! HOW DARE YOU TELL ME NOT TO TAKE IT PERSONALLY!
NNN!
MOM! EASE DOWN!
YOU SHOULD LISTEN TO YOUR BOY, MRS. MCGLADE. HE'S JUST TRYING TO LOOK OUT FOR YOU.
WHATEVER ELSE WE'VE LOST, WE'VE ALWAYS GOT FAMILY, RIGHT?

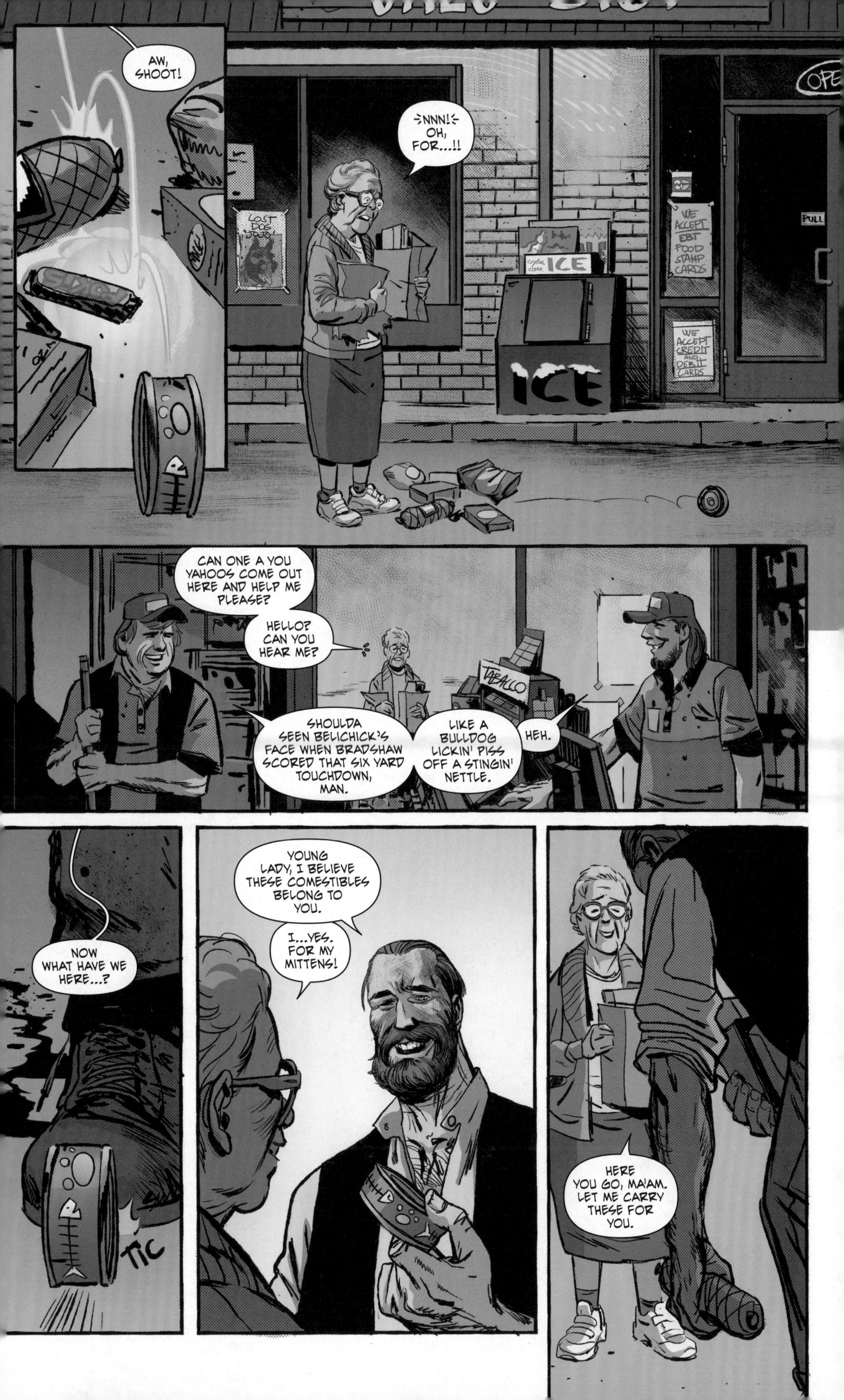
AW, SHOOT!
NNN! OH, FOR...!!
LOST DOG JOJO!
CRYSTAL CLEAR ICE
ICE
WE ACCEPT EBT FOOD STAMP CARDS
WE ACCEPT CREDIT AND DEBIT CARDS
PULL
CAN ONE A YOU YAHOOS COME OUT HERE AND HELP ME PLEASE?
HELLO? CAN YOU HEAR ME?
TABACCO
SHOULDA SEEN BELICHICK'S FACE WHEN BRADSHAW SCORED THAT SIX YARD TOUCHDOWN, MAN.
LIKE A BULLDOG LICKIN' PISS OFF A STINGIN' NETTLE.
HEH.
NOW WHAT HAVE WE HERE...?
TIC
YOUNG LADY, I BELIEVE THESE COMESTIBLES BELONG TO YOU.
I...YES. FOR MY MITTENS!
HERE YOU GO, MA'AM. LET ME CARRY THESE FOR YOU.

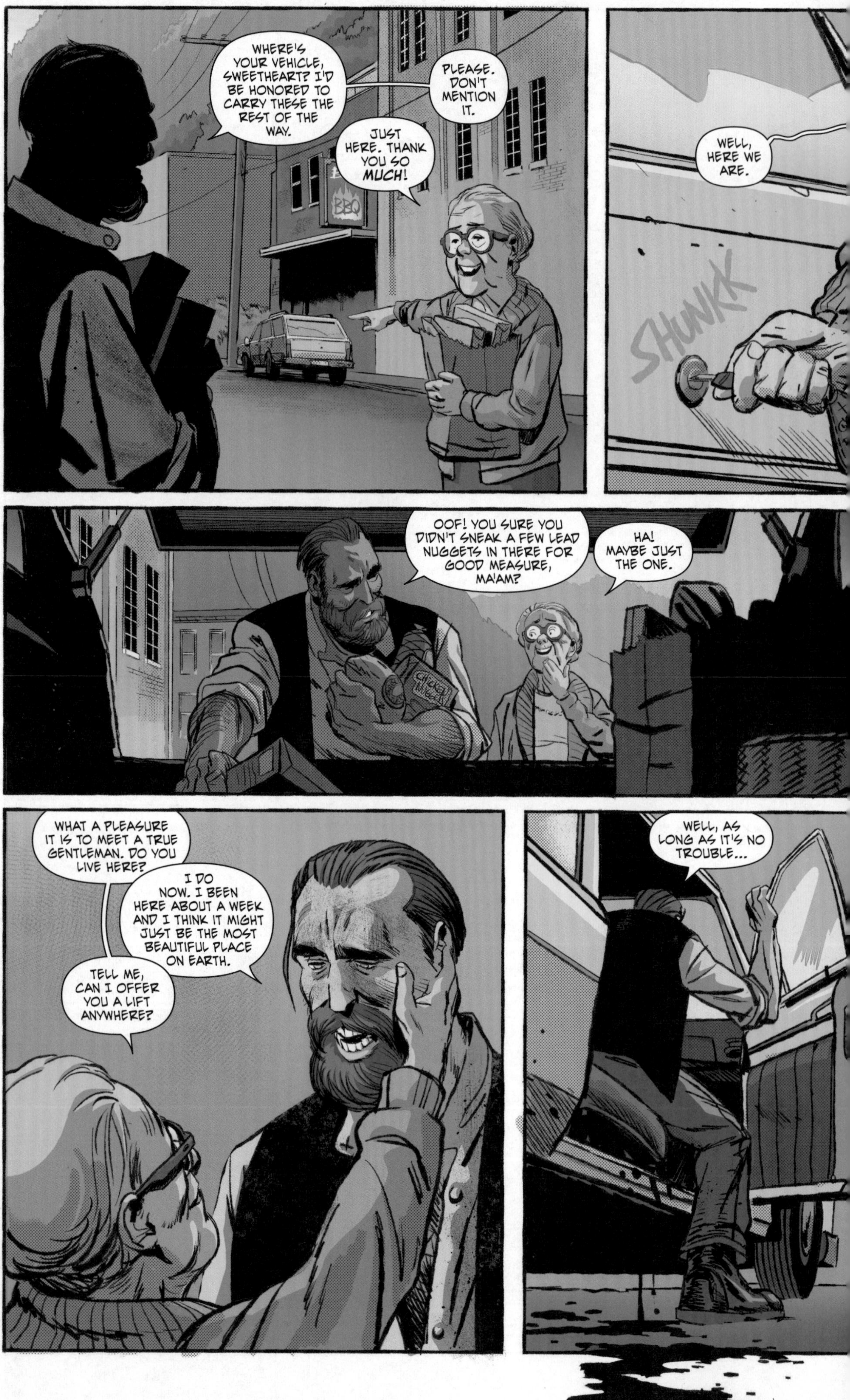
WHERE'S YOUR VEHICLE, SWEETHEART? I'D BE HONORED TO CARRY THESE THE REST OF THE WAY.
JUST HERE. THANK YOU SO MUCH!
PLEASE. DON'T MENTION IT.
BBQ
WELL, HERE WE ARE.
SHUNKK
OOF! YOU SURE YOU DIDN'T SNEAK A FEW LEAD NUGGETS IN THERE FOR GOOD MEASURE, MA'AM?
HA! MAYBE JUST THE ONE.
WHAT A PLEASURE IT IS TO MEET A TRUE GENTLEMAN. DO YOU LIVE HERE?
I DO NOW. I BEEN HERE ABOUT A WEEK AND I THINK IT MIGHT JUST BE THE MOST BEAUTIFUL PLACE ON EARTH.
TELL ME, CAN I OFFER YOU A LIFT ANYWHERE?
WELL, AS LONG AS IT'S NO TROUBLE...

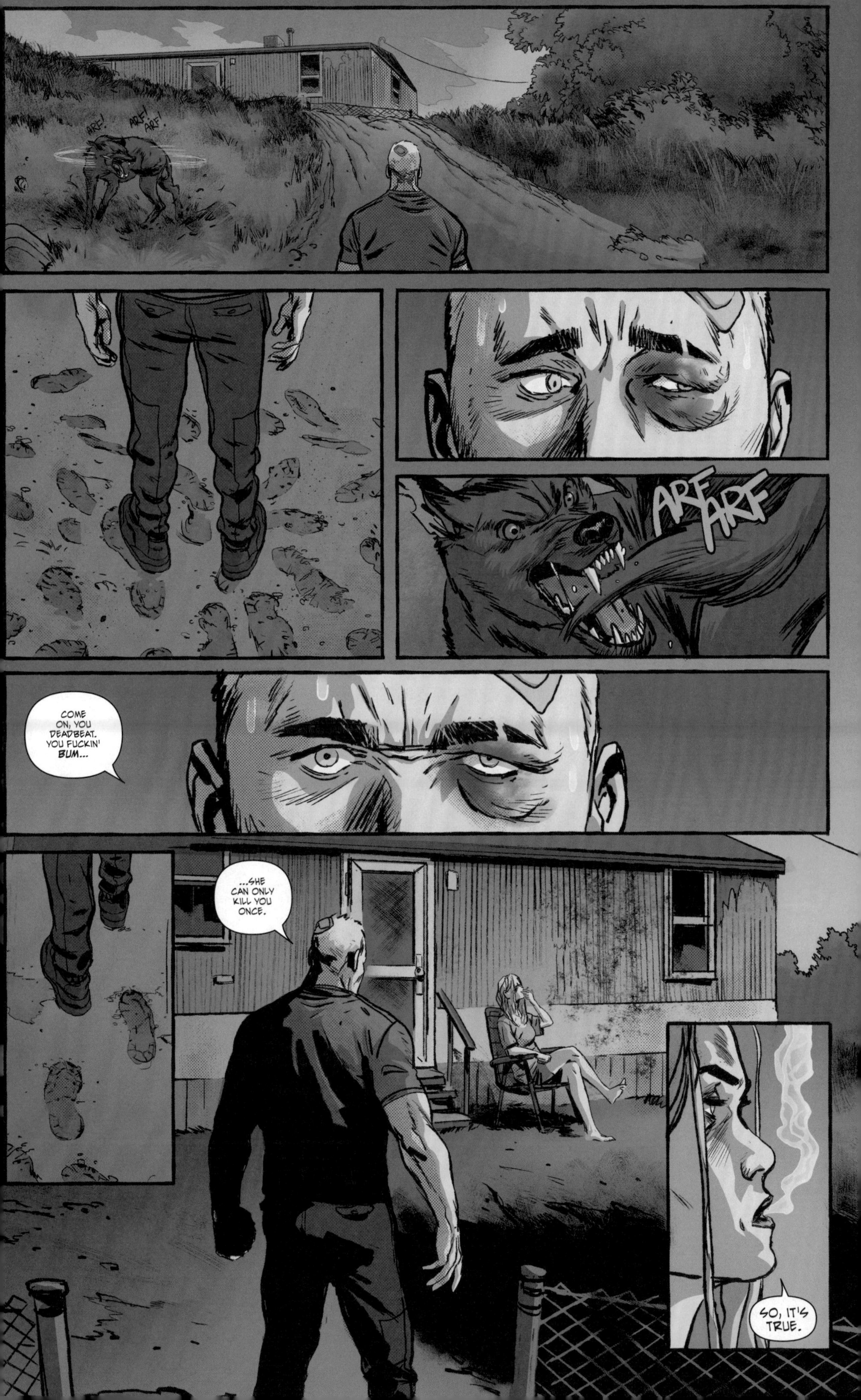
ARF! ARF! ARF!
ARF ARF
COME ON, YOU DEADBEAT. YOU FUCKIN' BUM...
...SHE CAN ONLY KILL YOU ONCE.
SO, IT'S TRUE.

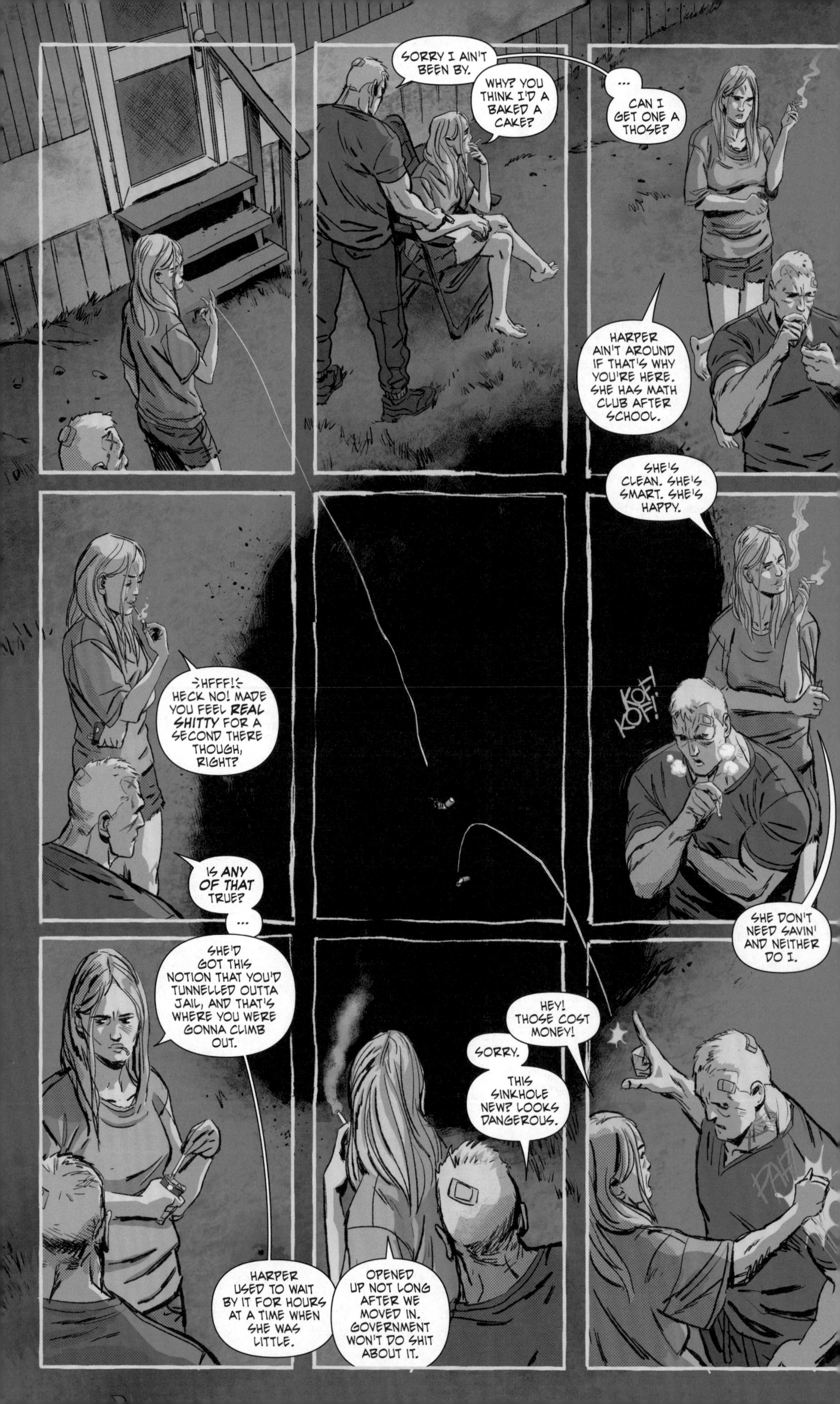

SORRY I AIN'T BEEN BY.
WHY? YOU THINK I'D A BAKED A CAKE?
...
CAN I GET ONE A THOSE?
HARPER AIN'T AROUND IF THAT'S WHY YOU'RE HERE. SHE HAS MATH CLUB AFTER SCHOOL.
SHE'S CLEAN. SHE'S SMART. SHE'S HAPPY.
KOF! KOF!
SHE DON'T NEED SAVIN' AND NEITHER DO I.
-HFFF!- HECK NO! MADE YOU FEEL REAL SHITTY FOR A SECOND THERE THOUGH, RIGHT?
IS ANY OF THAT TRUE?
...
SHE'D GOT THIS NOTION THAT YOU'D TUNNELLED OUTTA JAIL, AND THAT'S WHERE YOU WERE GONNA CLIMB OUT.
HARPER USED TO WAIT BY IT FOR HOURS AT A TIME WHEN SHE WAS LITTLE.
OPENED UP NOT LONG AFTER WE MOVED IN. GOVERNMENT WON'T DO SHIT ABOUT IT.
HEY! THOSE COST MONEY!
SORRY.
THIS SINKHOLE NEW? LOOKS DANGEROUS.
PAH

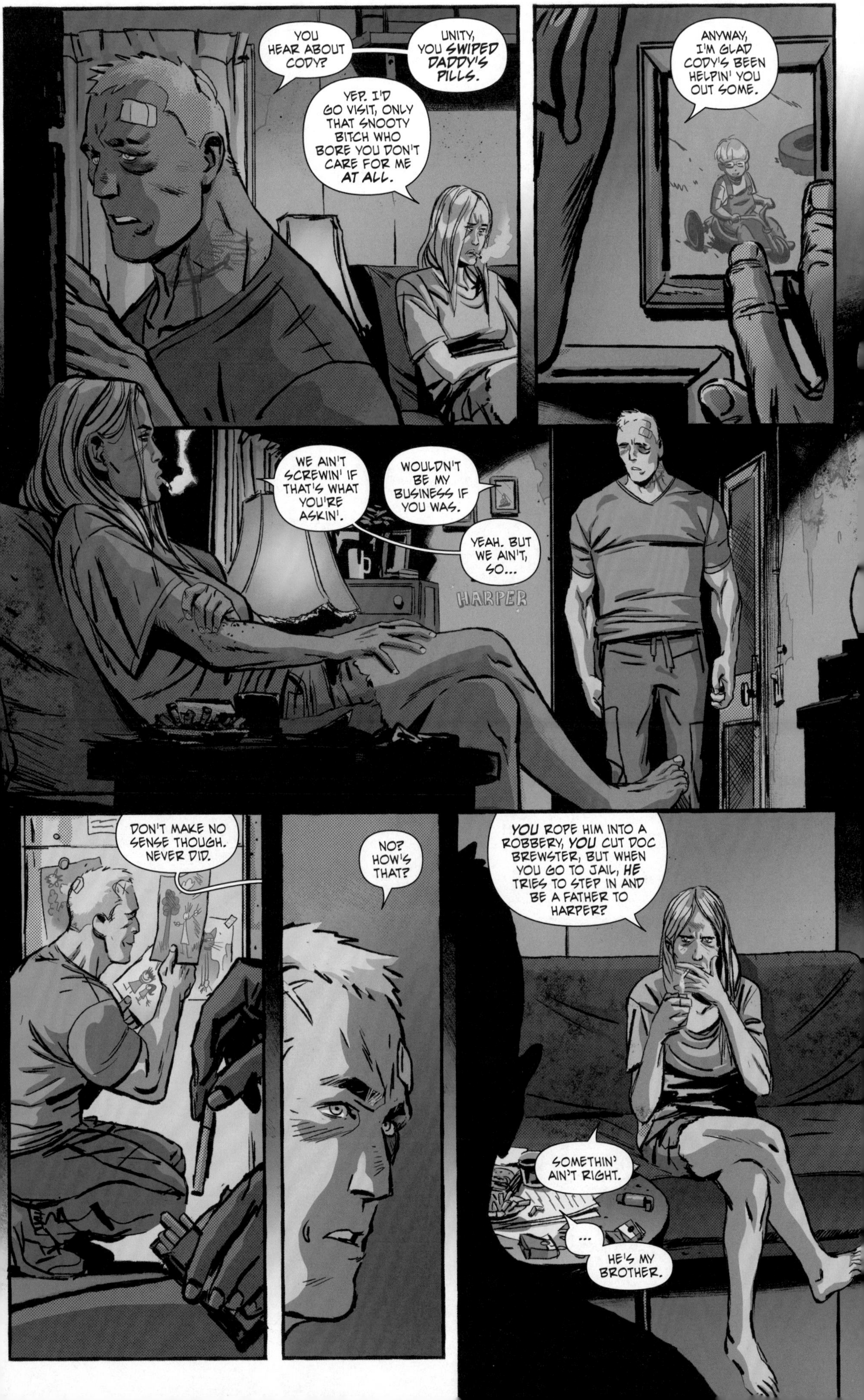
YOU HEAR ABOUT CODY?
UNITY, YOU SWIPED DADDY'S PILLS.
YEP. I'D GO VISIT, ONLY THAT SNOOTY BITCH WHO BORE YOU DON'T CARE FOR ME AT ALL.
ANYWAY, I'M GLAD CODY'S BEEN HELPIN' YOU OUT SOME.
WE AIN'T SCREWIN' IF THAT'S WHAT YOU'RE ASKIN'.
WOULDN'T BE MY BUSINESS IF YOU WAS.
YEAH. BUT WE AIN'T, SO...
HARPER
DON'T MAKE NO SENSE THOUGH. NEVER DID.
NO? HOW'S THAT?
YOU ROPE HIM INTO A ROBBERY, YOU CUT DOC BREWSTER, BUT WHEN YOU GO TO JAIL, HE TRIES TO STEP IN AND BE A FATHER TO HARPER?
SOMETHIN' AIN'T RIGHT.
...
HE'S MY BROTHER.

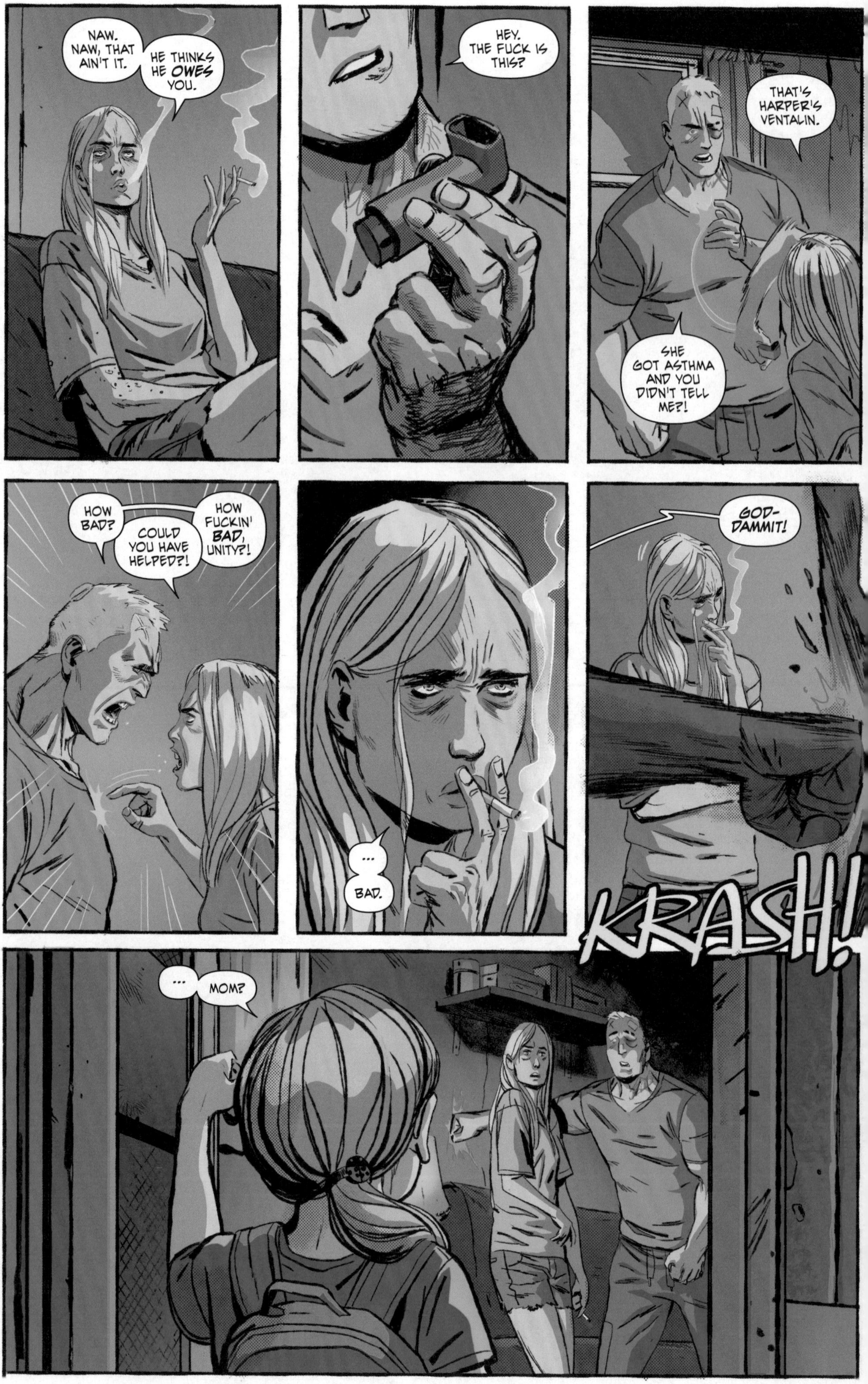
NAW. NAW, THAT AIN'T IT.
HE THINKS HE OWES YOU.
HEY. THE FUCK IS THIS?
THAT'S HARPER'S VENTALIN.
SHE GOT ASTHMA AND YOU DIDN'T TELL ME?!
HOW BAD?
COULD YOU HAVE HELPED?!
HOW FUCKIN' BAD, UNITY?!
...
BAD.
GOD-DAMMIT!
KRASH!
...
MOM?

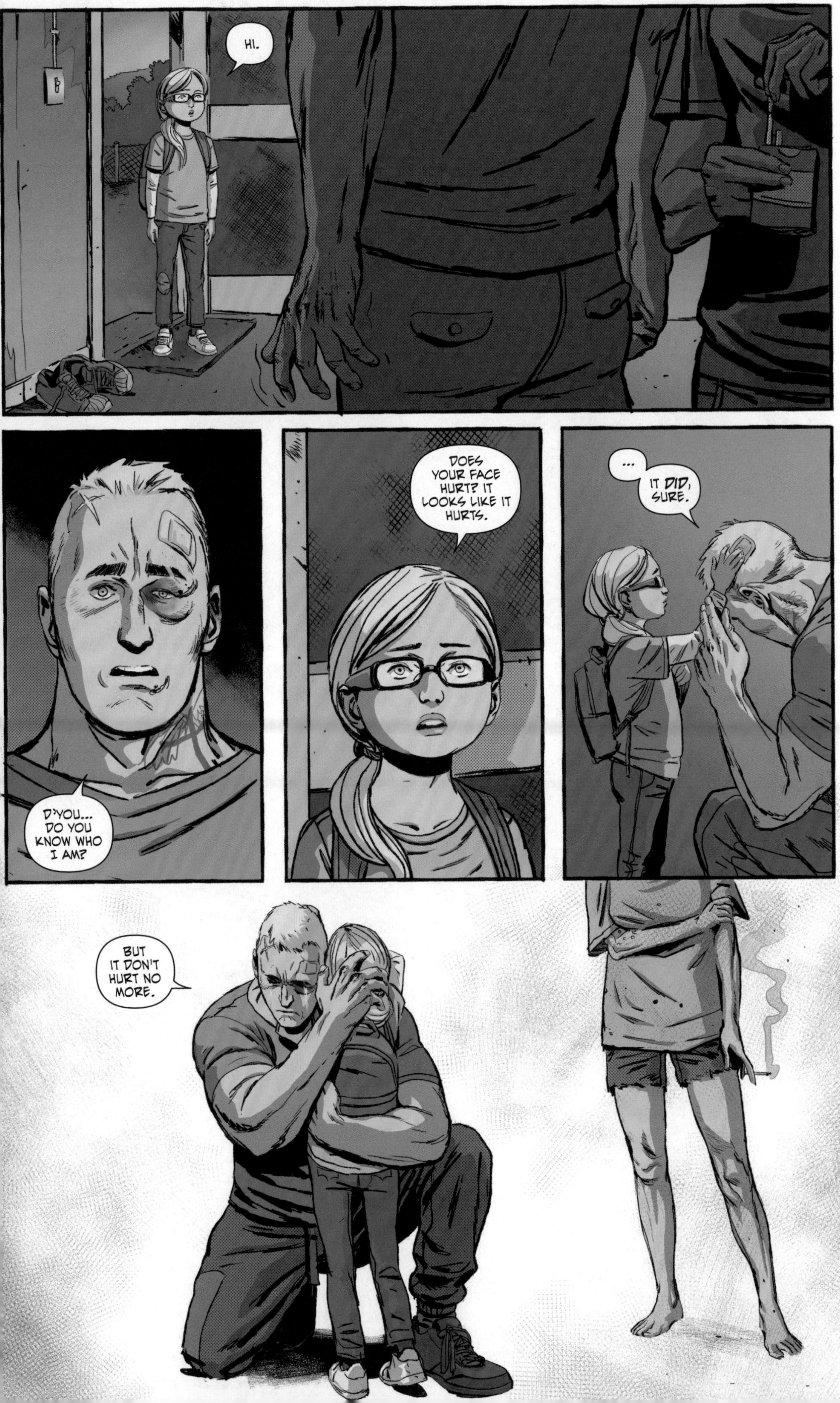
HI.
D'YOU... DO YOU KNOW WHO I AM?
DOES YOUR FACE HURT? IT LOOKS LIKE IT HURTS.
...
IT DID, SURE.
BUT IT DON'T HURT NO MORE.

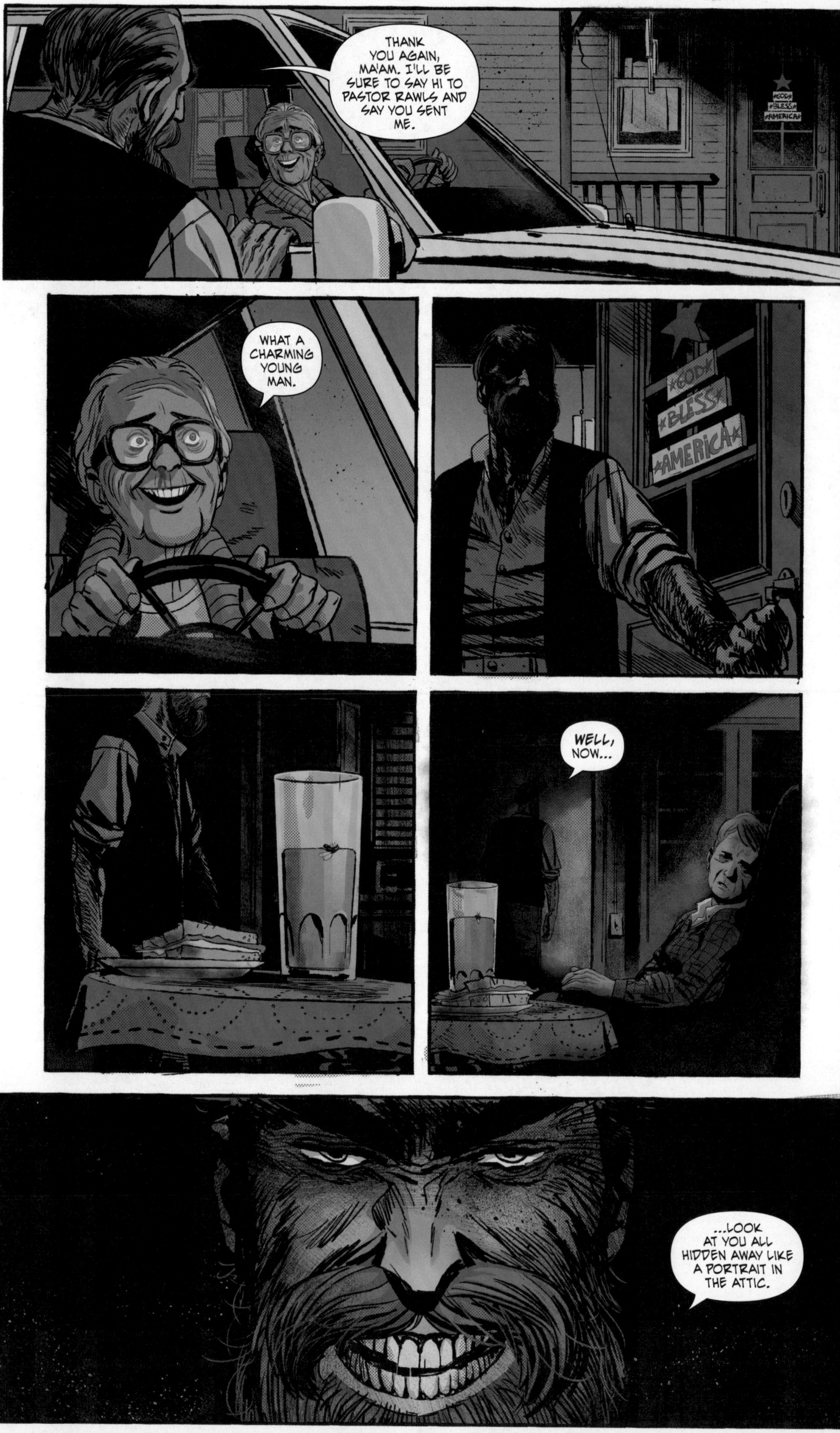
THANK YOU AGAIN, MA'AM. I'LL BE SURE TO SAY HI TO PASTOR RAWLS AND SAY YOU SENT ME.
GOD BLESS AMERICA
WHAT A CHARMING YOUNG MAN.
GOD BLESS AMERICA
WELL, NOW...
...LOOK AT YOU ALL HIDDEN AWAY LIKE A PORTRAIT IN THE ATTIC.

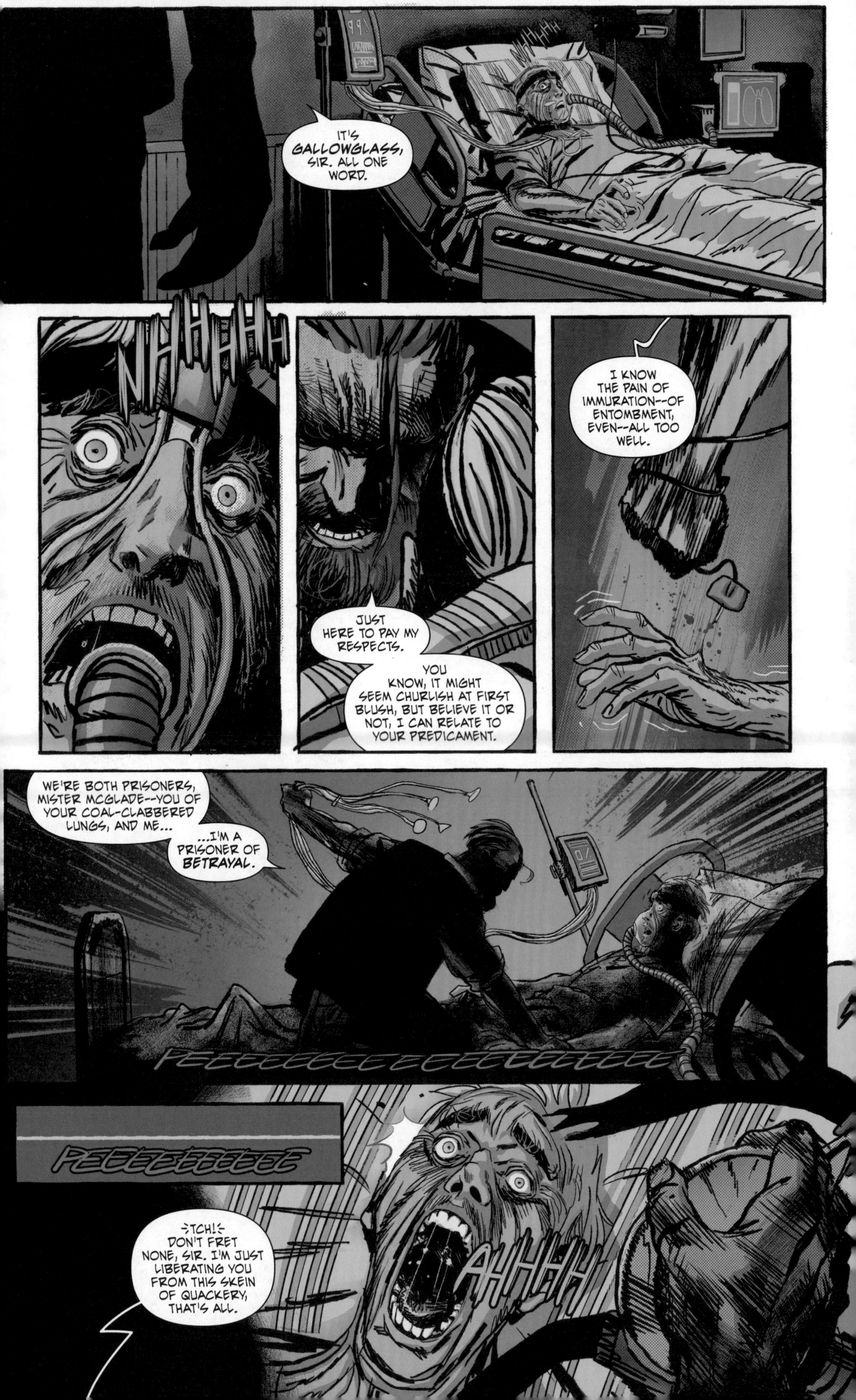
NHHHHH
IT'S GALLOWGLASS, SIR. ALL ONE WORD.
NHHHHH
JUST HERE TO PAY MY RESPECTS.
YOU KNOW, IT MIGHT SEEM CHURLISH AT FIRST BLUSH, BUT BELIEVE IT OR NOT, I CAN RELATE TO YOUR PREDICAMENT.
I KNOW THE PAIN OF IMMURATION--OF ENTOMBMENT, EVEN--ALL TOO WELL.
WE'RE BOTH PRISONERS, MISTER MCGLADE--YOU OF YOUR COAL-CLABBERED LUNGS, AND ME...
...I'M A PRISONER OF BETRAYAL.
PEEEEEEEEEEEEEEEEEEEEEEEEEE
PEEEEEEEEEEEE
TCH!
DON'T FRET NONE, SIR. I'M JUST LIBERATING YOU FROM THIS SKEIN OF QUACKERY, THAT'S ALL.
AHHHH

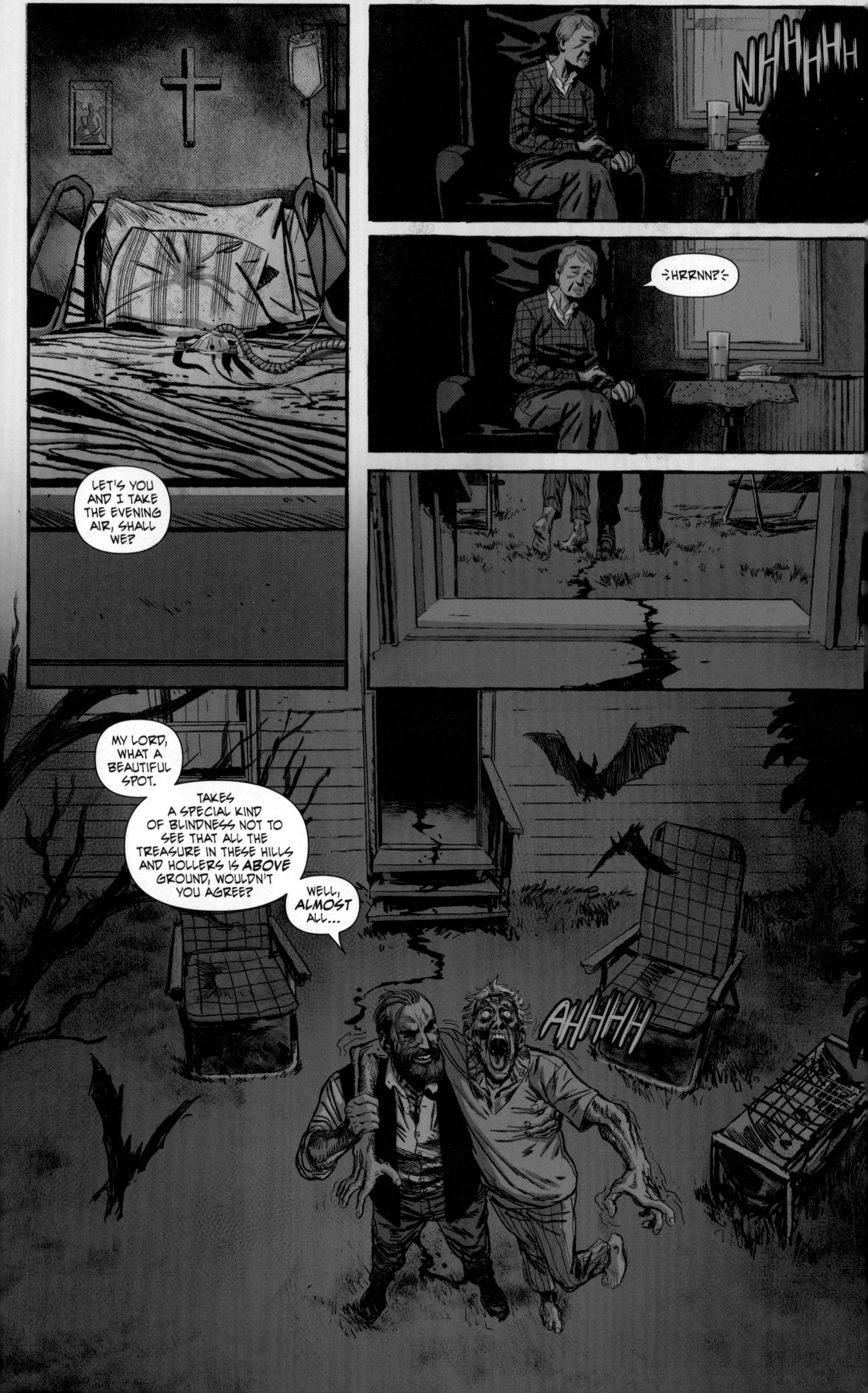
NHHHHH
HRRNN?
LET'S YOU AND I TAKE THE EVENING AIR, SHALL WE?
MY LORD, WHAT A BEAUTIFUL SPOT.
TAKES A SPECIAL KIND OF BLINDNESS NOT TO SEE THAT ALL THE TREASURE IN THESE HILLS AND HOLLERS IS ABOVE GROUND, WOULDN'T YOU AGREE?
WELL, ALMOST ALL...
AHHHH

I WAS CRAWLING AROUND UP THERE IN THOSE VOIDS FOR A *LONG TIME*, MISTER MCGLADE.

IT'S WHERE I MET YOUR BOY.

I WAS LOOKING FOR THIS. I CALL IT 'SNOW COAL.'

IT BURNS COLD AND WITHOUT SURCEASE, IN DEFIANCE OF ALL NATURE.

...BUCK?

A SINGLE INGOT CAN POWER A WHOLE TOWN...

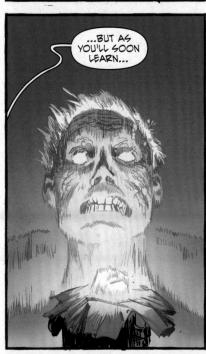

...BUT AS YOU'LL SOON LEARN...

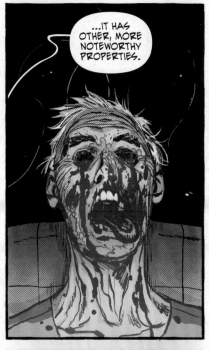

...IT HAS OTHER, MORE NOTEWORTHY PROPERTIES.

I'M HERE TO FIND THE LAST FIRE THE WORLD WILL EVER NEED, MISTER MCGLADE.

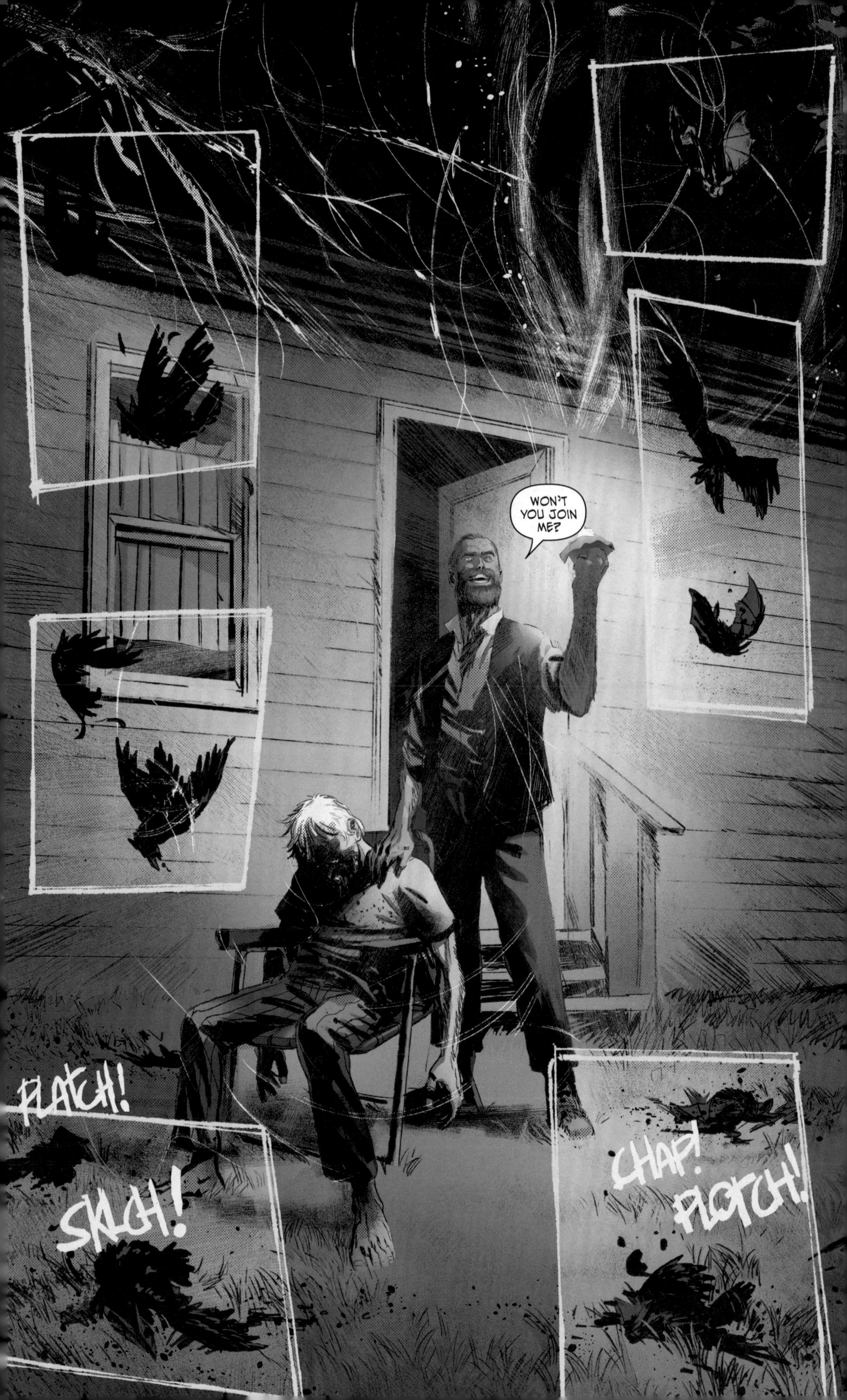
WON'T YOU JOIN ME?
FLATCH!
SKLCH!
CHAP!
PLOTCH!

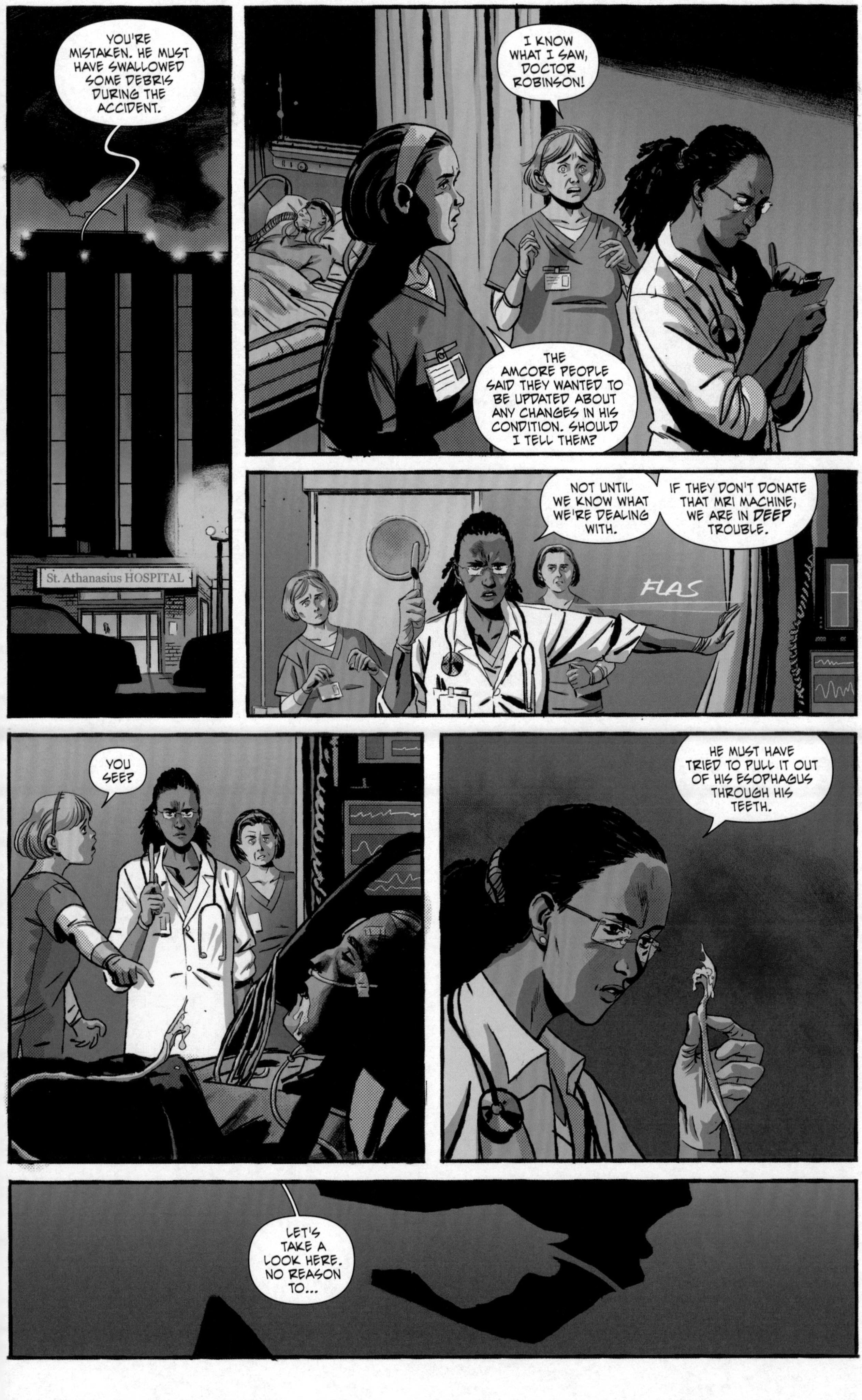
YOU'RE MISTAKEN. HE MUST HAVE SWALLOWED SOME DEBRIS DURING THE ACCIDENT.
St. Athanasius HOSPITAL
I KNOW WHAT I SAW, DOCTOR ROBINSON!
THE AMCORE PEOPLE SAID THEY WANTED TO BE UPDATED ABOUT ANY CHANGES IN HIS CONDITION. SHOULD I TELL THEM?
NOT UNTIL WE KNOW WHAT WE'RE DEALING WITH.
IF THEY DON'T DONATE THAT MRI MACHINE, WE ARE IN DEEP TROUBLE.
FLAS
YOU SEE?
HE MUST HAVE TRIED TO PULL IT OUT OF HIS ESOPHAGUS THROUGH HIS TEETH.
LET'S TAKE A LOOK HERE. NO REASON TO...

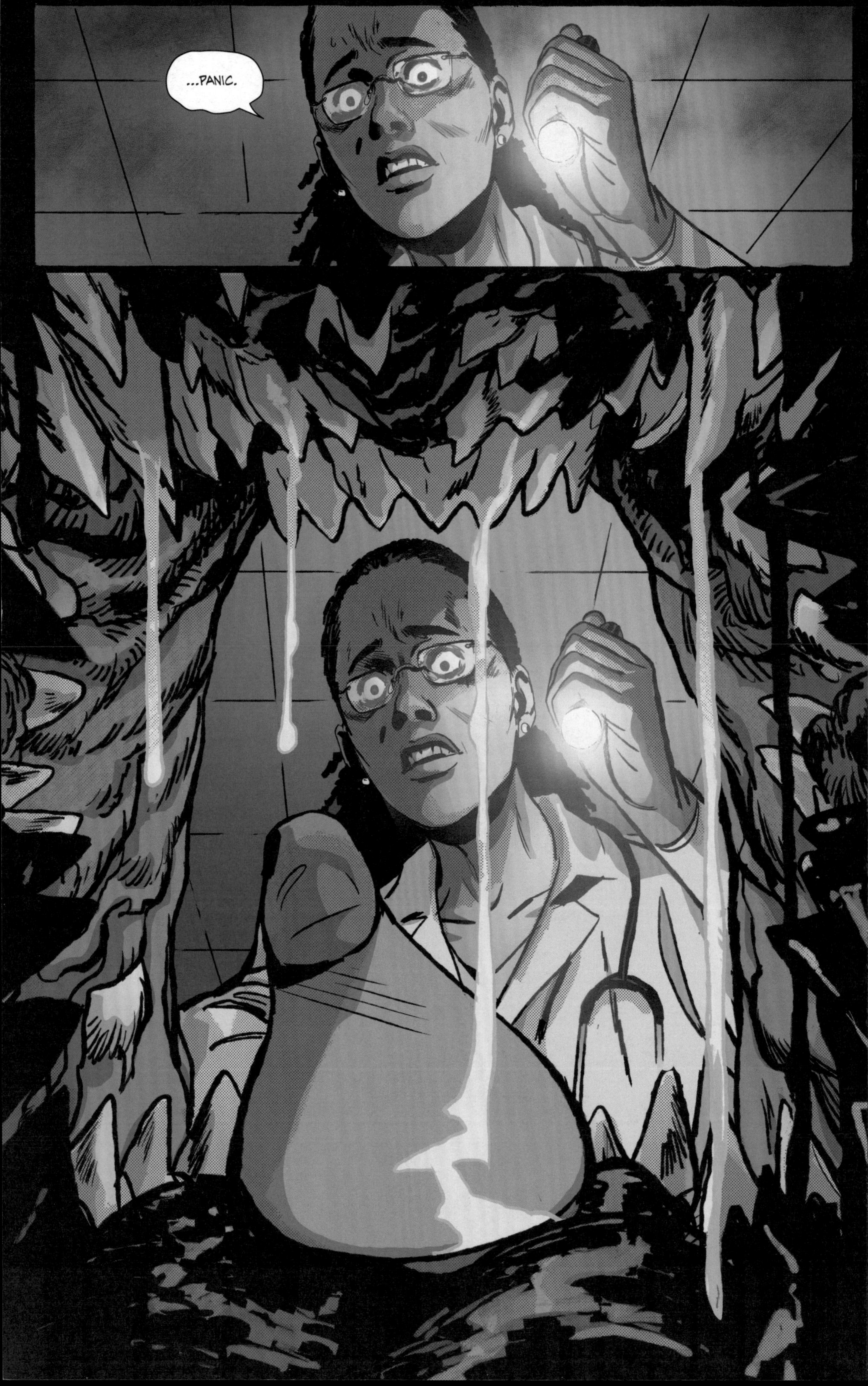
...PANIC.

CHAPTER 3

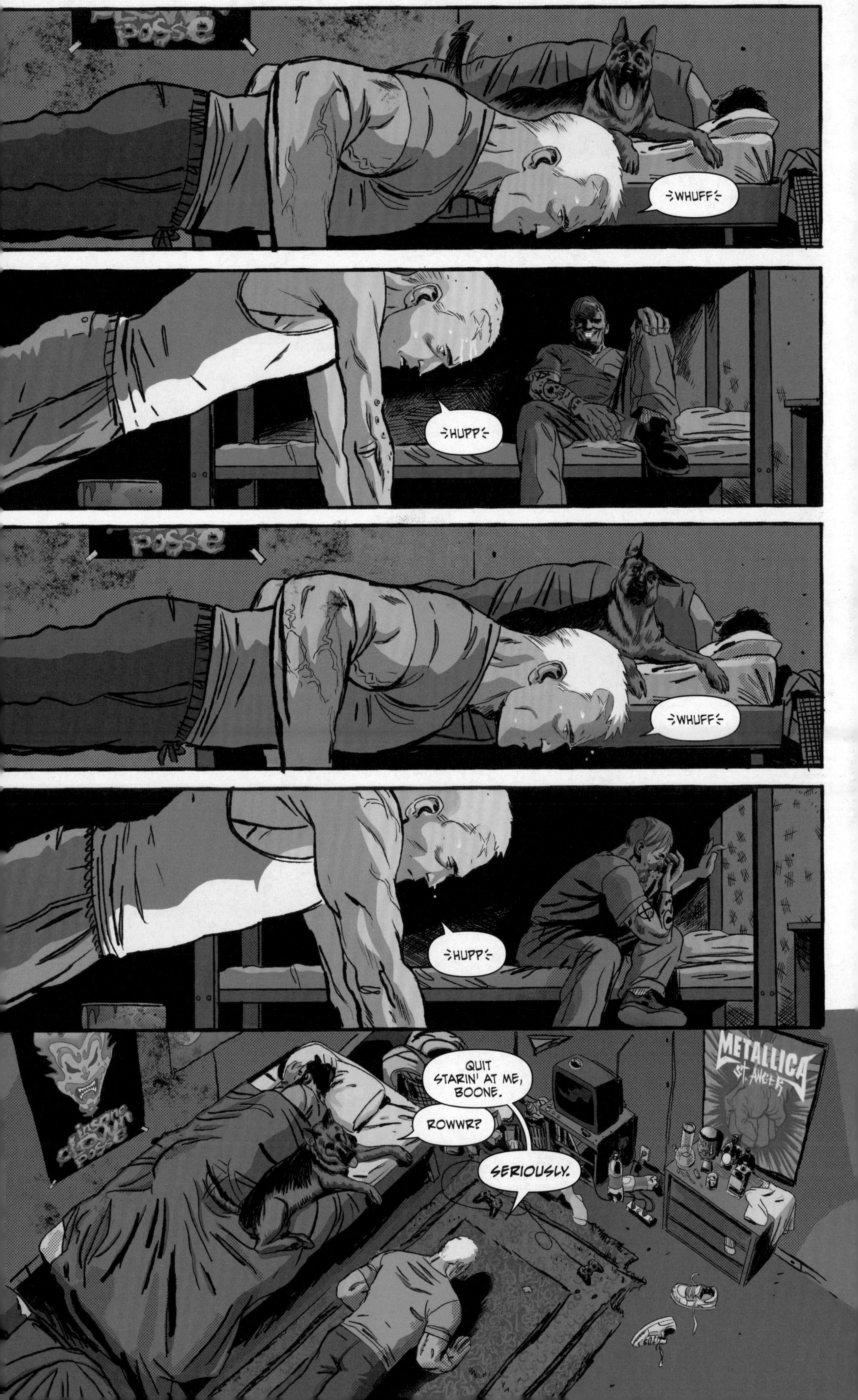
POSSE
WHUFF
HUPP
POSSE
WHUFF
HUPP
METALLICA
ST. ANGER
QUIT STARIN' AT ME, BOONE.
ROWWR?
SERIOUSLY.

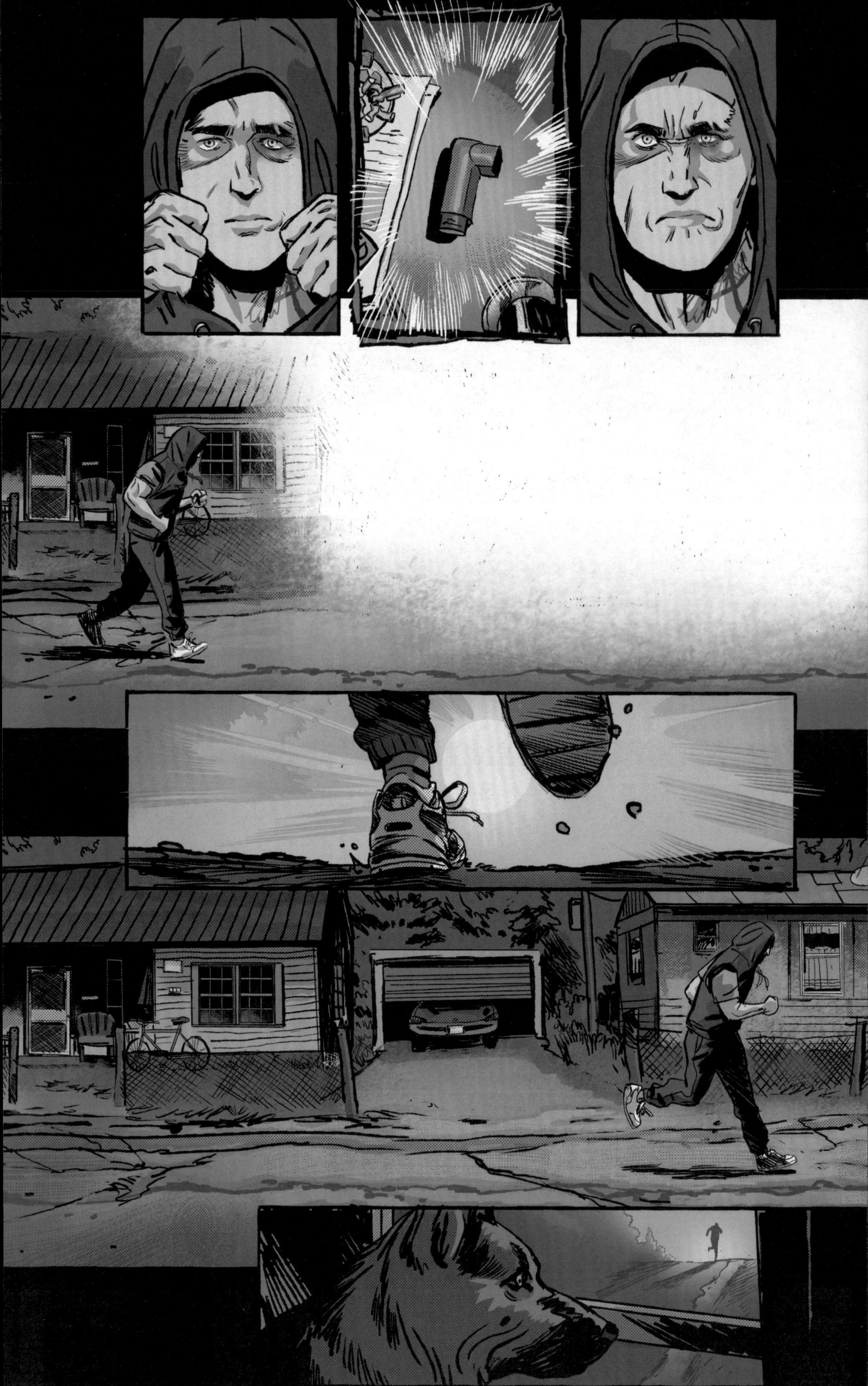

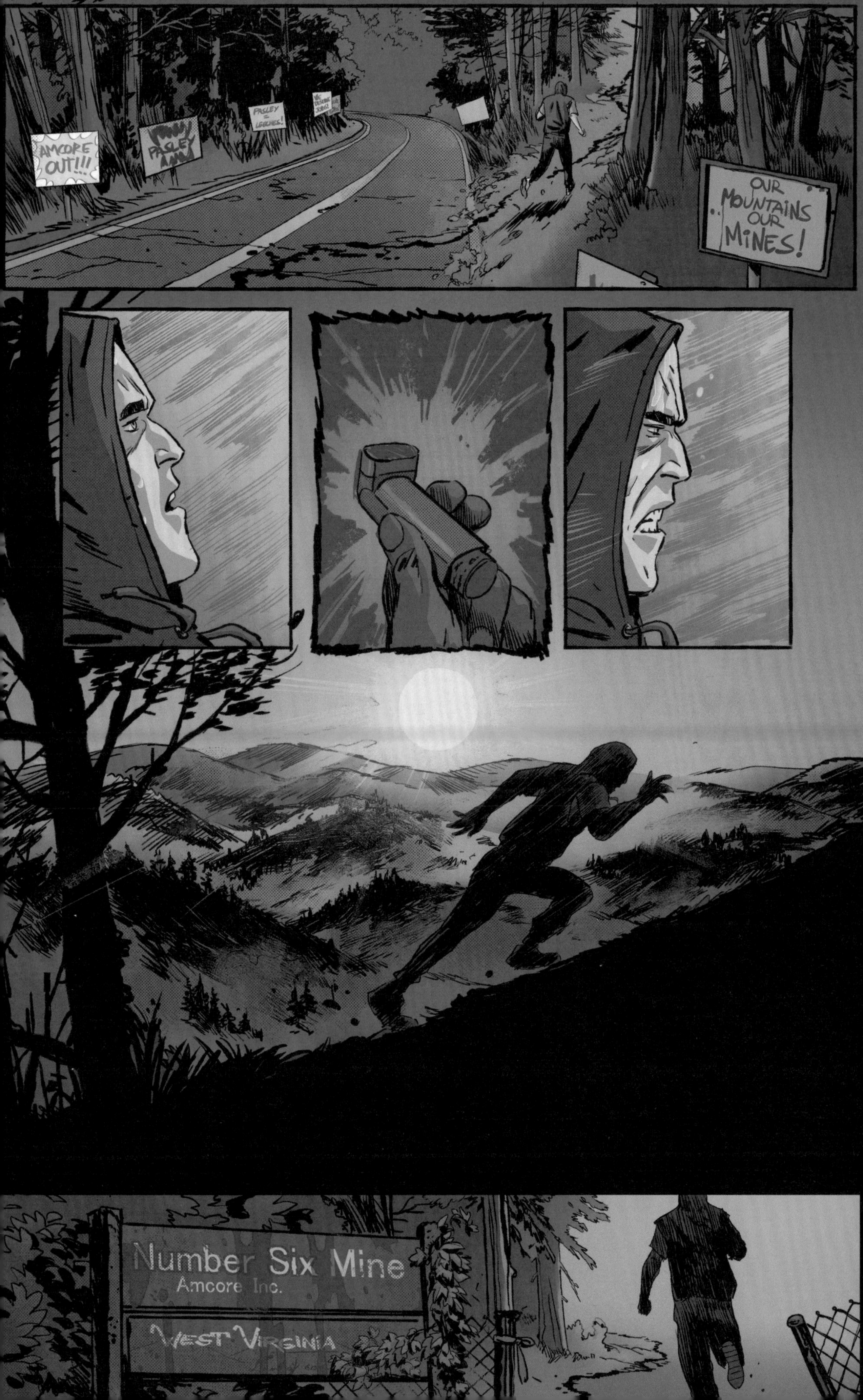
AMCORE OUT!!!
PASLEY
PASLEY = LEECHES!
WE DESERVE JOBS!
OUR MOUNTAINS OUR MINES!
Number Six Mine
Amcore Inc.
West Virginia

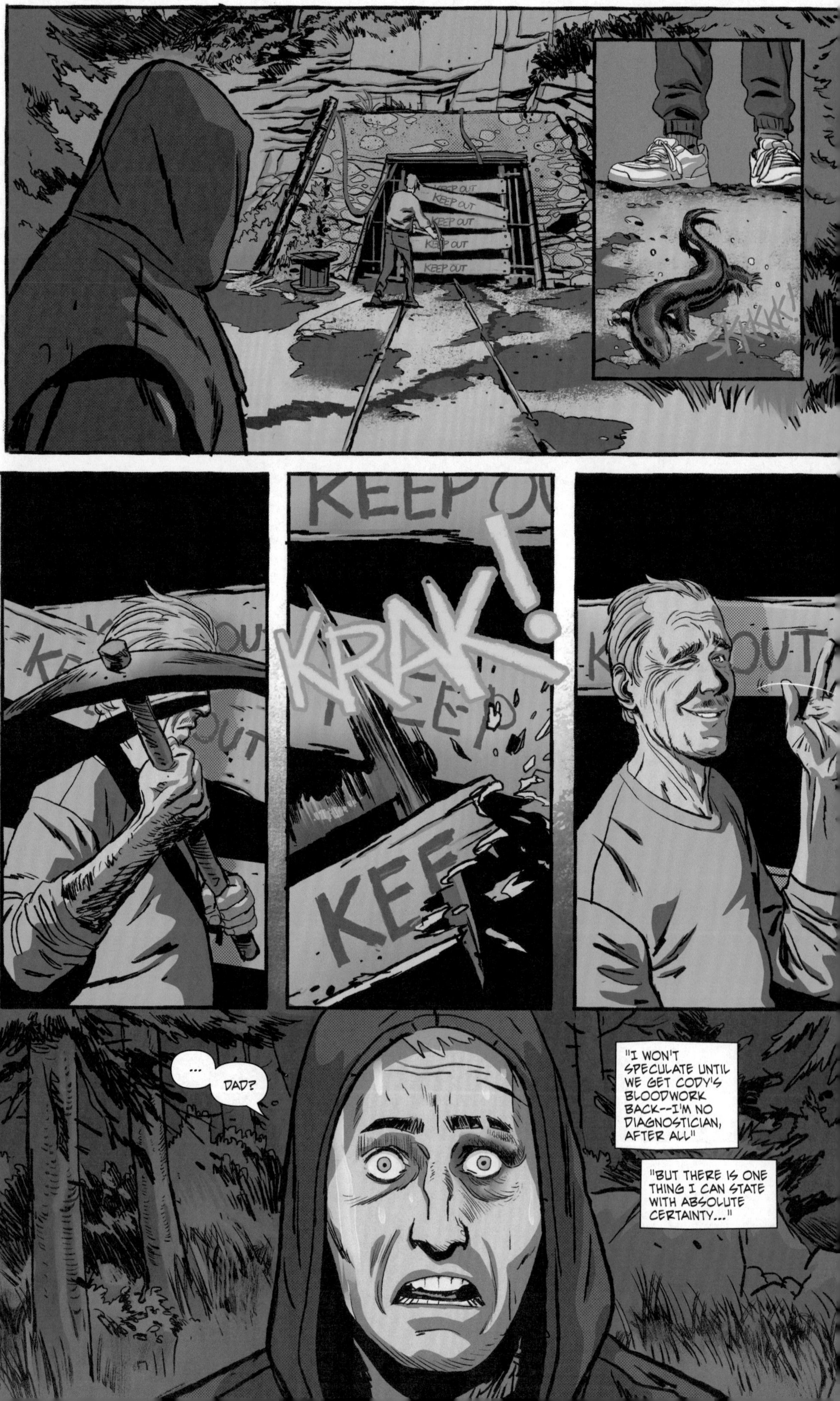
KEEP OUT
KEEP OUT
KEEP OUT
KEEP OUT
KEEP OUT
SKRKKK!
KEEP OUT
KRAK!
...
DAD?
"I WON'T SPECULATE UNTIL WE GET CODY'S BLOODWORK BACK--I'M NO DIAGNOSTICIAN, AFTER ALL"
"BUT THERE IS ONE THING I CAN STATE WITH ABSOLUTE CERTAINTY..."

...IN ALL MY 25 YEARS AS A CLINICIAN, I HAVE NEVER SEEN ANYTHING--*ANYTHING*--REMOTELY LIKE THIS.

MRS. MCGLADE?

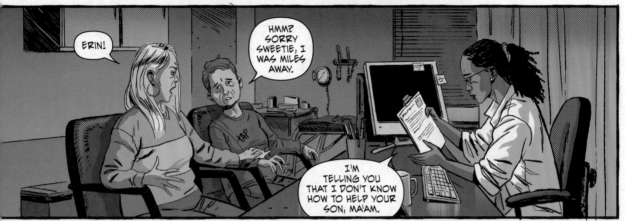

ERIN!

HMM? SORRY SWEETIE, I WAS MILES AWAY.

I'M TELLING YOU THAT I DON'T KNOW HOW TO HELP YOUR SON, MA'AM.

THE PHYSIOLOGICAL CHANGES CODY'S UNDERGOING AREN'T JUST COSMETIC, MRS. MCGLADE.

THE, UH... THE NECROSIS WE'RE SEEING IN HIS SOFT TISSUE IS ONLY THE MOST VISIBLE SYMPTOM OF WHAT APPEARS TO BE A SERIOUS *SOMATIC* EVENT.

I DON'T...

...I GOT REAL BAD TINNITUS, SO COULD YOU SAY ALL THAT AGAIN?

DOCTOR'S SAYING CODY'S GOT SOME NEW KINDA CANCER NOBODY'S SEEN BEFORE.

OH, LIKE EUNICE HART AFTER THAT BUSINESS WITH HER *WELL WATER*?

...

NO. NO, MA'AM.

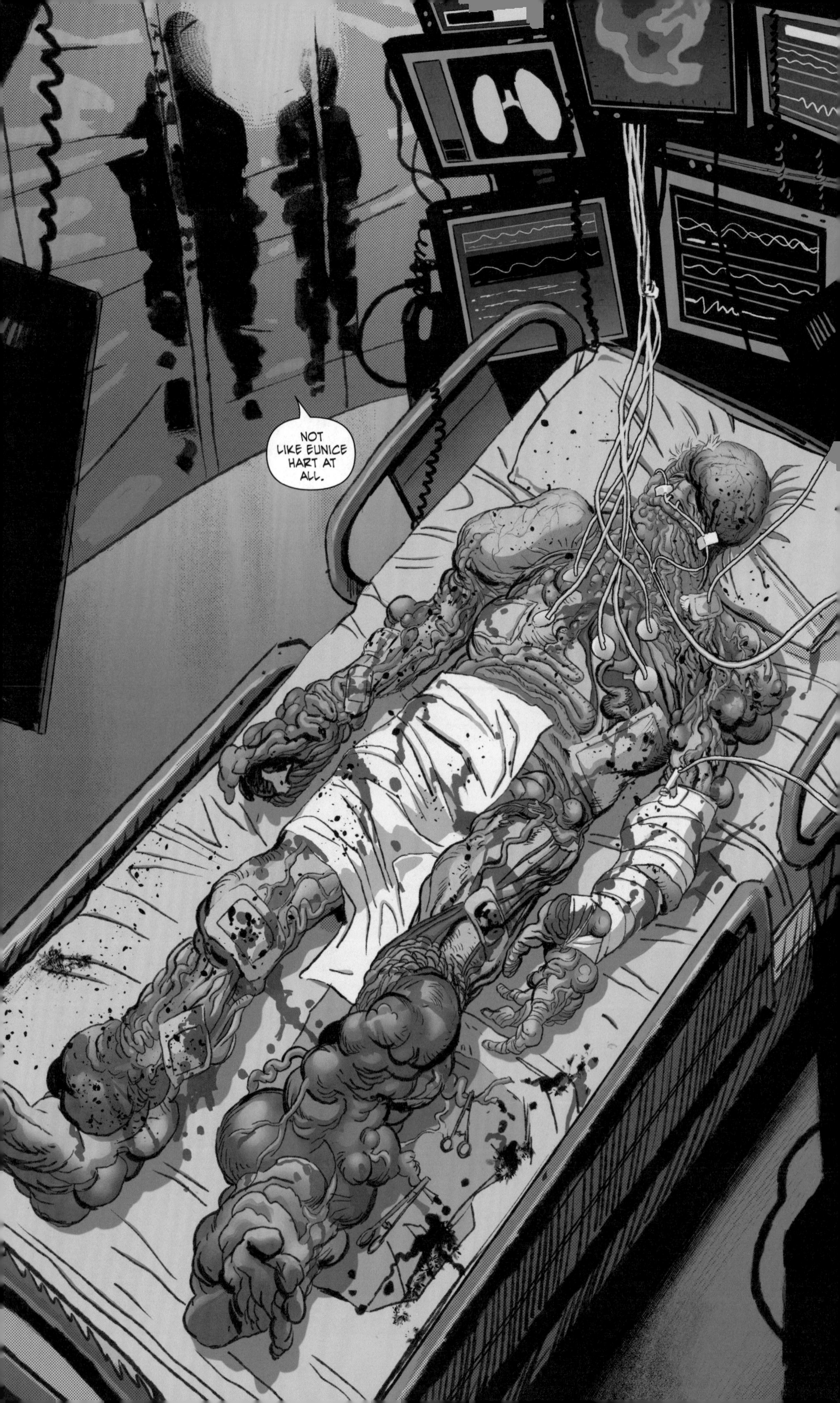
NOT LIKE EUNICE HART AT ALL.

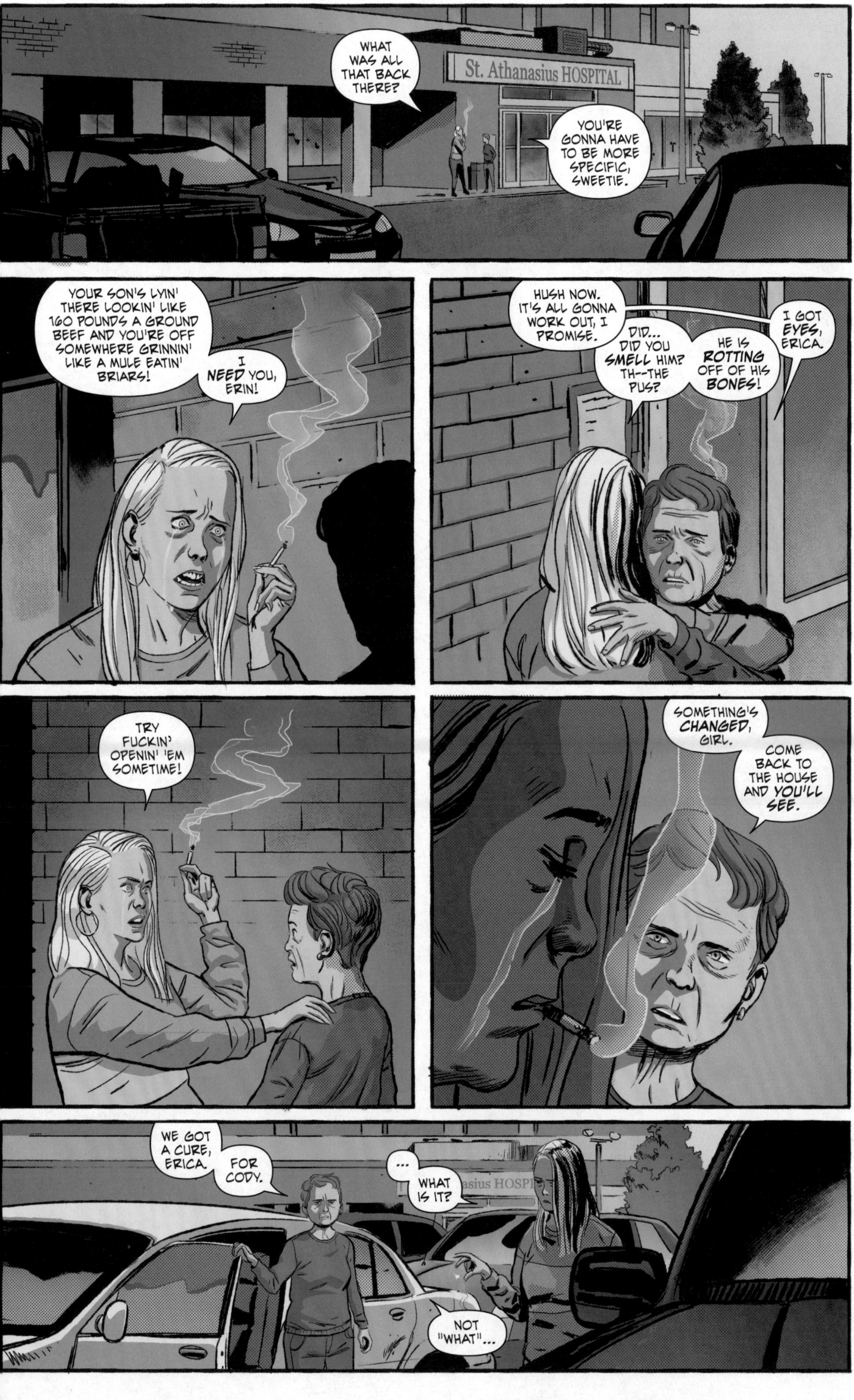

St. Athanasius HOSPITAL
WHAT WAS ALL THAT BACK THERE?
YOU'RE GONNA HAVE TO BE MORE SPECIFIC, SWEETIE.
YOUR SON'S LYIN' THERE LOOKIN' LIKE 160 POUNDS A GROUND BEEF AND YOU'RE OFF SOMEWHERE GRINNIN' LIKE A MULE EATIN' BRIARS!
I NEED YOU, ERIN!
HUSH NOW. IT'S ALL GONNA WORK OUT, I PROMISE.
DID... DID YOU SMELL HIM? TH--THE PUS?
HE IS ROTTING OFF OF HIS BONES!
I GOT EYES, ERICA.
TRY FUCKIN' OPENIN' 'EM SOMETIME!
SOMETHING'S CHANGED, GIRL.
COME BACK TO THE HOUSE AND YOU'LL SEE.
WE GOT A CURE, ERICA.
FOR CODY.
...
WHAT IS IT?
asius HOSP
NOT "WHAT"...

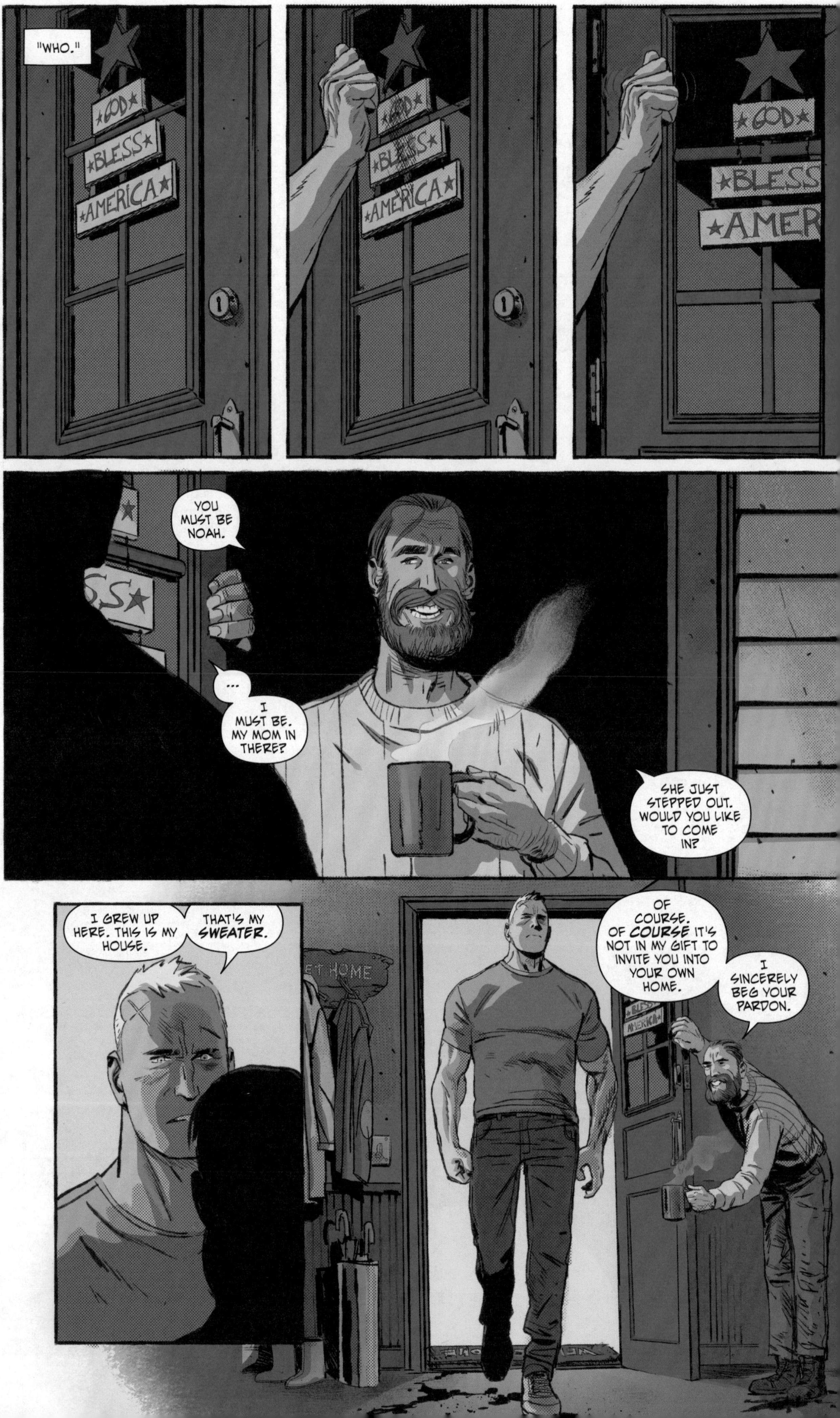
"WHO."
GOD BLESS AMERICA
YOU MUST BE NOAH.
...
I MUST BE. MY MOM IN THERE?
SHE JUST STEPPED OUT. WOULD YOU LIKE TO COME IN?
I GREW UP HERE. THIS IS MY HOUSE.
THAT'S MY SWEATER.
OF COURSE. OF COURSE IT'S NOT IN MY GIFT TO INVITE YOU INTO YOUR OWN HOME.
I SINCERELY BEG YOUR PARDON.

MIGHT WE START OVER?

HOW'S THIS--MAY I COME IN?

CUTE.

SORRY, COULDN'T RESIST.

I'M A FRIEND OF YOUR PARENTS'. NAME'S GALLOWGLASS.

GIVEN NAME OR SURNAME?

...

NOM DE GUERRE.

"I'M GONNA GO CHECK IN ON MY DAD."

"I, UH...FEAR YOU MAY BE STYMIED IN THAT ENDEAVOR."

"'STYMIED', HUH? WELL, WE WOULDN'T WANT THAT NOW, WOULD WE?"

SO IT'S TRUE.

MY MOM KNOW ABOUT THIS?

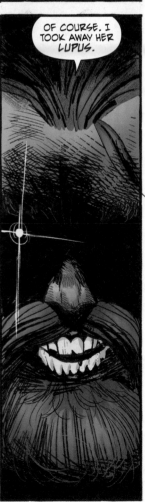

OF COURSE. I TOOK AWAY HER LUPUS.

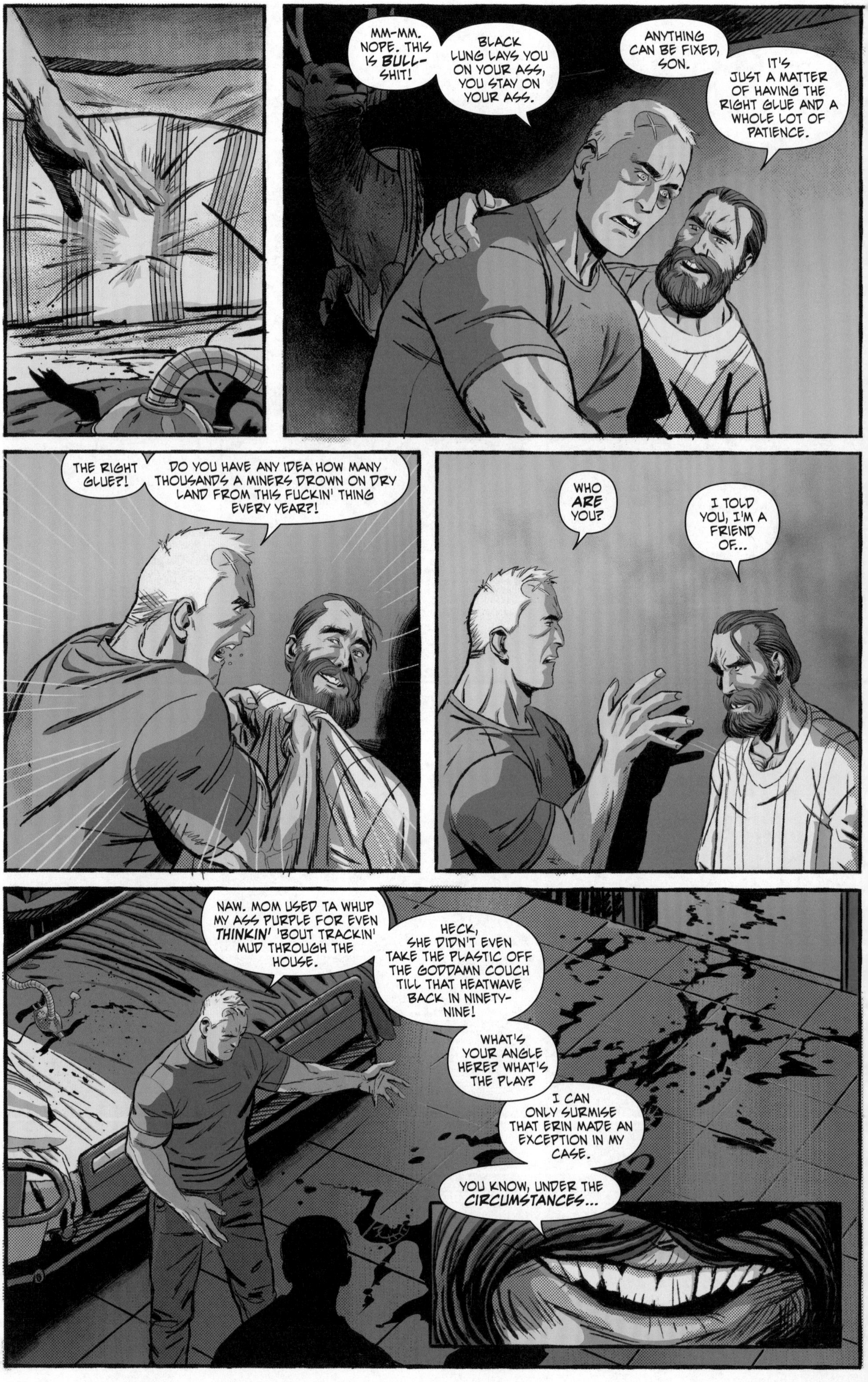
MM-MM. NOPE. THIS IS BULL-SHIT!
BLACK LUNG LAYS YOU ON YOUR ASS, YOU STAY ON YOUR ASS.
ANYTHING CAN BE FIXED, SON.
IT'S JUST A MATTER OF HAVING THE RIGHT GLUE AND A WHOLE LOT OF PATIENCE.
THE RIGHT GLUE?!
DO YOU HAVE ANY IDEA HOW MANY THOUSANDS A MINERS DROWN ON DRY LAND FROM THIS FUCKIN' THING EVERY YEAR?!
WHO ARE YOU?
I TOLD YOU, I'M A FRIEND OF...
NAW. MOM USED TA WHUP MY ASS PURPLE FOR EVEN THINKIN' 'BOUT TRACKIN' MUD THROUGH THE HOUSE.
HECK, SHE DIDN'T EVEN TAKE THE PLASTIC OFF THE GODDAMN COUCH TILL THAT HEATWAVE BACK IN NINETY-NINE!
WHAT'S YOUR ANGLE HERE? WHAT'S THE PLAY?
I CAN ONLY SURMISE THAT ERIN MADE AN EXCEPTION IN MY CASE.
YOU KNOW, UNDER THE CIRCUMSTANCES...

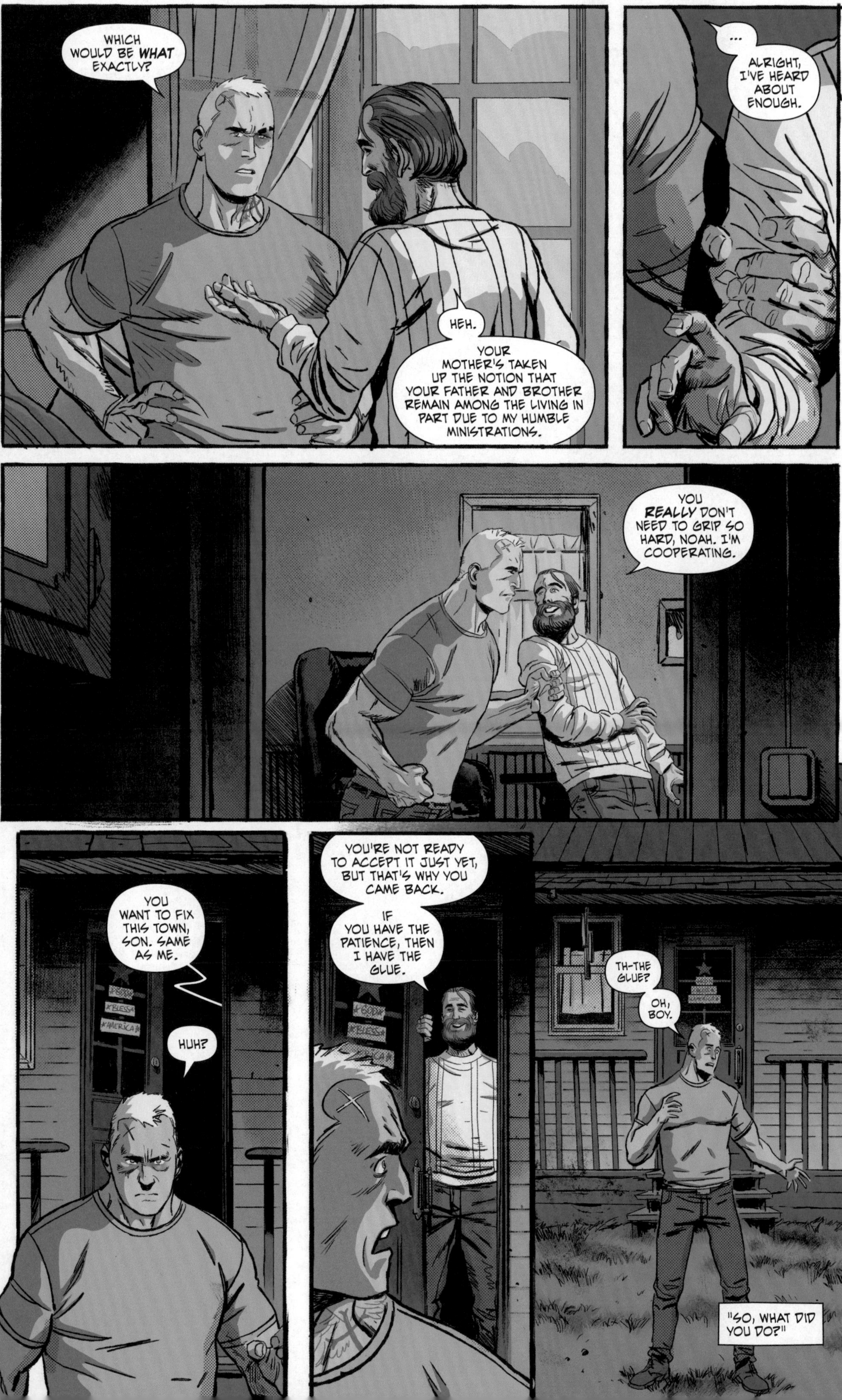
WHICH WOULD BE **WHAT** EXACTLY?
HEH.
YOUR MOTHER'S TAKEN UP THE NOTION THAT YOUR FATHER AND BROTHER REMAIN AMONG THE LIVING IN PART DUE TO MY HUMBLE MINISTRATIONS.
...
ALRIGHT, I'VE HEARD ABOUT ENOUGH.
YOU **REALLY** DON'T NEED TO GRIP SO HARD, NOAH. I'M COOPERATING.
YOU WANT TO FIX THIS TOWN, SON. SAME AS ME.
HUH?
YOU'RE NOT READY TO ACCEPT IT JUST YET, BUT THAT'S WHY YOU CAME BACK.
IF YOU HAVE THE PATIENCE, THEN I HAVE THE GLUE.
TH-THE GLUE?
OH, BOY.
"SO, WHAT DID YOU DO?"

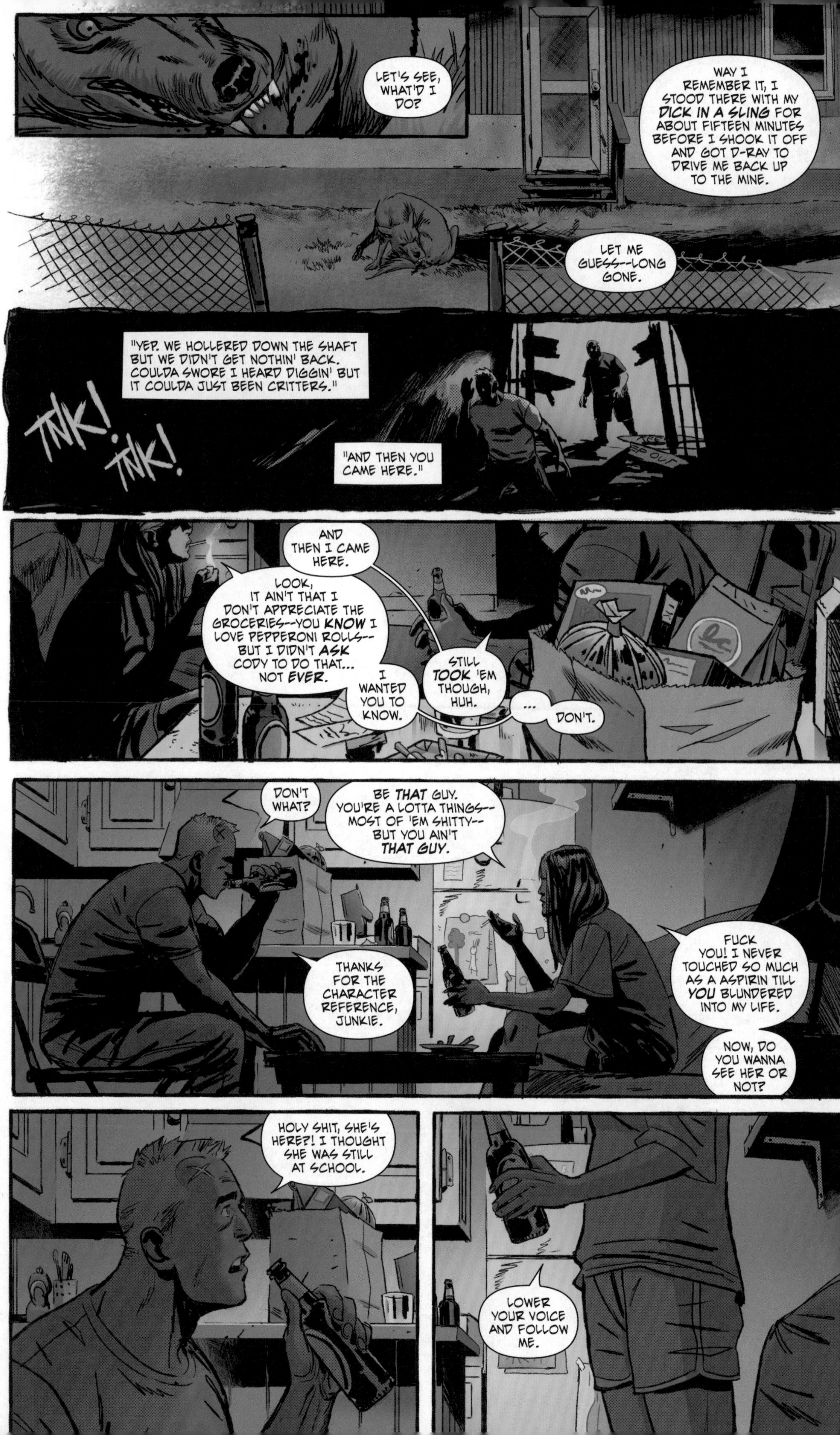
LET'S SEE, WHAT'D I DO?
WAY I REMEMBER IT, I STOOD THERE WITH MY DICK IN A SLING FOR ABOUT FIFTEEN MINUTES BEFORE I SHOOK IT OFF AND GOT D-RAY TO DRIVE ME BACK UP TO THE MINE.
LET ME GUESS--LONG GONE.
"YEP. WE HOLLERED DOWN THE SHAFT BUT WE DIDN'T GET NOTHIN' BACK. COULDA SWORE I HEARD DIGGIN' BUT IT COULDA JUST BEEN CRITTERS."
TNK! TNK!
"AND THEN YOU CAME HERE."
AND THEN I CAME HERE.
LOOK, IT AIN'T THAT I DON'T APPRECIATE THE GROCERIES--YOU KNOW I LOVE PEPPERONI ROLLS--BUT I DIDN'T ASK CODY TO DO THAT... NOT EVER.
I WANTED YOU TO KNOW.
STILL TOOK 'EM THOUGH, HUH.
...
DON'T.
DON'T WHAT?
BE THAT GUY. YOU'RE A LOTTA THINGS--MOST OF 'EM SHITTY--BUT YOU AIN'T THAT GUY.
THANKS FOR THE CHARACTER REFERENCE, JUNKIE.
FUCK YOU! I NEVER TOUCHED SO MUCH AS A ASPIRIN TILL YOU BLUNDERED INTO MY LIFE.
NOW, DO YOU WANNA SEE HER OR NOT?
HOLY SHIT, SHE'S HERE?! I THOUGHT SHE WAS STILL AT SCHOOL.
LOWER YOUR VOICE AND FOLLOW ME.

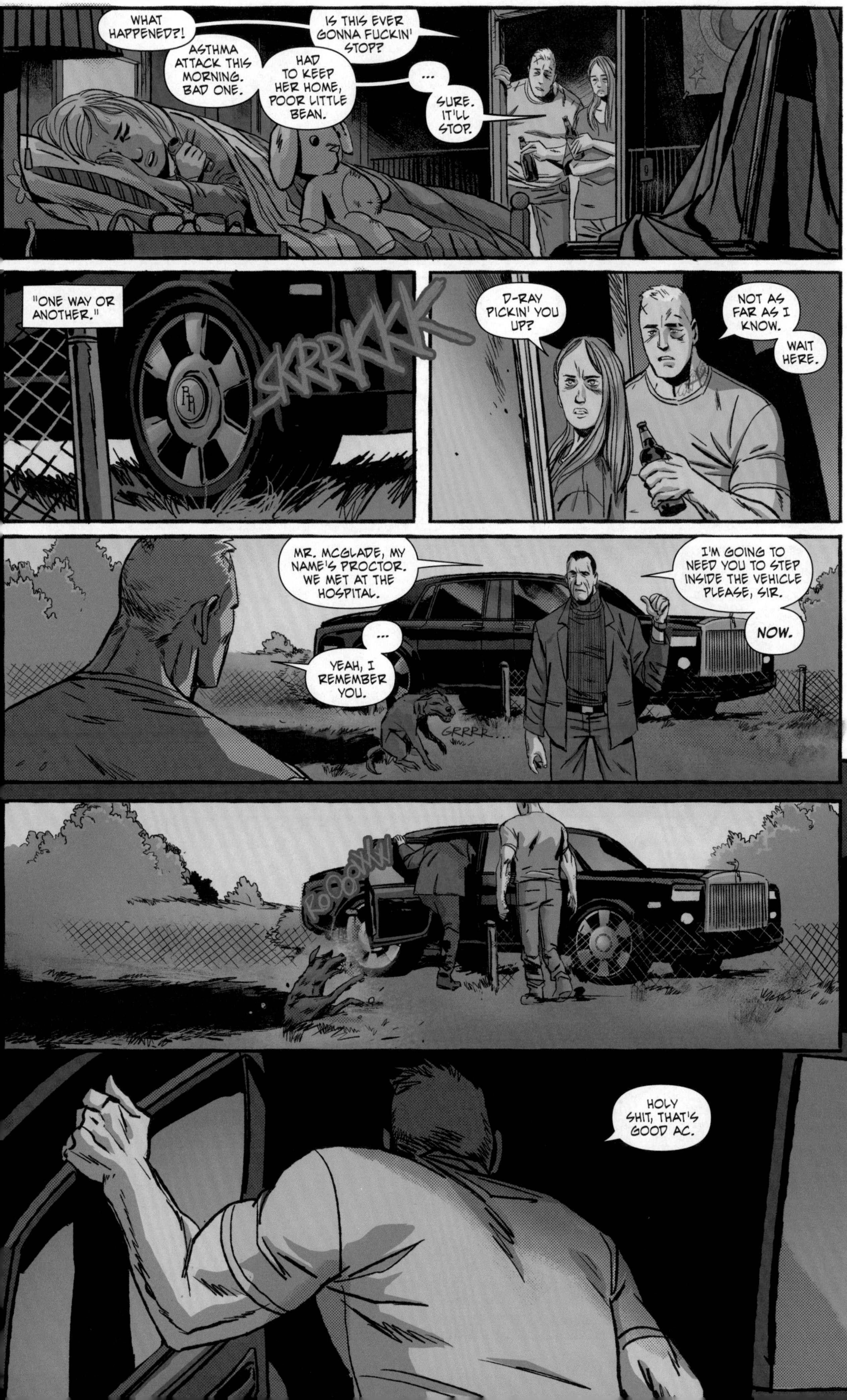
WHAT HAPPENED?!
IS THIS EVER GONNA FUCKIN' STOP?
ASTHMA ATTACK THIS MORNING. BAD ONE.
HAD TO KEEP HER HOME, POOR LITTLE BEAN.
...
SURE. IT'LL STOP.
"ONE WAY OR ANOTHER."
SKRRKKK
D-RAY PICKIN' YOU UP?
NOT AS FAR AS I KNOW.
WAIT HERE.
MR. MCGLADE, MY NAME'S PROCTOR. WE MET AT THE HOSPITAL.
...
YEAH, I REMEMBER YOU.
I'M GOING TO NEED YOU TO STEP INSIDE THE VEHICLE PLEASE, SIR.
NOW.
GRRRR...
KOOOWW!
HOLY SHIT, THAT'S GOOD AC.

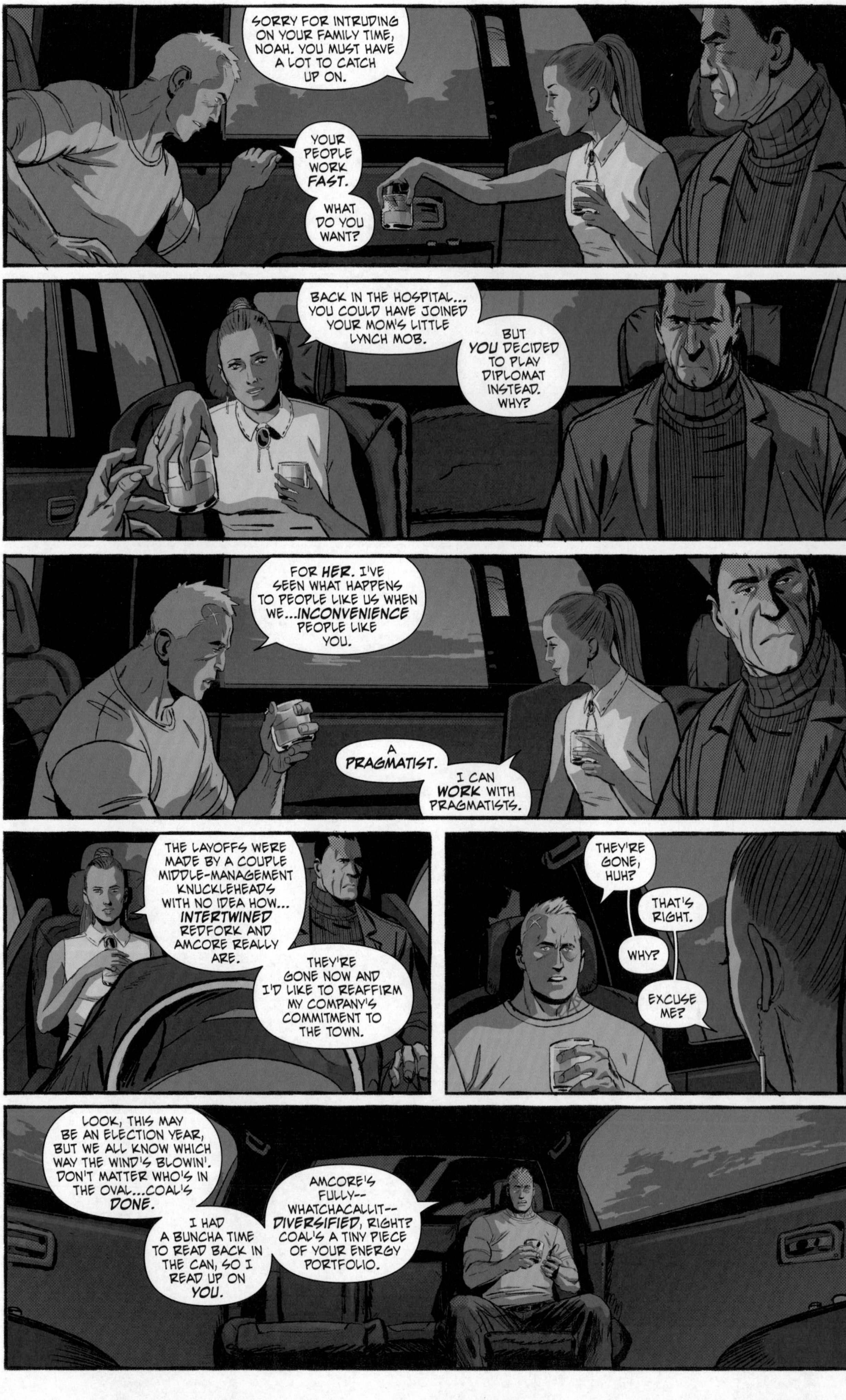
SORRY FOR INTRUDING ON YOUR FAMILY TIME, NOAH. YOU MUST HAVE A LOT TO CATCH UP ON.
YOUR PEOPLE WORK FAST.
WHAT DO YOU WANT?
BACK IN THE HOSPITAL... YOU COULD HAVE JOINED YOUR MOM'S LITTLE LYNCH MOB.
BUT YOU DECIDED TO PLAY DIPLOMAT INSTEAD. WHY?
FOR HER. I'VE SEEN WHAT HAPPENS TO PEOPLE LIKE US WHEN WE...INCONVENIENCE PEOPLE LIKE YOU.
A PRAGMATIST.
I CAN WORK WITH PRAGMATISTS.
THE LAYOFFS WERE MADE BY A COUPLE MIDDLE-MANAGEMENT KNUCKLEHEADS WITH NO IDEA HOW... INTERTWINED REDFORK AND AMCORE REALLY ARE.
THEY'RE GONE NOW AND I'D LIKE TO REAFFIRM MY COMPANY'S COMMITMENT TO THE TOWN.
THEY'RE GONE, HUH?
THAT'S RIGHT.
WHY?
EXCUSE ME?
LOOK, THIS MAY BE AN ELECTION YEAR, BUT WE ALL KNOW WHICH WAY THE WIND'S BLOWIN'. DON'T MATTER WHO'S IN THE OVAL...COAL'S DONE.
I HAD A BUNCHA TIME TO READ BACK IN THE CAN, SO I READ UP ON YOU.
AMCORE'S FULLY--WHATCHACALLIT--DIVERSIFIED, RIGHT? COAL'S A TINY PIECE OF YOUR ENERGY PORTFOLIO.

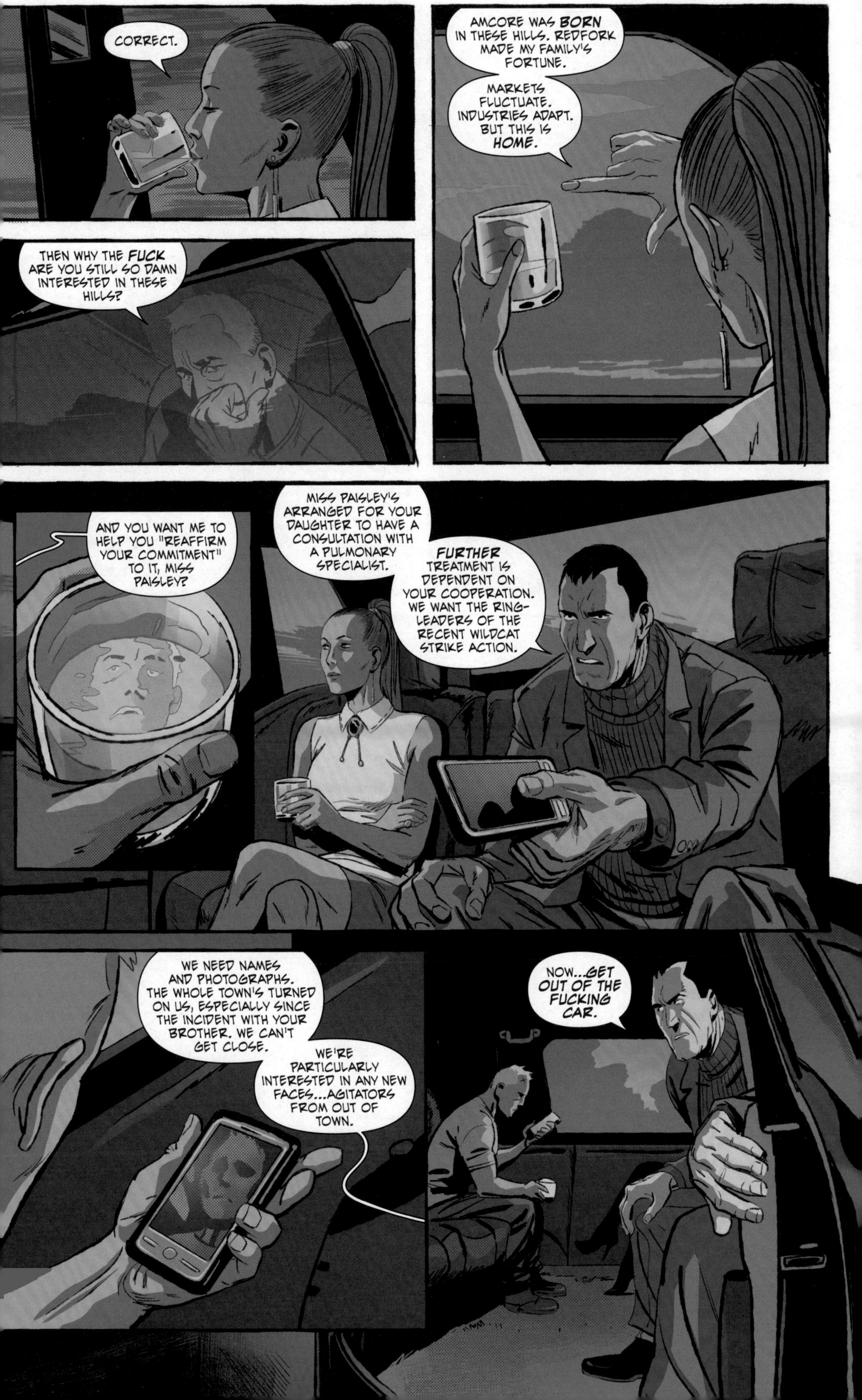
CORRECT.
AMCORE WAS BORN IN THESE HILLS. REDFORK MADE MY FAMILY'S FORTUNE.
MARKETS FLUCTUATE. INDUSTRIES ADAPT. BUT THIS IS HOME.
THEN WHY THE FUCK ARE YOU STILL SO DAMN INTERESTED IN THESE HILLS?
AND YOU WANT ME TO HELP YOU "REAFFIRM YOUR COMMITMENT" TO IT, MISS PAISLEY?
MISS PAISLEY'S ARRANGED FOR YOUR DAUGHTER TO HAVE A CONSULTATION WITH A PULMONARY SPECIALIST.
FURTHER TREATMENT IS DEPENDENT ON YOUR COOPERATION. WE WANT THE RING-LEADERS OF THE RECENT WILDCAT STRIKE ACTION.
WE NEED NAMES AND PHOTOGRAPHS. THE WHOLE TOWN'S TURNED ON US, ESPECIALLY SINCE THE INCIDENT WITH YOUR BROTHER. WE CAN'T GET CLOSE.
WE'RE PARTICULARLY INTERESTED IN ANY NEW FACES...AGITATORS FROM OUT OF TOWN.
NOW...GET OUT OF THE FUCKING CAR.

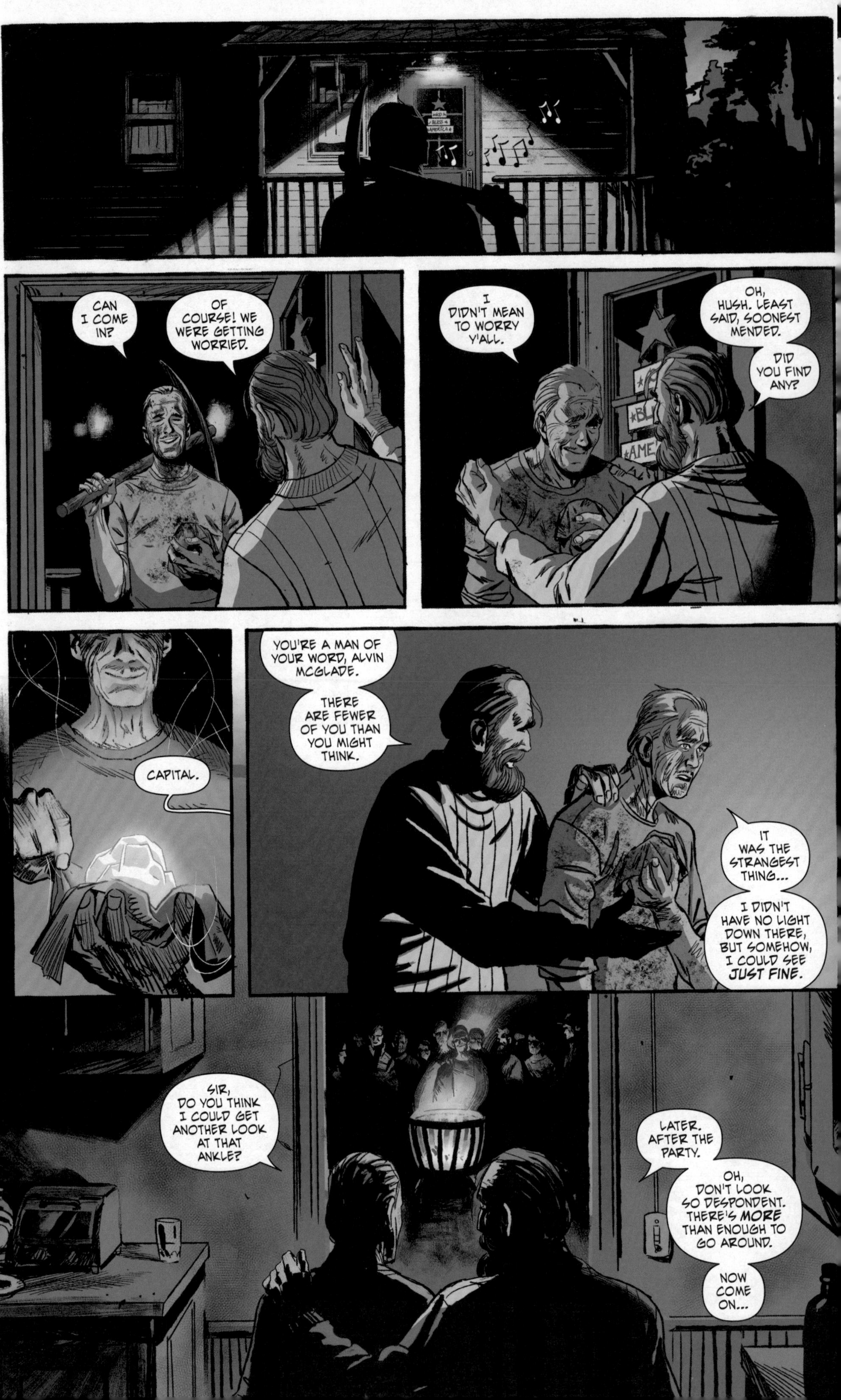
GOD BLESS AMERICA
CAN I COME IN?
OF COURSE! WE WERE GETTING WORRIED.
I DIDN'T MEAN TO WORRY Y'ALL.
OH, HUSH. LEAST SAID, SOONEST MENDED.
DID YOU FIND ANY?
CAPITAL.
YOU'RE A MAN OF YOUR WORD, ALVIN MCGLADE.
THERE ARE FEWER OF YOU THAN YOU MIGHT THINK.
IT WAS THE STRANGEST THING...
I DIDN'T HAVE NO LIGHT DOWN THERE, BUT SOMEHOW, I COULD SEE **JUST FINE**.
SIR, DO YOU THINK I COULD GET ANOTHER LOOK AT THAT ANKLE?
LATER. AFTER THE PARTY.
OH, DON'T LOOK SO DESPONDENT. THERE'S ***MORE*** THAN ENOUGH TO GO AROUND.
NOW COME ON...

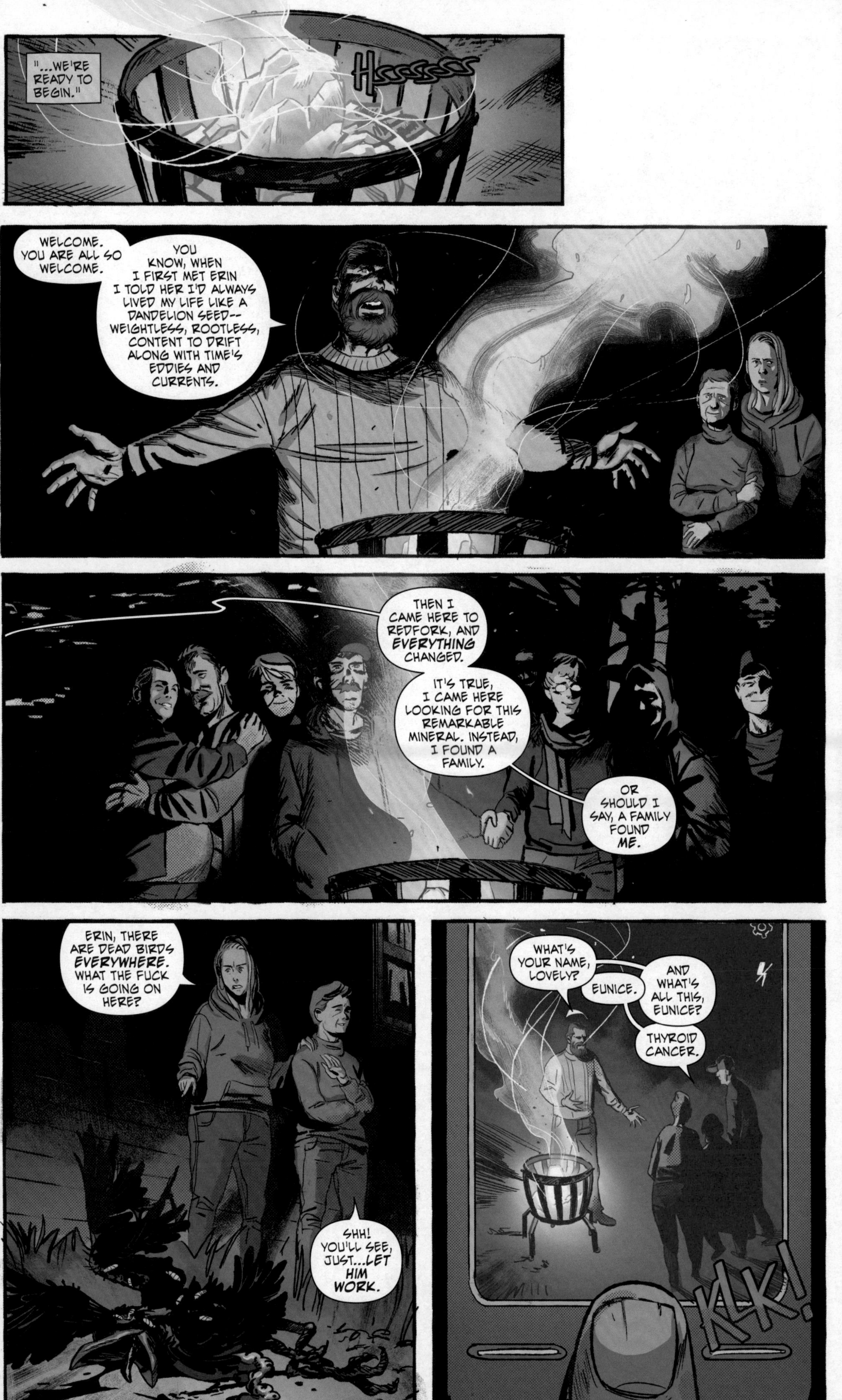
"...WE'RE READY TO BEGIN."
HSSSSSSS
WELCOME. YOU ARE ALL SO WELCOME.
YOU KNOW, WHEN I FIRST MET ERIN I TOLD HER I'D ALWAYS LIVED MY LIFE LIKE A DANDELION SEED-- WEIGHTLESS, ROOTLESS, CONTENT TO DRIFT ALONG WITH TIME'S EDDIES AND CURRENTS.
THEN I CAME HERE TO REDFORK, AND **EVERYTHING** CHANGED.
IT'S TRUE, I CAME HERE LOOKING FOR THIS REMARKABLE MINERAL. INSTEAD, I FOUND A FAMILY.
OR SHOULD I SAY, A FAMILY FOUND **ME**.
ERIN, THERE ARE DEAD BIRDS **EVERYWHERE**. WHAT THE FUCK IS GOING ON HERE?
SHH! YOU'LL SEE, JUST...**LET HIM WORK**.
WHAT'S YOUR NAME, LOVELY?
EUNICE.
AND WHAT'S ALL THIS, EUNICE?
THYROID CANCER.
KLK!

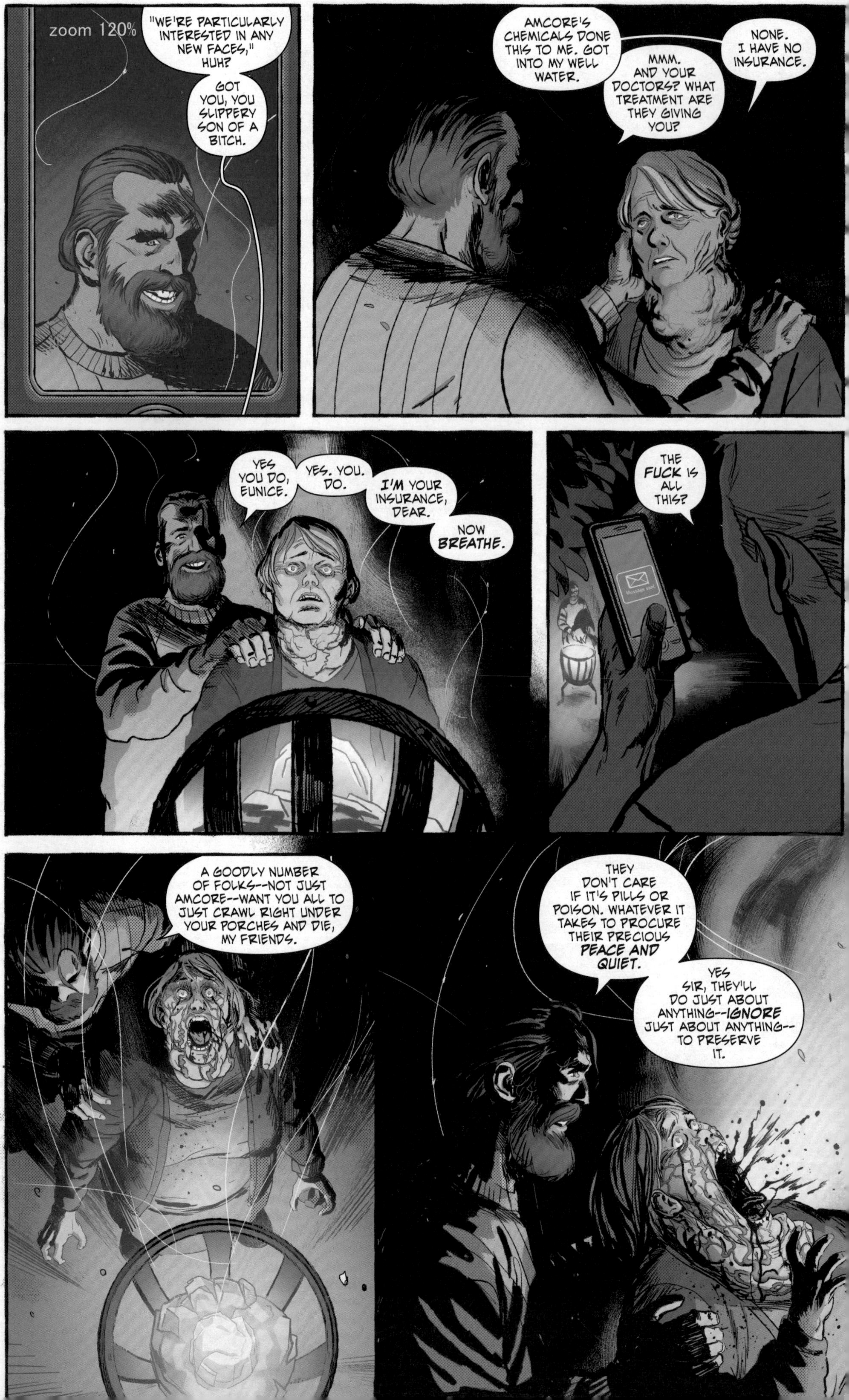
zoom 120%
"WE'RE PARTICULARLY INTERESTED IN ANY NEW FACES," HUH?
GOT YOU, YOU SLIPPERY SON OF A BITCH.
AMCORE'S CHEMICALS DONE THIS TO ME. GOT INTO MY WELL WATER.
MMM. AND YOUR DOCTORS? WHAT TREATMENT ARE THEY GIVING YOU?
NONE. I HAVE NO INSURANCE.
YES YOU DO, EUNICE.
YES. YOU. DO.
I'M YOUR INSURANCE, DEAR.
NOW BREATHE.
THE FUCK IS ALL THIS?
A GOODLY NUMBER OF FOLKS--NOT JUST AMCORE--WANT YOU ALL TO JUST CRAWL RIGHT UNDER YOUR PORCHES AND DIE, MY FRIENDS.
THEY DON'T CARE IF IT'S PILLS OR POISON. WHATEVER IT TAKES TO PROCURE THEIR PRECIOUS PEACE AND QUIET.
YES SIR, THEY'LL DO JUST ABOUT ANYTHING--IGNORE JUST ABOUT ANYTHING--TO PRESERVE IT.

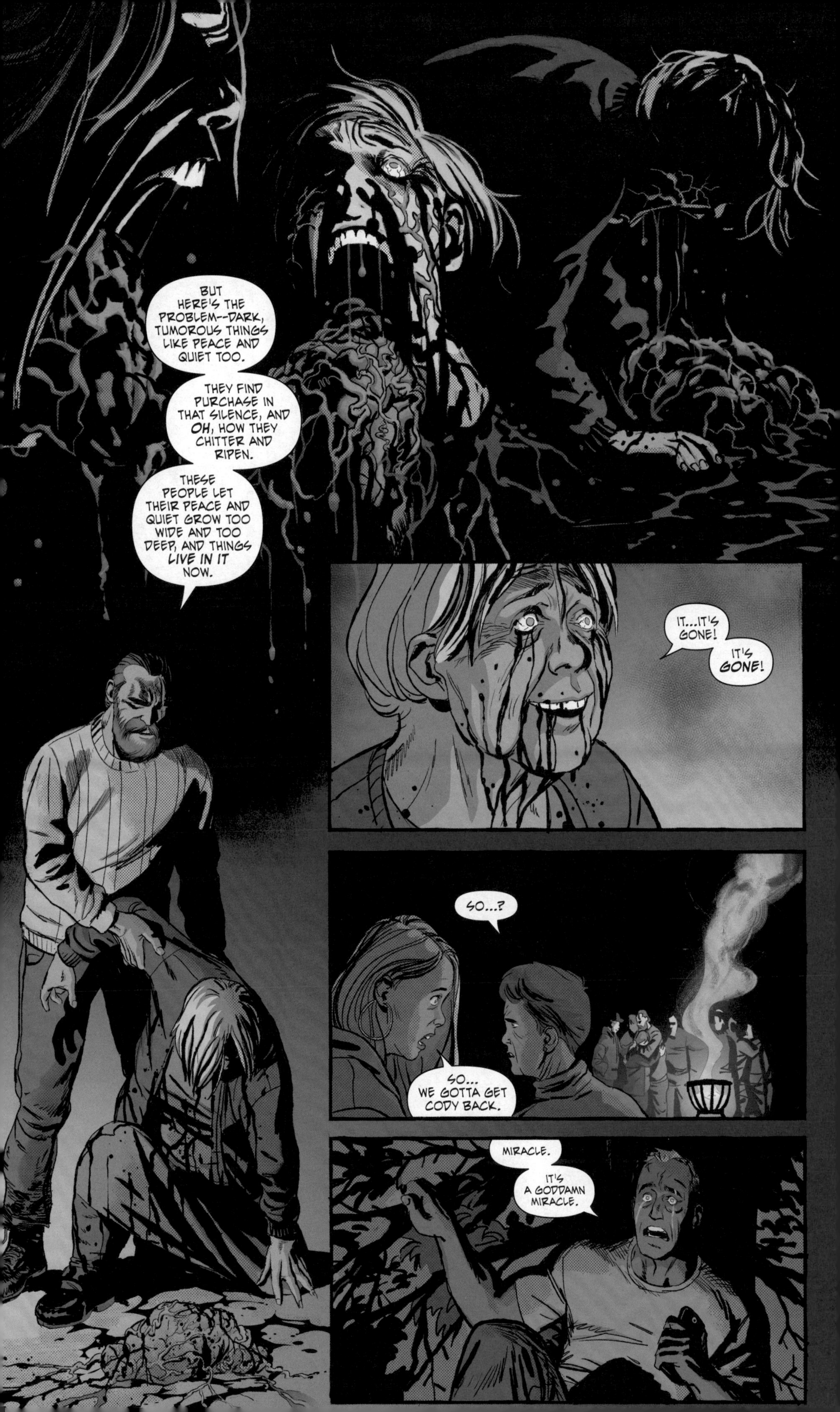
BUT HERE'S THE PROBLEM--DARK, TUMOROUS THINGS LIKE PEACE AND QUIET TOO.
THEY FIND PURCHASE IN THAT SILENCE, AND OH, HOW THEY CHITTER AND RIPEN.
THESE PEOPLE LET THEIR PEACE AND QUIET GROW TOO WIDE AND TOO DEEP, AND THINGS LIVE IN IT NOW.
IT...IT'S GONE!
IT'S GONE!
SO...?
SO... WE GOTTA GET CODY BACK.
MIRACLE.
IT'S A GODDAMN MIRACLE.

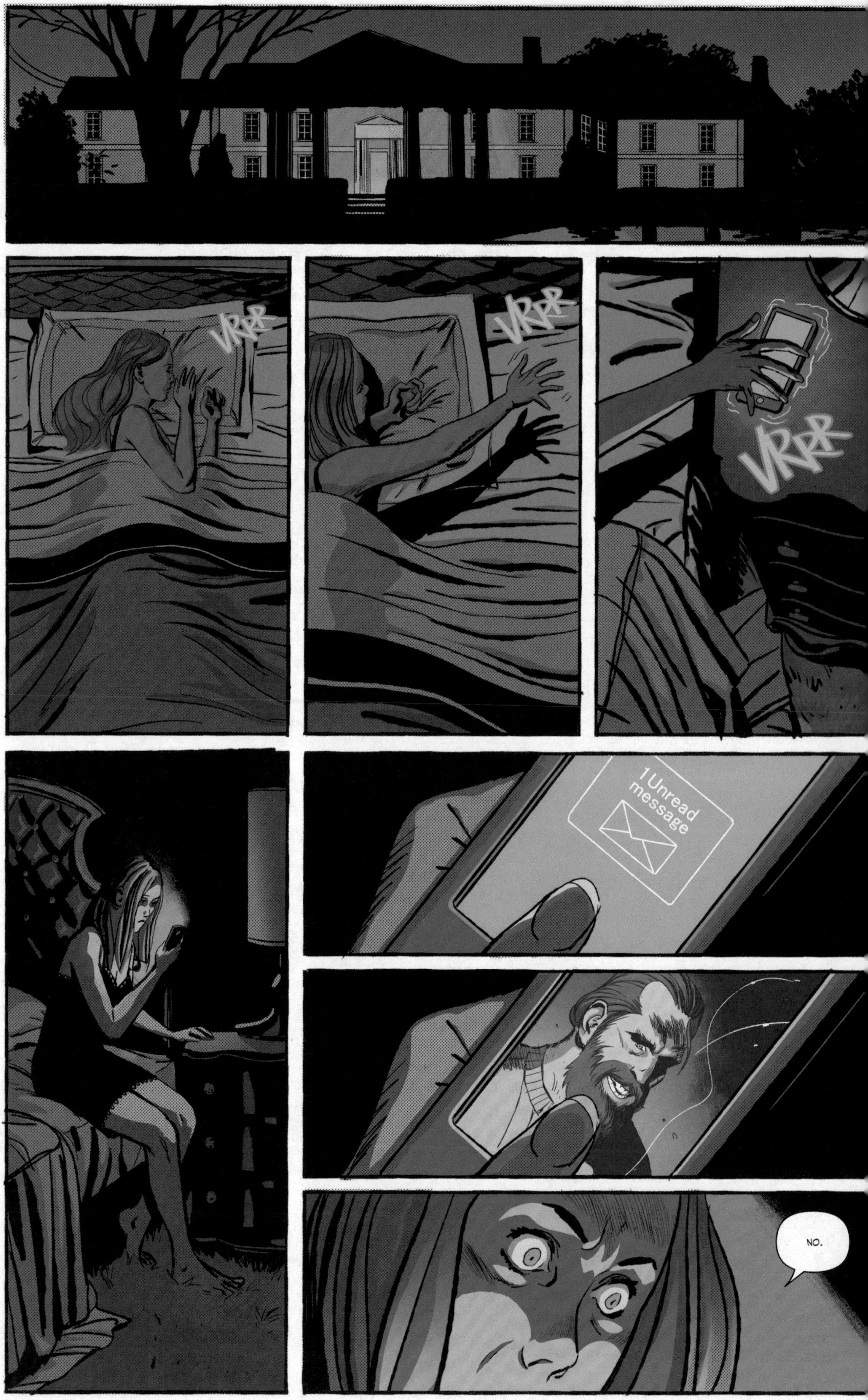
VRRR
VRRR
VRRR
1 Unread message
NO.

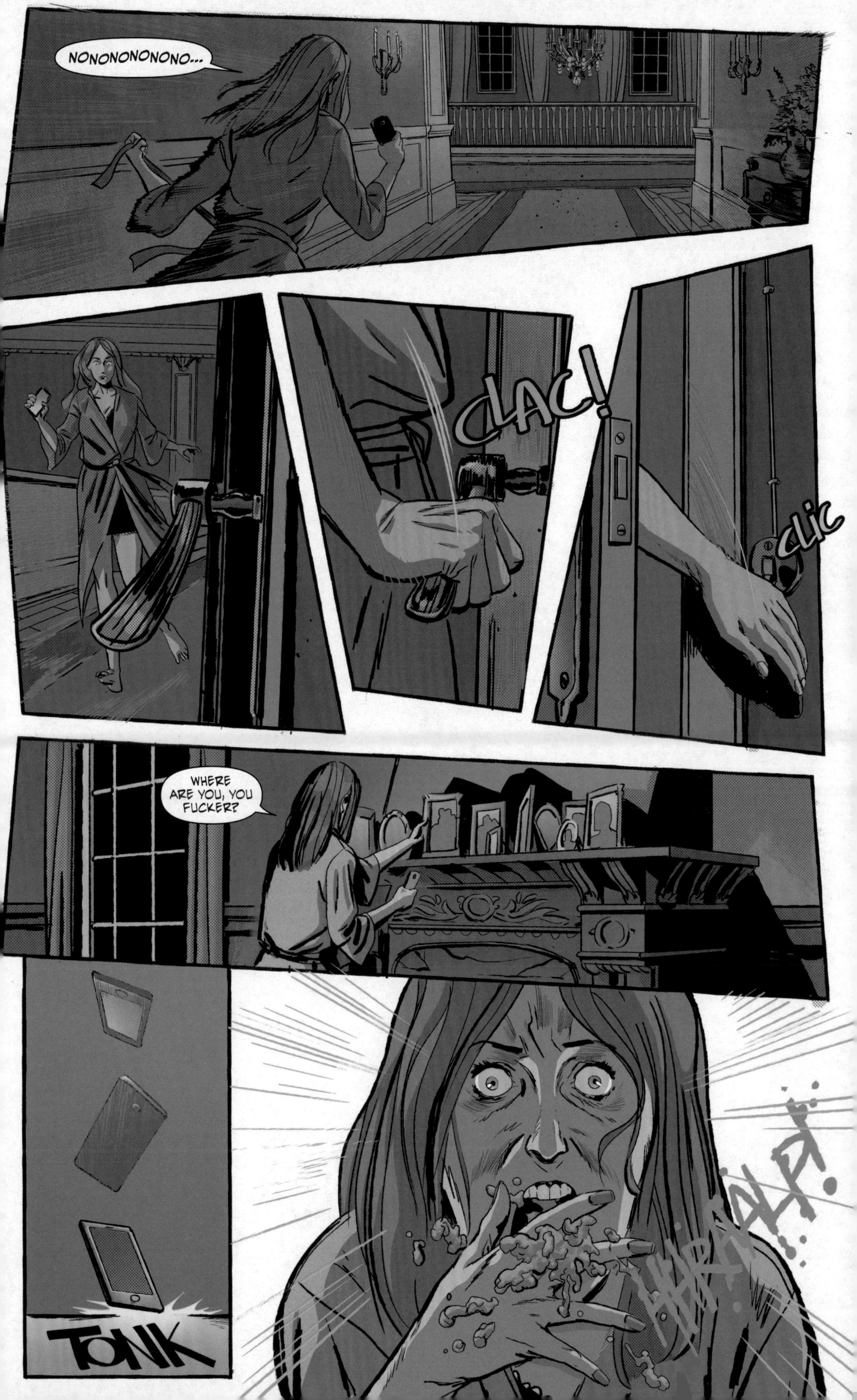
NONONONONONO...
CLAC!
CLIC
WHERE ARE YOU, YOU FUCKER?
TONK

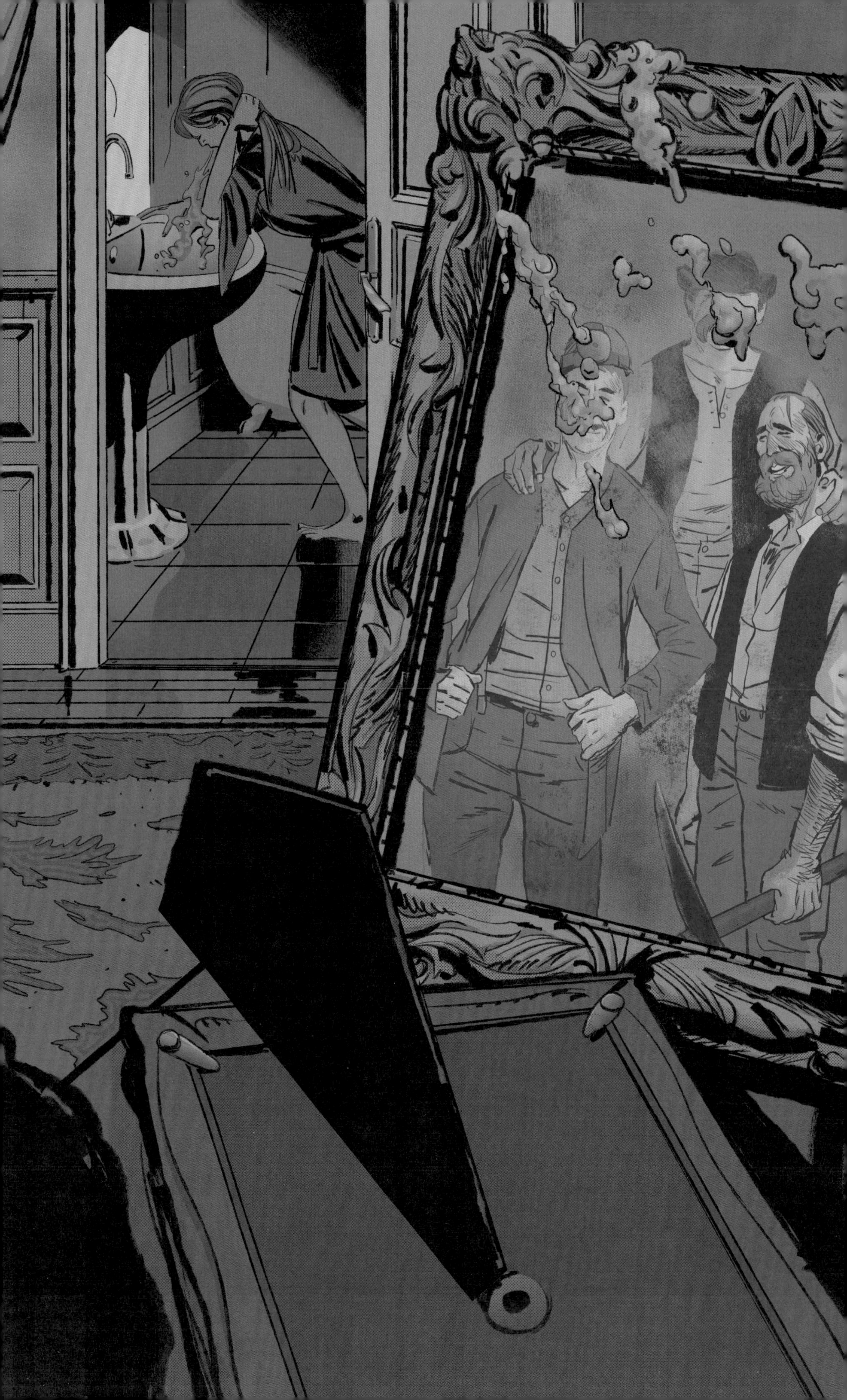

CHAPTER 4

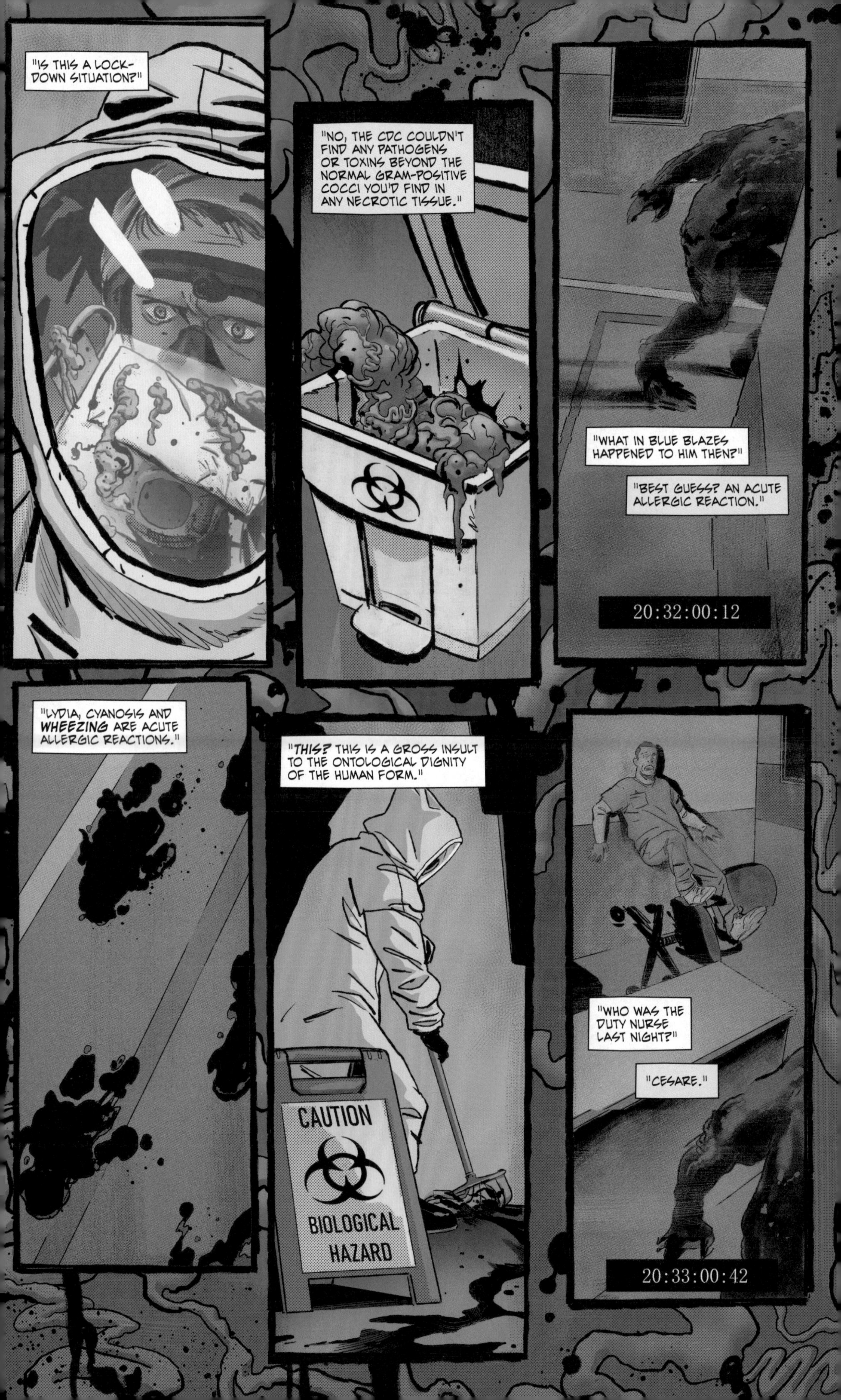
"IS THIS A LOCK-DOWN SITUATION?"
"NO, THE CDC COULDN'T FIND ANY PATHOGENS OR TOXINS BEYOND THE NORMAL GRAM-POSITIVE COCCI YOU'D FIND IN ANY NECROTIC TISSUE."
"WHAT IN BLUE BLAZES HAPPENED TO HIM THEN?"
"BEST GUESS? AN ACUTE ALLERGIC REACTION."
20:32:00:12
"LYDIA, CYANOSIS AND WHEEZING ARE ACUTE ALLERGIC REACTIONS."
"THIS? THIS IS A GROSS INSULT TO THE ONTOLOGICAL DIGNITY OF THE HUMAN FORM."
CAUTION
BIOLOGICAL HAZARD
"WHO WAS THE DUTY NURSE LAST NIGHT?"
"CESARE."
20:33:00:42

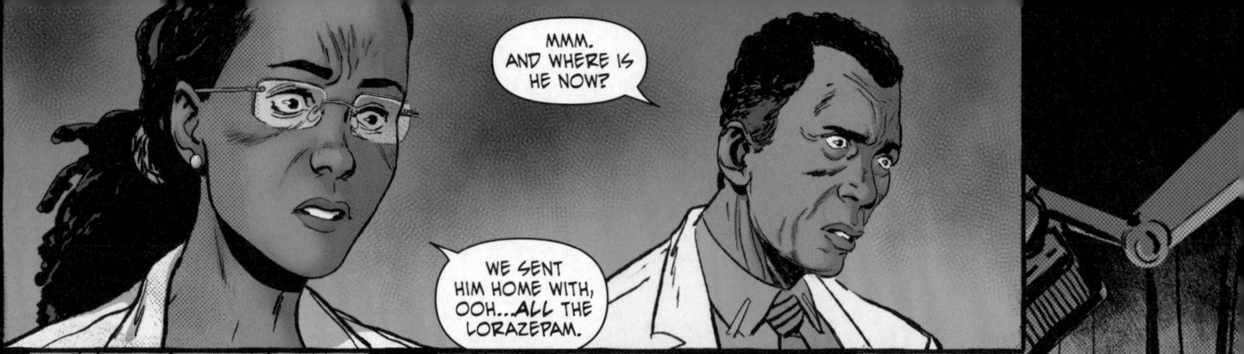
MMM. AND WHERE IS HE NOW?
WE SENT HIM HOME WITH, OOH...ALL THE LORAZEPAM.

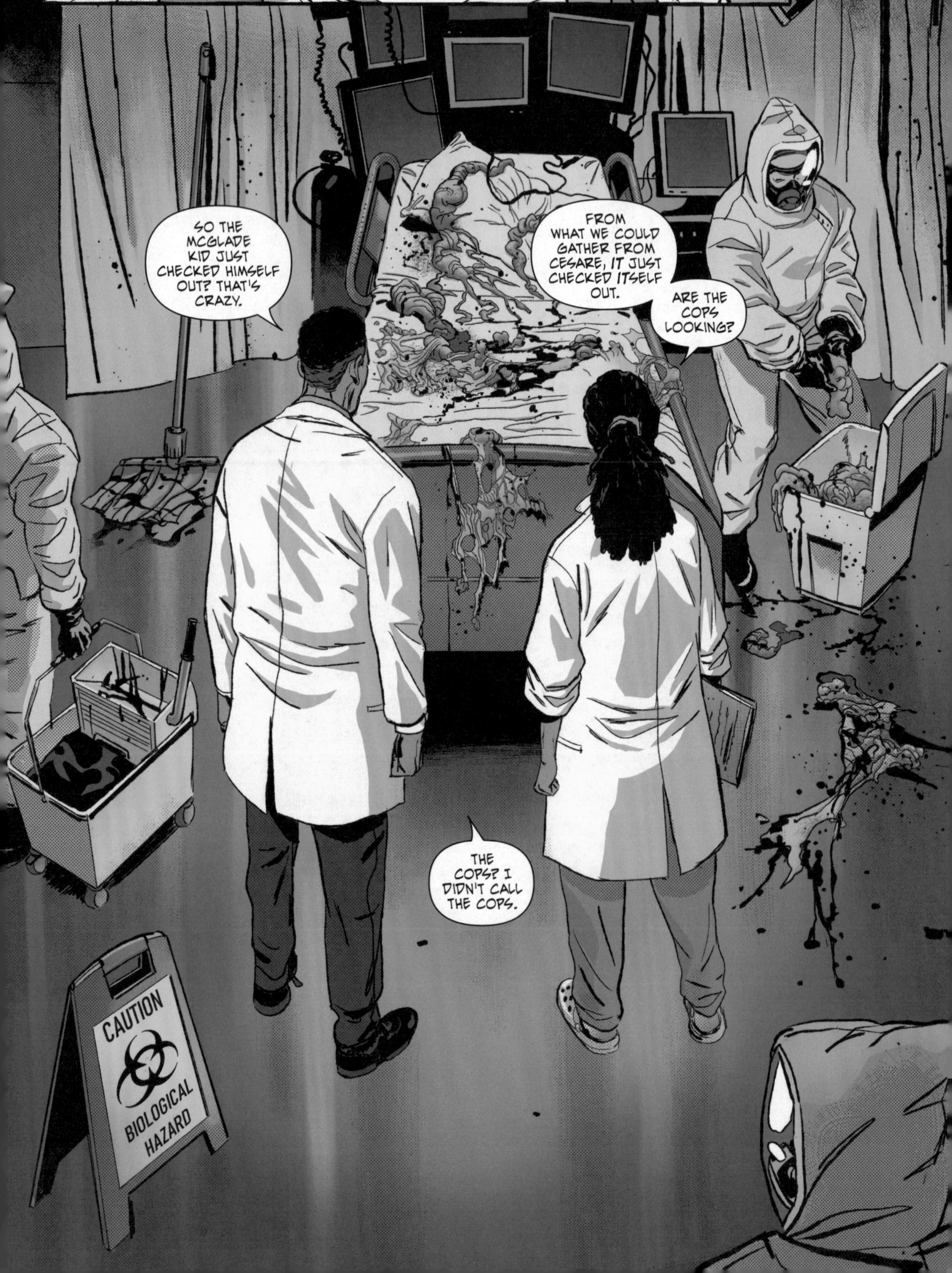
SO THE MCGLADE KID JUST CHECKED HIMSELF OUT? THAT'S CRAZY.
FROM WHAT WE COULD GATHER FROM CESARE, IT JUST CHECKED ITSELF OUT.
ARE THE COPS LOOKING?
THE COPS? I DIDN'T CALL THE COPS.
CAUTION
BIOLOGICAL HAZARD

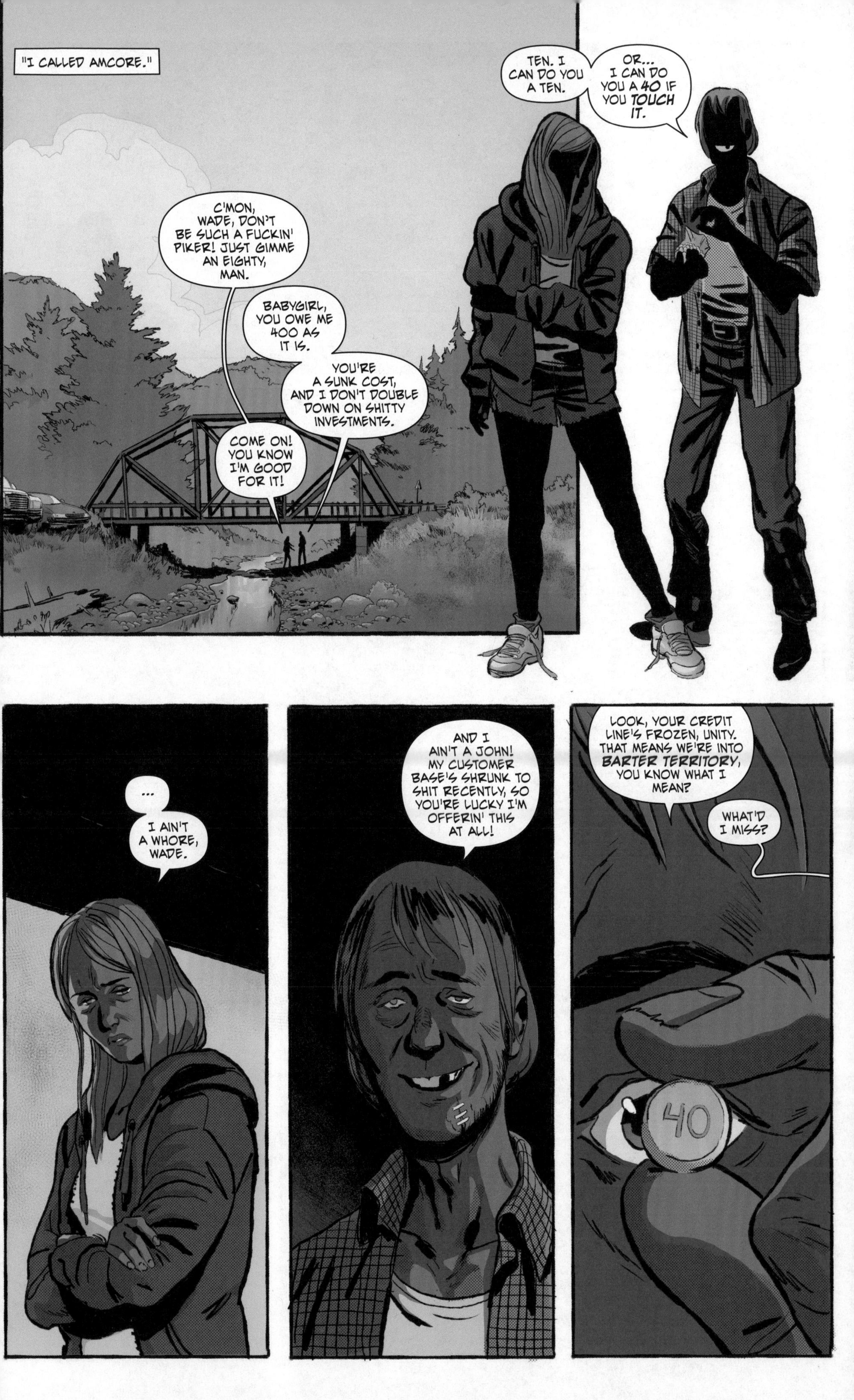
"I CALLED AMCORE."
C'MON, WADE, DON'T BE SUCH A FUCKIN' PIKER! JUST GIMME AN EIGHTY, MAN.
BABYGIRL, YOU OWE ME 400 AS IT IS.
YOU'RE A SUNK COST, AND I DON'T DOUBLE DOWN ON SHITTY INVESTMENTS.
COME ON! YOU KNOW I'M GOOD FOR IT!
TEN. I CAN DO YOU A TEN.
OR... I CAN DO YOU A 40 IF YOU TOUCH IT.
...
I AIN'T A WHORE, WADE.
AND I AIN'T A JOHN! MY CUSTOMER BASE'S SHRUNK TO SHIT RECENTLY, SO YOU'RE LUCKY I'M OFFERIN' THIS AT ALL!
LOOK, YOUR CREDIT LINE'S FROZEN, UNITY. THAT MEANS WE'RE INTO BARTER TERRITORY, YOU KNOW WHAT I MEAN?
WHAT'D I MISS?
40

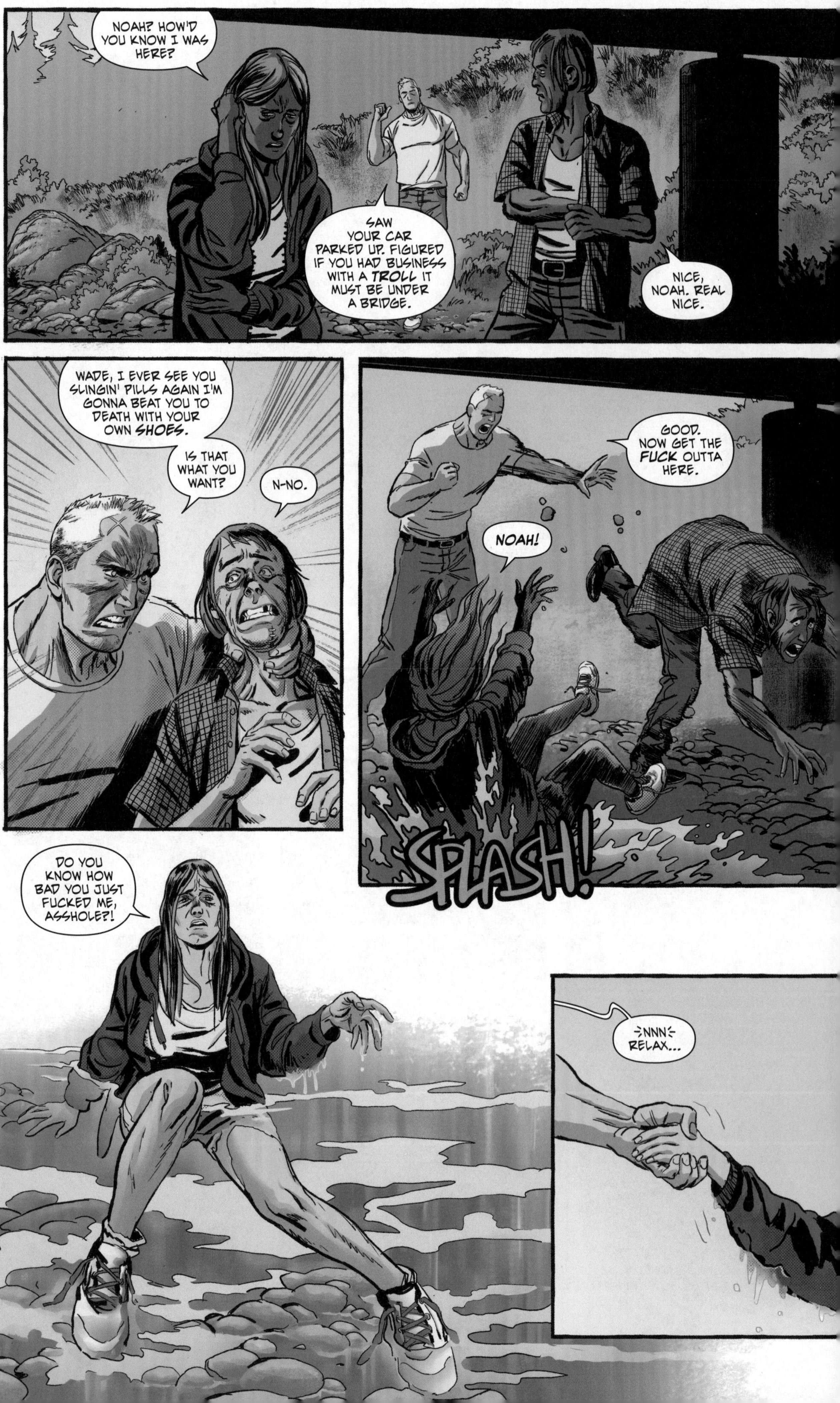
NOAH? HOW'D YOU KNOW I WAS HERE?
SAW YOUR CAR PARKED UP. FIGURED IF YOU HAD BUSINESS WITH A TROLL IT MUST BE UNDER A BRIDGE.
NICE, NOAH. REAL NICE.
WADE, I EVER SEE YOU SLINGIN' PILLS AGAIN I'M GONNA BEAT YOU TO DEATH WITH YOUR OWN SHOES.
IS THAT WHAT YOU WANT?
N-NO.
GOOD. NOW GET THE FUCK OUTTA HERE.
NOAH!
SPLASH!
DO YOU KNOW HOW BAD YOU JUST FUCKED ME, ASSHOLE?!
NNN
RELAX...

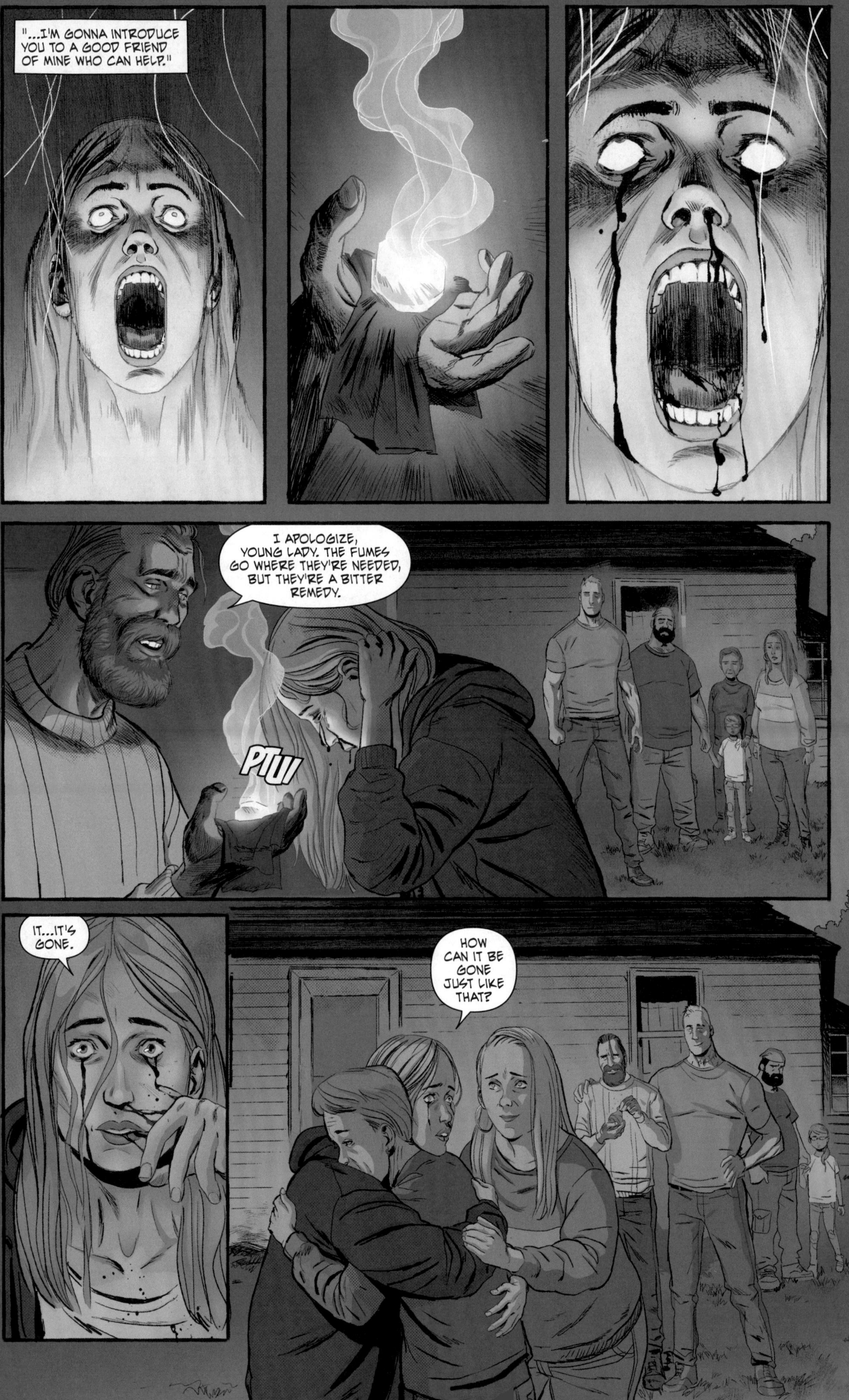
"...I'M GONNA INTRODUCE YOU TO A GOOD FRIEND OF MINE WHO CAN HELP."
I APOLOGIZE, YOUNG LADY. THE FUMES GO WHERE THEY'RE NEEDED, BUT THEY'RE A BITTER REMEDY.
PTUI
IT...IT'S GONE.
HOW CAN IT BE GONE JUST LIKE THAT?

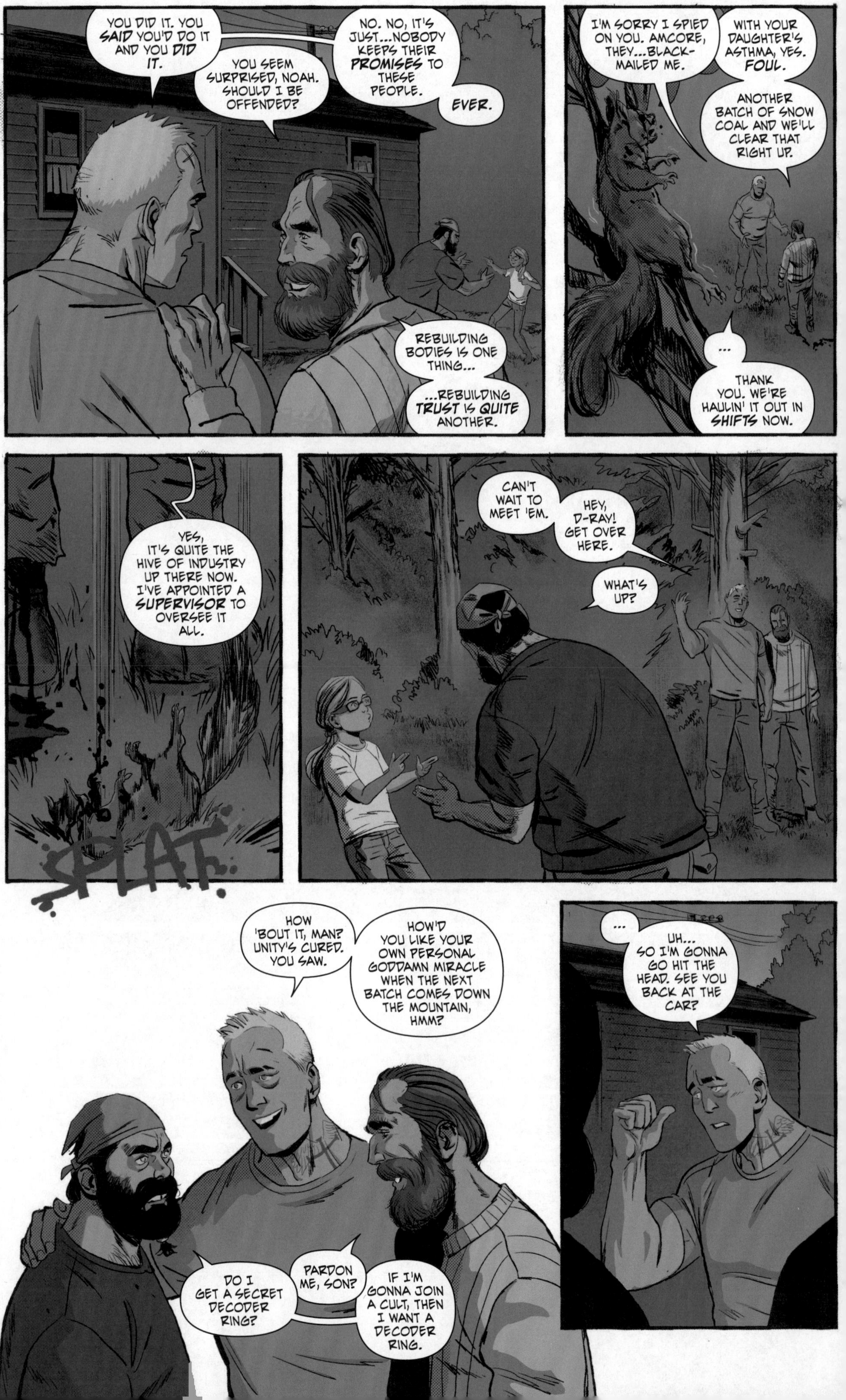
YOU DID IT. YOU SAID YOU'D DO IT AND YOU DID IT.
YOU SEEM SURPRISED, NOAH. SHOULD I BE OFFENDED?
NO. NO, IT'S JUST...NOBODY KEEPS THEIR PROMISES TO THESE PEOPLE.
EVER.
REBUILDING BODIES IS ONE THING...
...REBUILDING TRUST IS QUITE ANOTHER.
I'M SORRY I SPIED ON YOU. AMCORE, THEY...BLACK-MAILED ME.
WITH YOUR DAUGHTER'S ASTHMA, YES. FOUL.
ANOTHER BATCH OF SNOW COAL AND WE'LL CLEAR THAT RIGHT UP.
...
THANK YOU. WE'RE HAULIN' IT OUT IN SHIFTS NOW.
YES, IT'S QUITE THE HIVE OF INDUSTRY UP THERE NOW. I'VE APPOINTED A SUPERVISOR TO OVERSEE IT ALL.
SPLAT.
CAN'T WAIT TO MEET 'EM.
HEY, D-RAY! GET OVER HERE.
WHAT'S UP?
HOW 'BOUT IT, MAN? UNITY'S CURED. YOU SAW.
HOW'D YOU LIKE YOUR OWN PERSONAL GODDAMN MIRACLE WHEN THE NEXT BATCH COMES DOWN THE MOUNTAIN, HMM?
DO I GET A SECRET DECODER RING?
PARDON ME, SON?
IF I'M GONNA JOIN A CULT, THEN I WANT A DECODER RING.
...
UH... SO I'M GONNA GO HIT THE HEAD. SEE YOU BACK AT THE CAR?

‹TTT›

YOU'RE OKAY. HECK, YOU'RE *BETTER'N* OKAY.

EVERYTHIN'S BACK ON TRACK.

WHAKK!

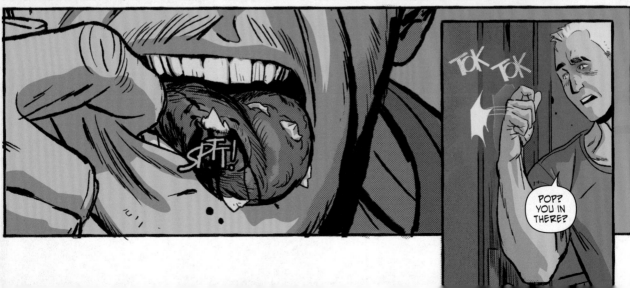

SPTT!

TOK TOK

POP? YOU IN THERE?

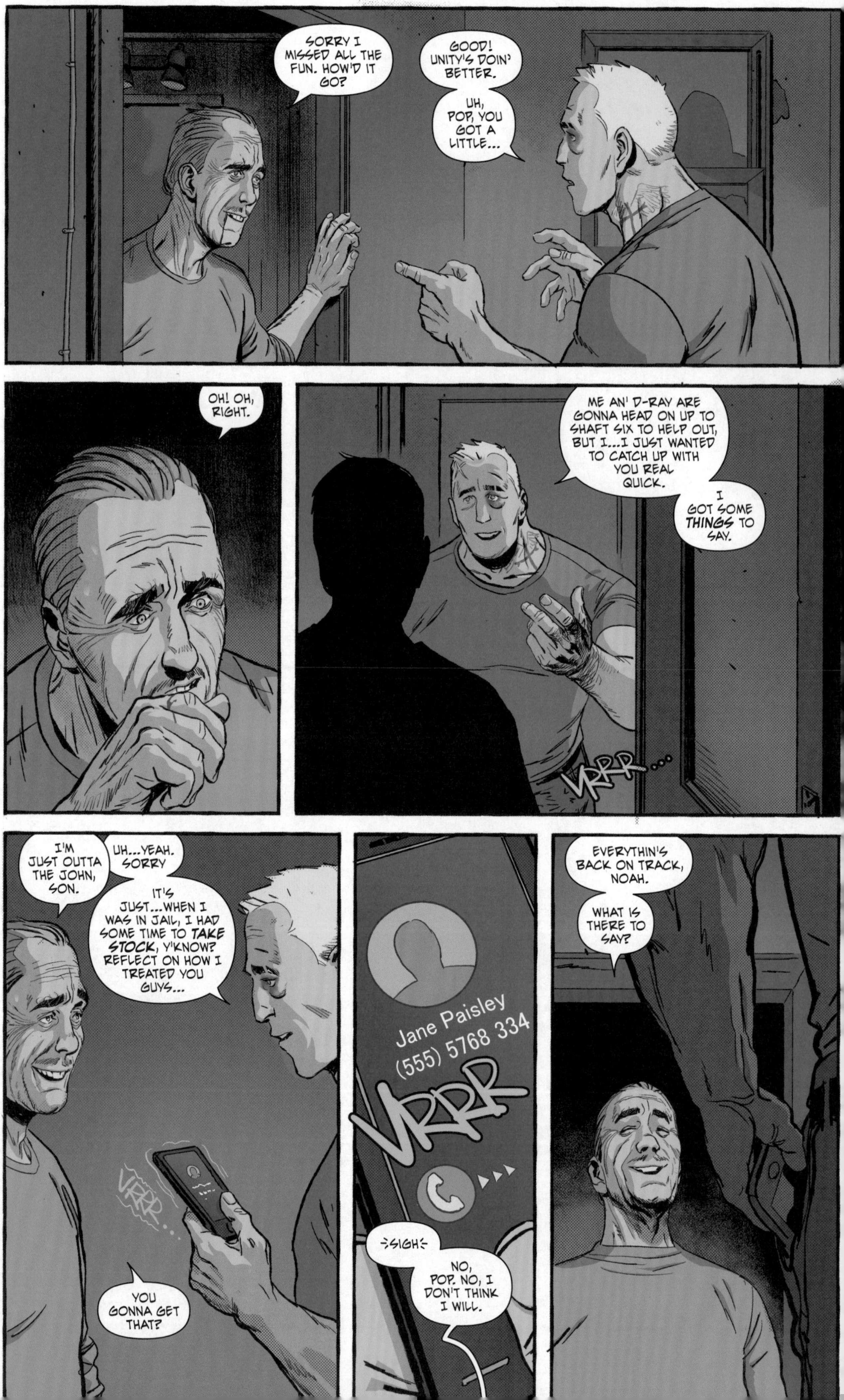
SORRY I MISSED ALL THE FUN. HOW'D IT GO?
GOOD! UNITY'S DOIN' BETTER.
UH, POP, YOU GOT A LITTLE...
OH! OH, RIGHT.
ME AN' D-RAY ARE GONNA HEAD ON UP TO SHAFT SIX TO HELP OUT, BUT I...I JUST WANTED TO CATCH UP WITH YOU REAL QUICK.
I GOT SOME THINGS TO SAY.
VRRR...
I'M JUST OUTTA THE JOHN, SON.
UH...YEAH. SORRY
IT'S JUST...WHEN I WAS IN JAIL, I HAD SOME TIME TO TAKE STOCK, Y'KNOW? REFLECT ON HOW I TREATED YOU GUYS...
VRRR...
YOU GONNA GET THAT?
Jane Paisley
(555) 5768 334
VRRR
-SIGH-
NO, POP. NO, I DON'T THINK I WILL.
EVERYTHIN'S BACK ON TRACK, NOAH.
WHAT IS THERE TO SAY?

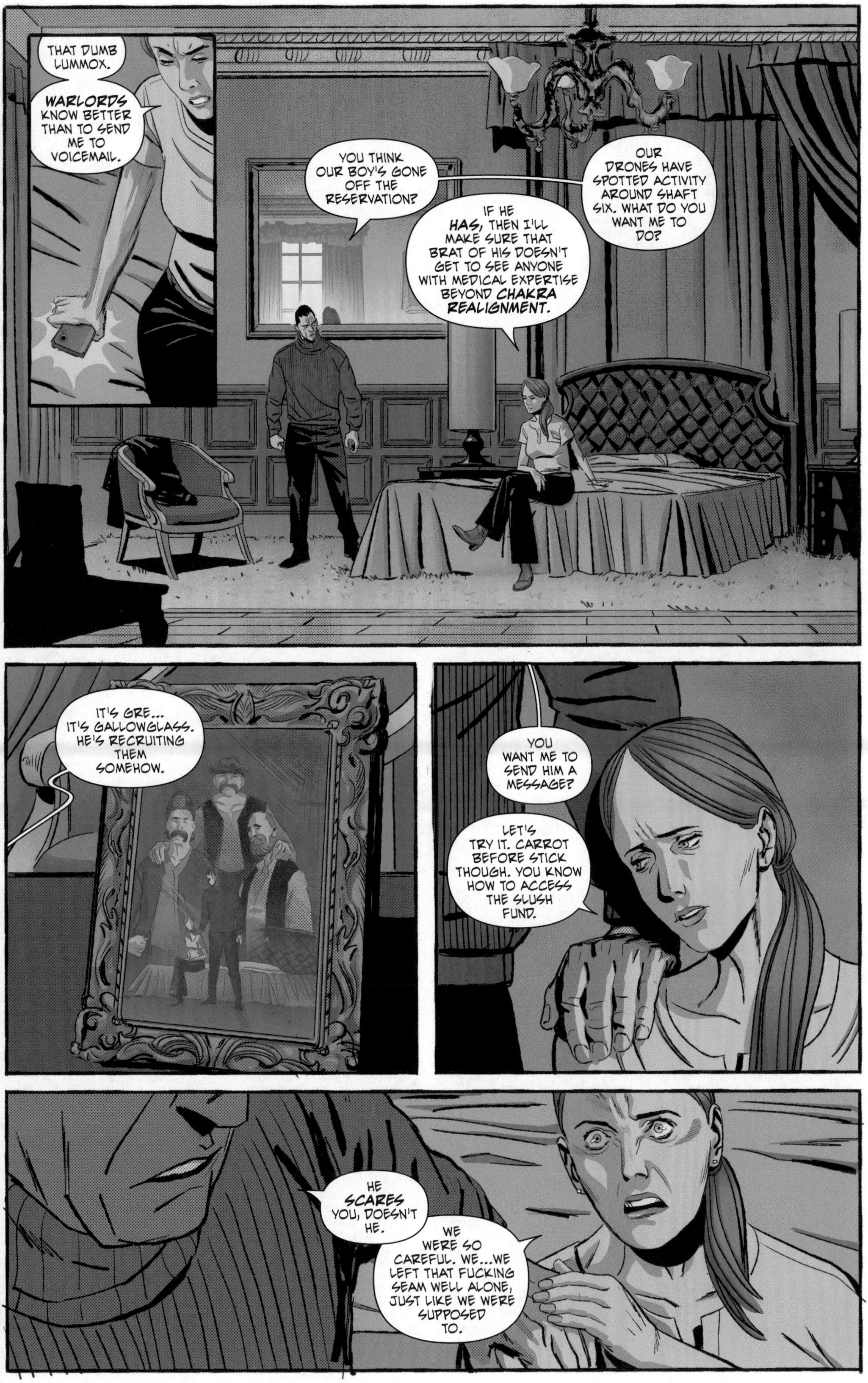
THAT DUMB LUMMOX.
WARLORDS KNOW BETTER THAN TO SEND ME TO VOICEMAIL.
YOU THINK OUR BOY'S GONE OFF THE RESERVATION?
OUR DRONES HAVE SPOTTED ACTIVITY AROUND SHAFT SIX. WHAT DO YOU WANT ME TO DO?
IF HE HAS, THEN I'LL MAKE SURE THAT BRAT OF HIS DOESN'T GET TO SEE ANYONE WITH MEDICAL EXPERTISE BEYOND CHAKRA REALIGNMENT.
IT'S GRE... IT'S GALLOWGLASS. HE'S RECRUITING THEM SOMEHOW.
YOU WANT ME TO SEND HIM A MESSAGE?
LET'S TRY IT. CARROT BEFORE STICK THOUGH. YOU KNOW HOW TO ACCESS THE SLUSH FUND.
HE SCARES YOU, DOESN'T HE.
WE WERE SO CAREFUL. WE...WE LEFT THAT FUCKING SEAM WELL ALONE, JUST LIKE WE WERE SUPPOSED TO.

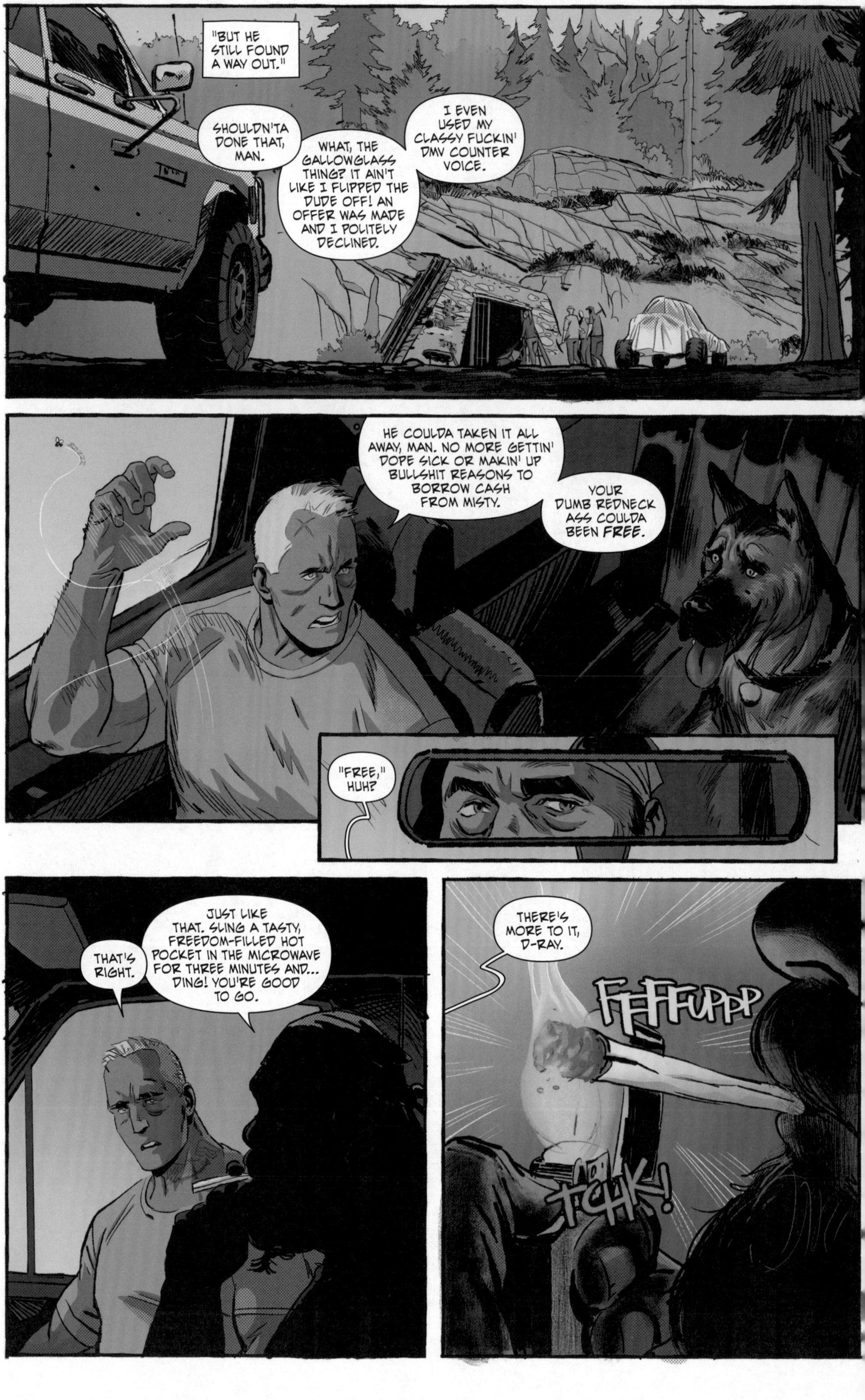
"BUT HE STILL FOUND A WAY OUT."
SHOULDN'TA DONE THAT, MAN.
WHAT, THE GALLOWGLASS THING? IT AIN'T LIKE I FLIPPED THE DUDE OFF! AN OFFER WAS MADE AND I POLITELY DECLINED.
I EVEN USED MY CLASSY FUCKIN' DMV COUNTER VOICE.
HE COULDA TAKEN IT ALL AWAY, MAN. NO MORE GETTIN' DOPE SICK OR MAKIN' UP BULLSHIT REASONS TO BORROW CASH FROM MISTY.
YOUR DUMB REDNECK ASS COULDA BEEN FREE.
"FREE," HUH?
THAT'S RIGHT.
JUST LIKE THAT. SLING A TASTY, FREEDOM-FILLED HOT POCKET IN THE MICROWAVE FOR THREE MINUTES AND... DING! YOU'RE GOOD TO GO.
THERE'S MORE TO IT, D-RAY.
FFFFUPPP
TCHK!

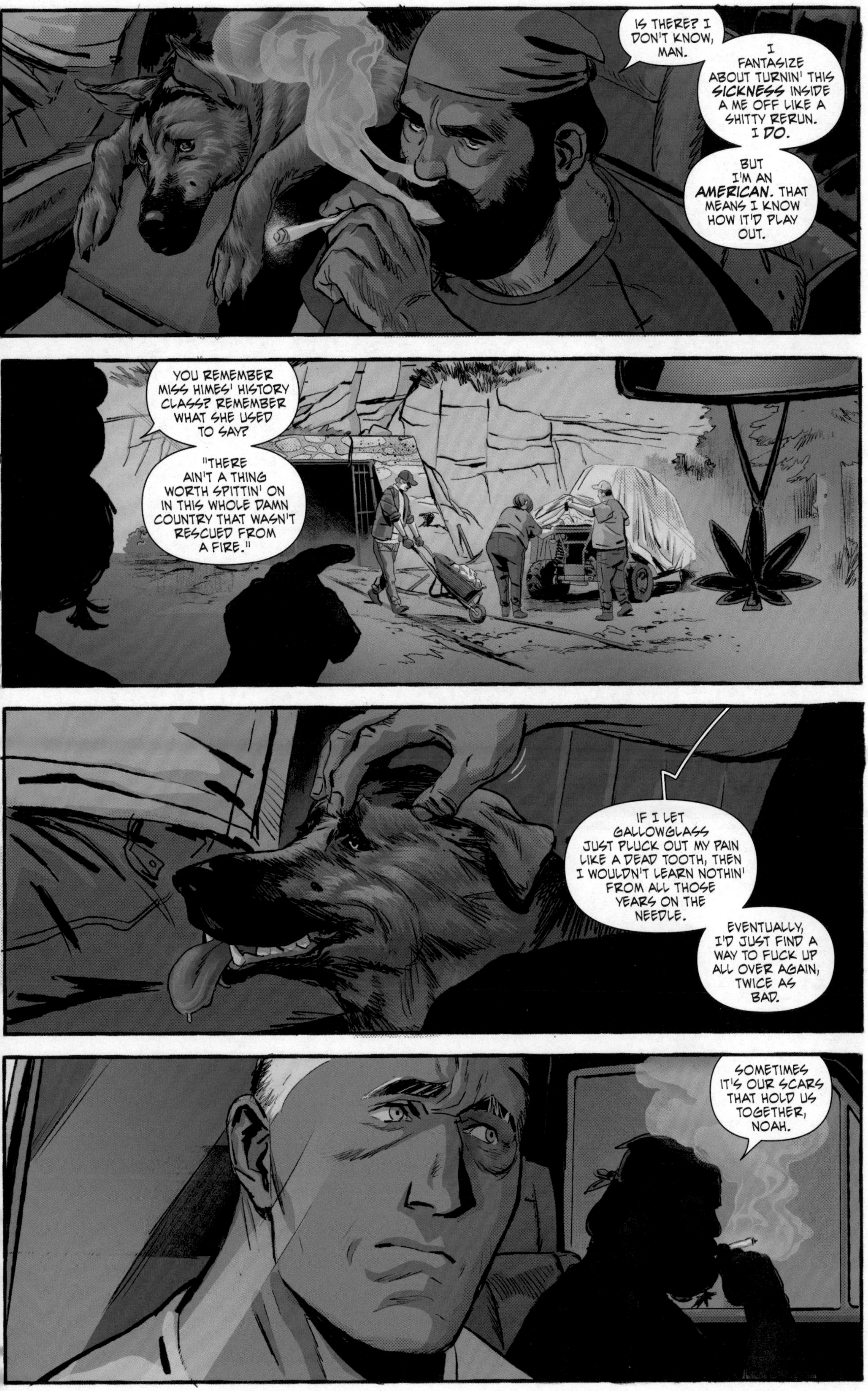
IS THERE? I DON'T KNOW, MAN.
I FANTASIZE ABOUT TURNIN' THIS SICKNESS INSIDE A ME OFF LIKE A SHITTY RERUN. I DO.
BUT I'M AN AMERICAN. THAT MEANS I KNOW HOW IT'D PLAY OUT.
YOU REMEMBER MISS HIMES' HISTORY CLASS? REMEMBER WHAT SHE USED TO SAY?
"THERE AIN'T A THING WORTH SPITTIN' ON IN THIS WHOLE DAMN COUNTRY THAT WASN'T RESCUED FROM A FIRE."
IF I LET GALLOWGLASS JUST PLUCK OUT MY PAIN LIKE A DEAD TOOTH, THEN I WOULDN'T LEARN NOTHIN' FROM ALL THOSE YEARS ON THE NEEDLE.
EVENTUALLY, I'D JUST FIND A WAY TO FUCK UP ALL OVER AGAIN, TWICE AS BAD.
SOMETIMES IT'S OUR SCARS THAT HOLD US TOGETHER, NOAH.

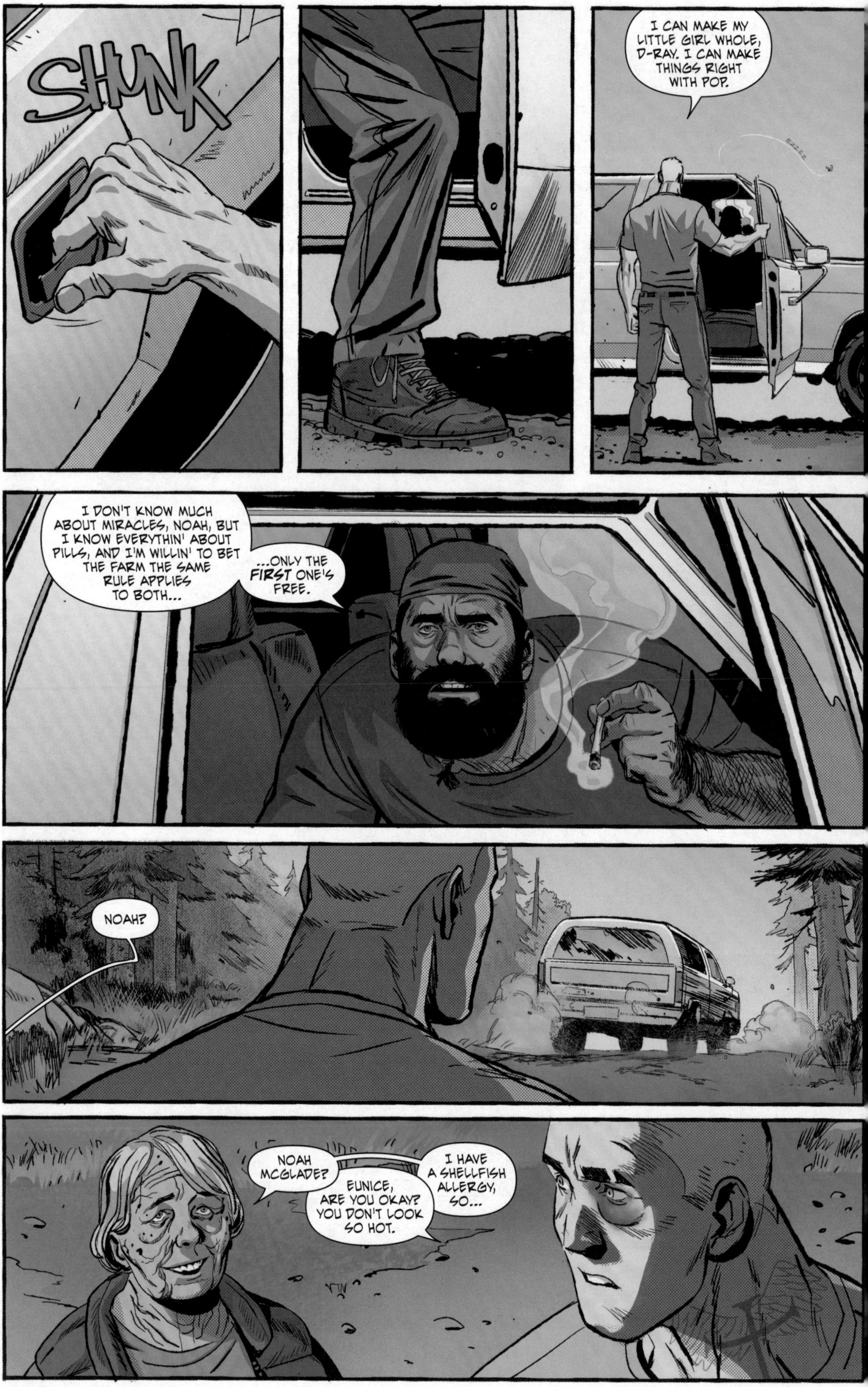
SHUNK
I CAN MAKE MY LITTLE GIRL WHOLE, D-RAY. I CAN MAKE THINGS RIGHT WITH POP.
I DON'T KNOW MUCH ABOUT MIRACLES, NOAH, BUT I KNOW EVERYTHIN' ABOUT PILLS, AND I'M WILLIN' TO BET THE FARM THE SAME RULE APPLIES TO BOTH...
...ONLY THE FIRST ONE'S FREE.
NOAH?
NOAH MCGLADE?
I HAVE A SHELLFISH ALLERGY, SO...
EUNICE, ARE YOU OKAY? YOU DON'T LOOK SO HOT.

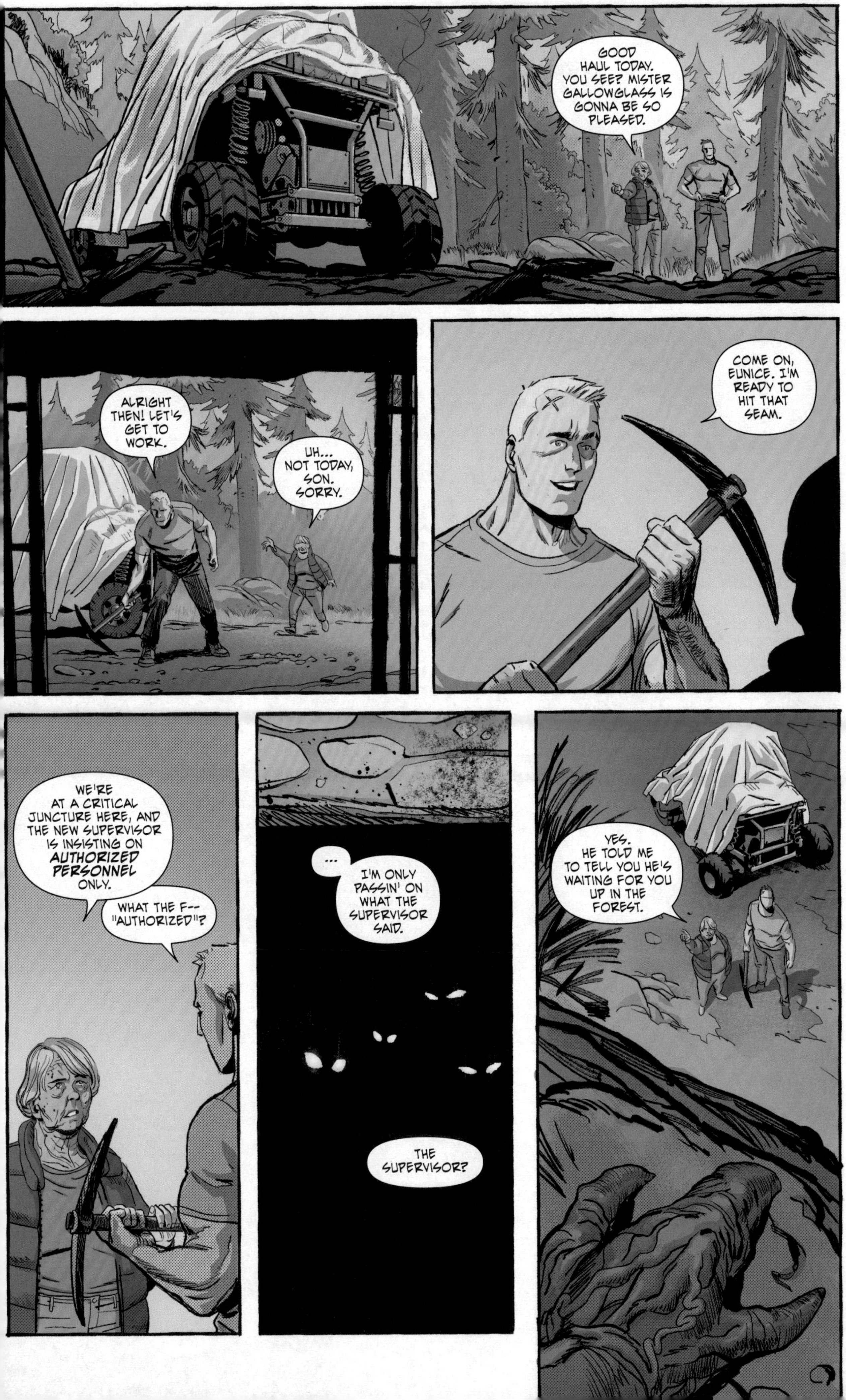
GOOD HAUL TODAY. YOU SEE? MISTER GALLOWGLASS IS GONNA BE SO PLEASED.
ALRIGHT THEN! LET'S GET TO WORK.
UH... NOT TODAY, SON. SORRY.
COME ON, EUNICE. I'M READY TO HIT THAT SEAM.
WE'RE AT A CRITICAL JUNCTURE HERE, AND THE NEW SUPERVISOR IS INSISTING ON AUTHORIZED PERSONNEL ONLY.
WHAT THE F-- "AUTHORIZED"?
...
I'M ONLY PASSIN' ON WHAT THE SUPERVISOR SAID.
THE SUPERVISOR?
YES. HE TOLD ME TO TELL YOU HE'S WAITING FOR YOU UP IN THE FOREST.

SKREEEE

GOOD MORNING, GENTLEMEN!

WHAT POSSESSED YOU TO *DRIVE* UP TO THIS BEAUTIFUL SPOT ON A DAY LIKE THIS, FRIENDS?

THIS MOUNTAIN AIR REALLY OPENS UP THE LUNGS DOESN'T IT?

DO YOU KNOW WHO WE WORK FOR?

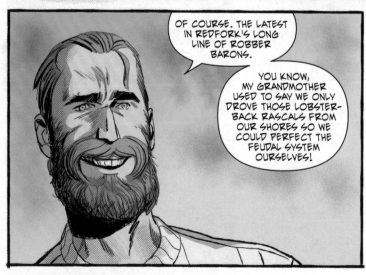

OF COURSE. THE LATEST IN REDFORK'S LONG LINE OF ROBBER BARONS.

YOU KNOW, MY GRANDMOTHER USED TO SAY WE ONLY DROVE THOSE LOBSTER-BACK RASCALS FROM OUR SHORES SO WE COULD PERFECT THE FEUDAL SYSTEM OURSELVES!

OPEN IT.

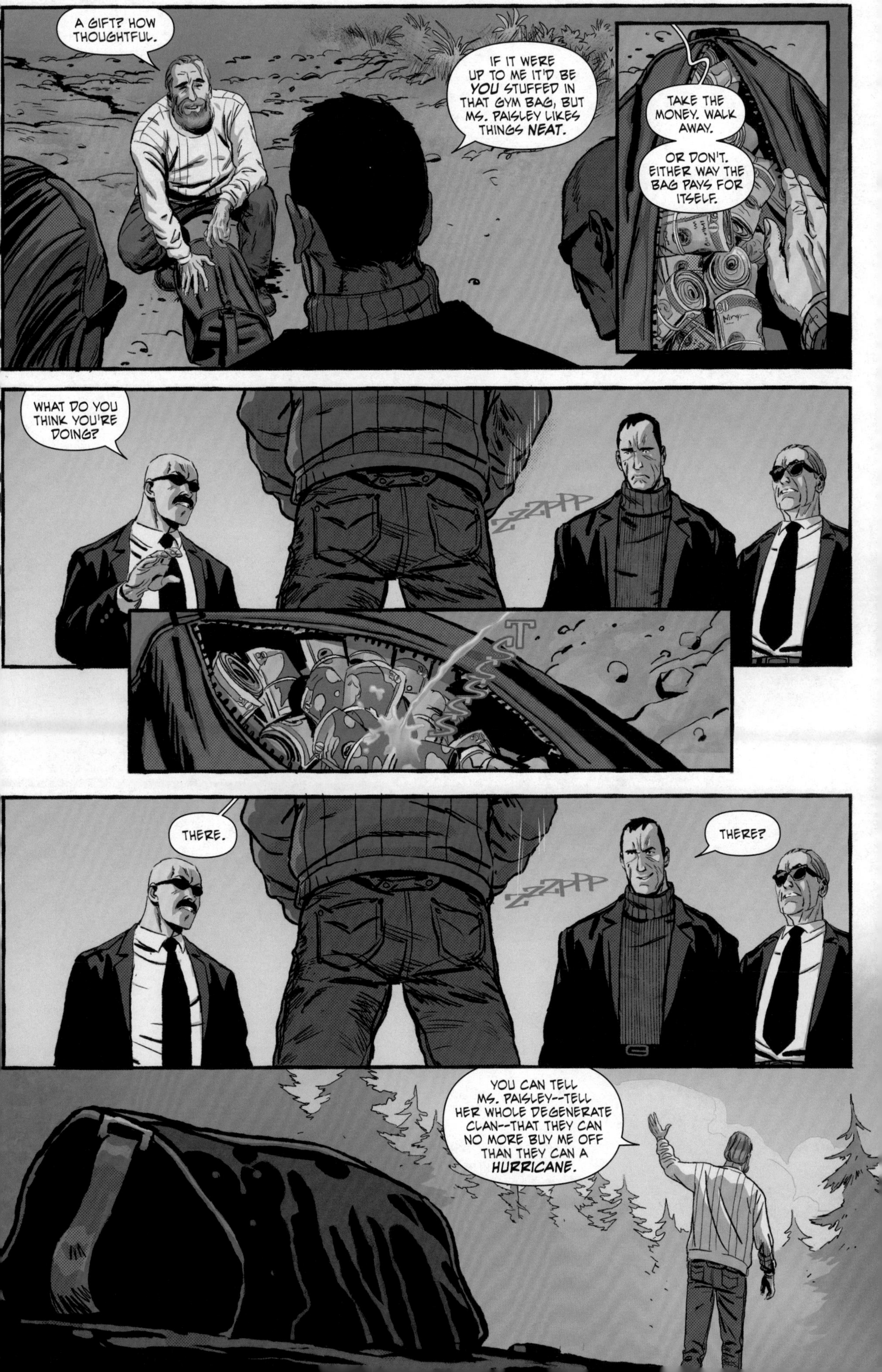
A GIFT? HOW THOUGHTFUL.
IF IT WERE UP TO ME IT'D BE YOU STUFFED IN THAT GYM BAG, BUT MS. PAISLEY LIKES THINGS NEAT.
TAKE THE MONEY. WALK AWAY.
OR DON'T. EITHER WAY THE BAG PAYS FOR ITSELF.
WHAT DO YOU THINK YOU'RE DOING?
ZZZPPP
T
THERE.
THERE?
ZZZPPP
YOU CAN TELL MS. PAISLEY--TELL HER WHOLE DEGENERATE CLAN--THAT THEY CAN NO MORE BUY ME OFF THAN THEY CAN A HURRICANE.

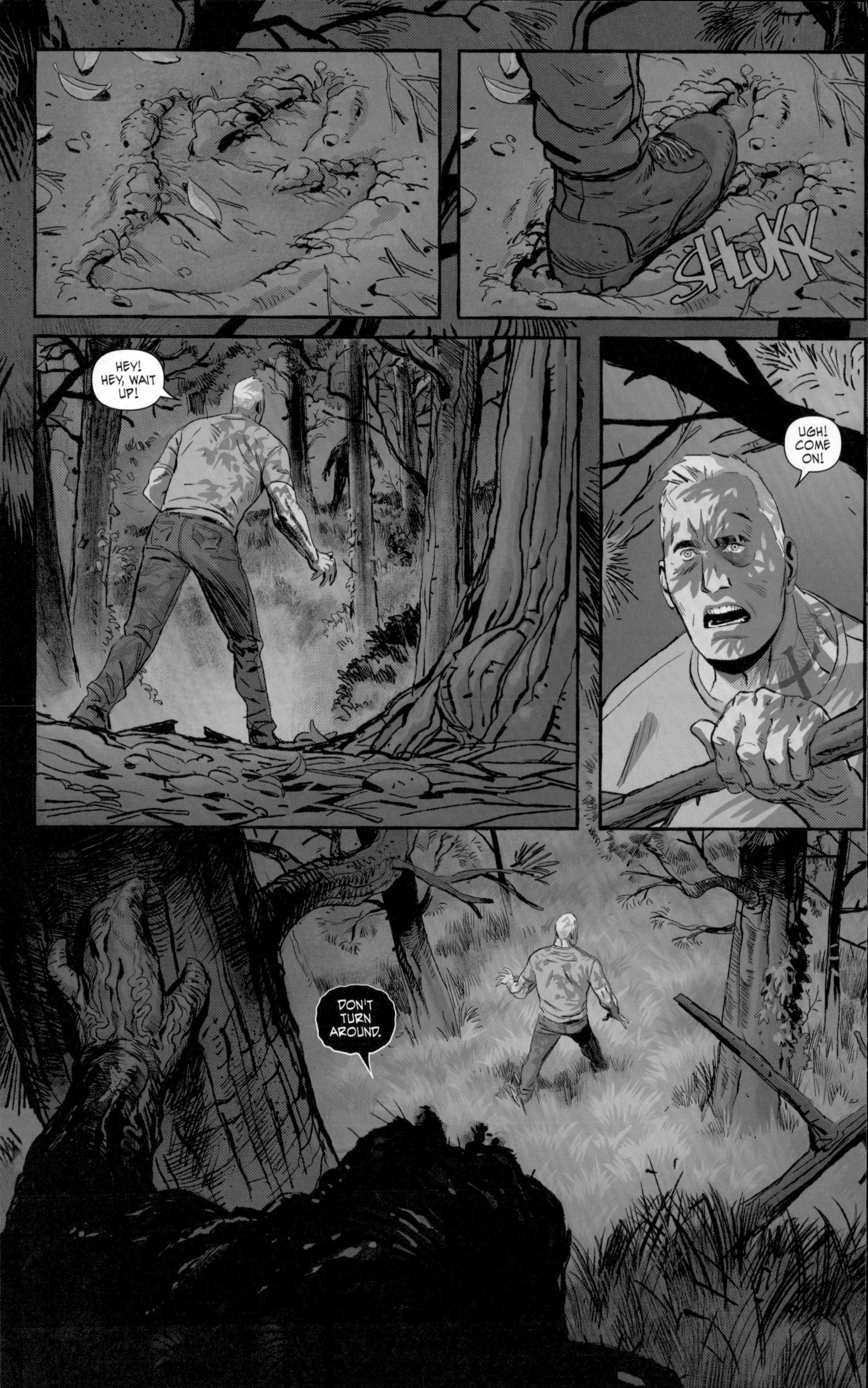
SHLUKK
HEY! HEY, WAIT UP!
UGH! COME ON!
DON'T TURN AROUND.

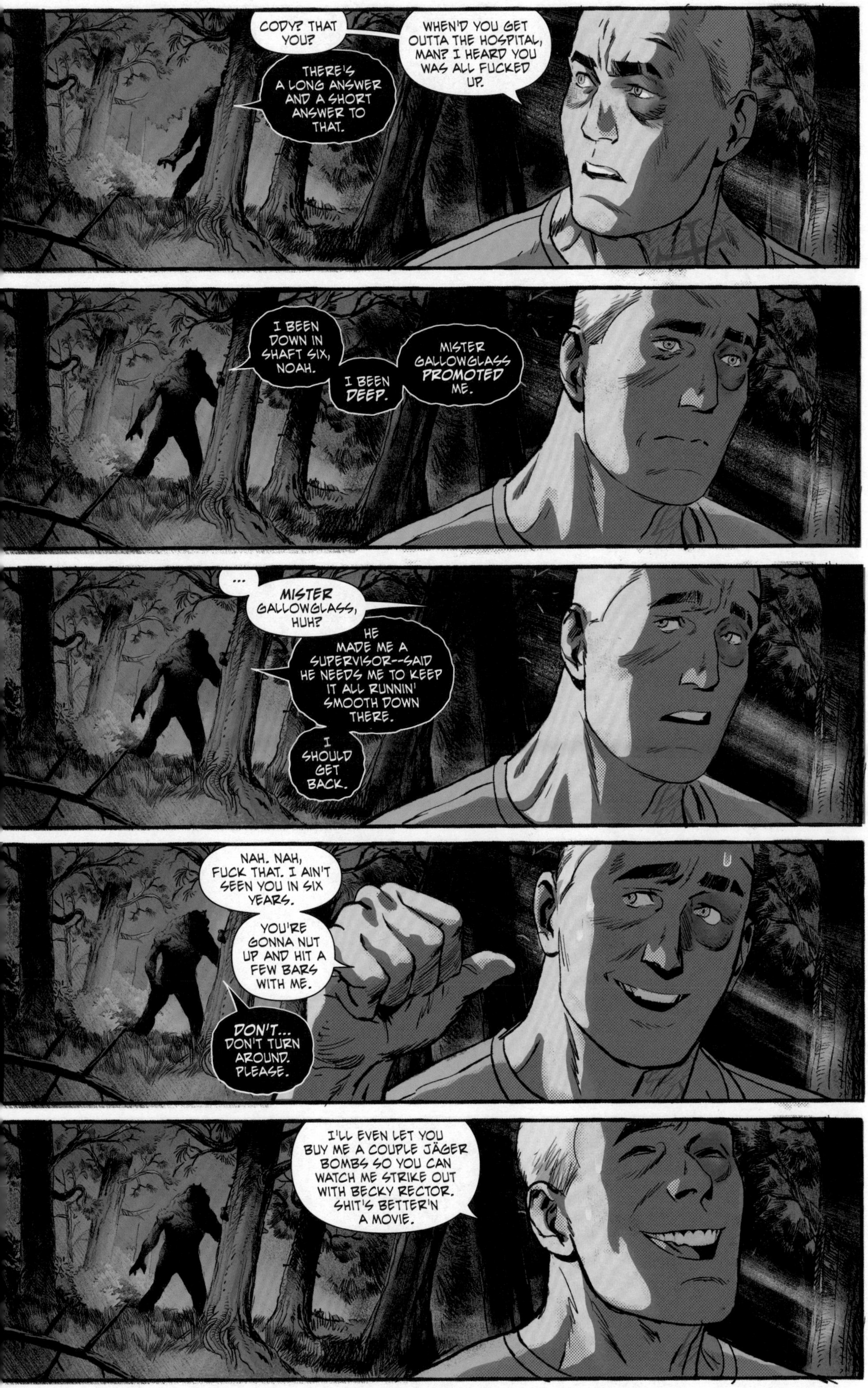

CODY? THAT YOU?
WHEN'D YOU GET OUTTA THE HOSPITAL, MAN? I HEARD YOU WAS ALL FUCKED UP.
THERE'S A LONG ANSWER AND A SHORT ANSWER TO THAT.
I BEEN DOWN IN SHAFT SIX, NOAH.
I BEEN DEEP.
MISTER GALLOWGLASS PROMOTED ME.
...
MISTER GALLOWGLASS, HUH?
HE MADE ME A SUPERVISOR--SAID HE NEEDS ME TO KEEP IT ALL RUNNIN' SMOOTH DOWN THERE.
I SHOULD GET BACK.
NAH. NAH, FUCK THAT. I AIN'T SEEN YOU IN SIX YEARS.
YOU'RE GONNA NUT UP AND HIT A FEW BARS WITH ME.
DON'T... DON'T TURN AROUND. PLEASE.
I'LL EVEN LET YOU BUY ME A COUPLE JÄGER BOMBS SO YOU CAN WATCH ME STRIKE OUT WITH BECKY RECTOR. SHIT'S BETTER'N A MOVIE.

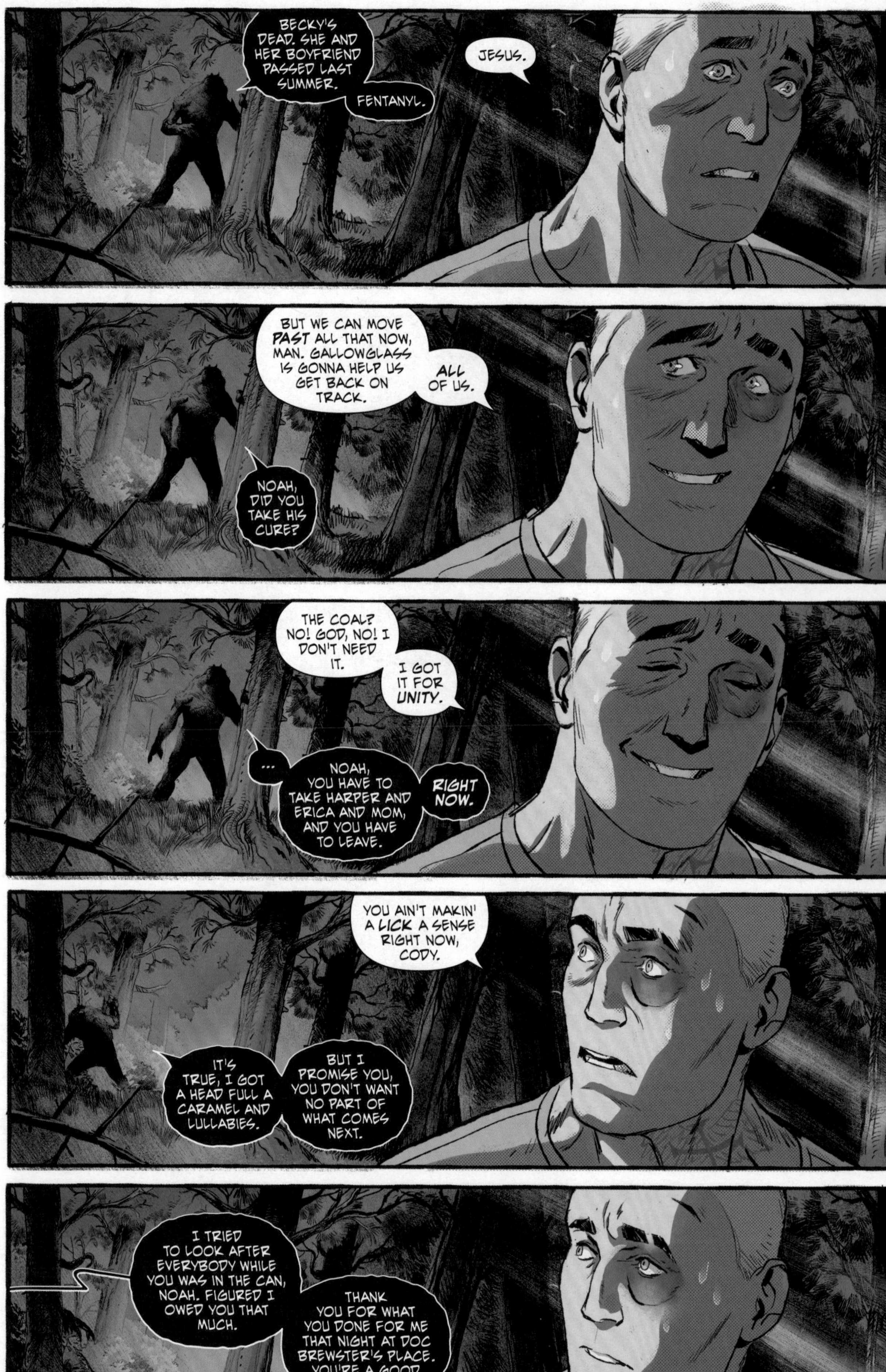
BECKY'S DEAD. SHE AND HER BOYFRIEND PASSED LAST SUMMER.
FENTANYL.
JESUS.
BUT WE CAN MOVE PAST ALL THAT NOW, MAN. GALLOWGLASS IS GONNA HELP US GET BACK ON TRACK.
ALL OF US.
NOAH, DID YOU TAKE HIS CURE?
THE COAL? NO! GOD, NO! I DON'T NEED IT.
I GOT IT FOR UNITY.
...
NOAH, YOU HAVE TO TAKE HARPER AND ERICA AND MOM, AND YOU HAVE TO LEAVE.
RIGHT NOW.
YOU AIN'T MAKIN' A LICK A SENSE RIGHT NOW, CODY.
IT'S TRUE, I GOT A HEAD FULL A CARAMEL AND LULLABIES.
BUT I PROMISE YOU, YOU DON'T WANT NO PART OF WHAT COMES NEXT.
I TRIED TO LOOK AFTER EVERYBODY WHILE YOU WAS IN THE CAN, NOAH. FIGURED I OWED YOU THAT MUCH.
THANK YOU FOR WHAT YOU DONE FOR ME THAT NIGHT AT DOC BREWSTER'S PLACE. YOU'RE A GOOD BROTHER.

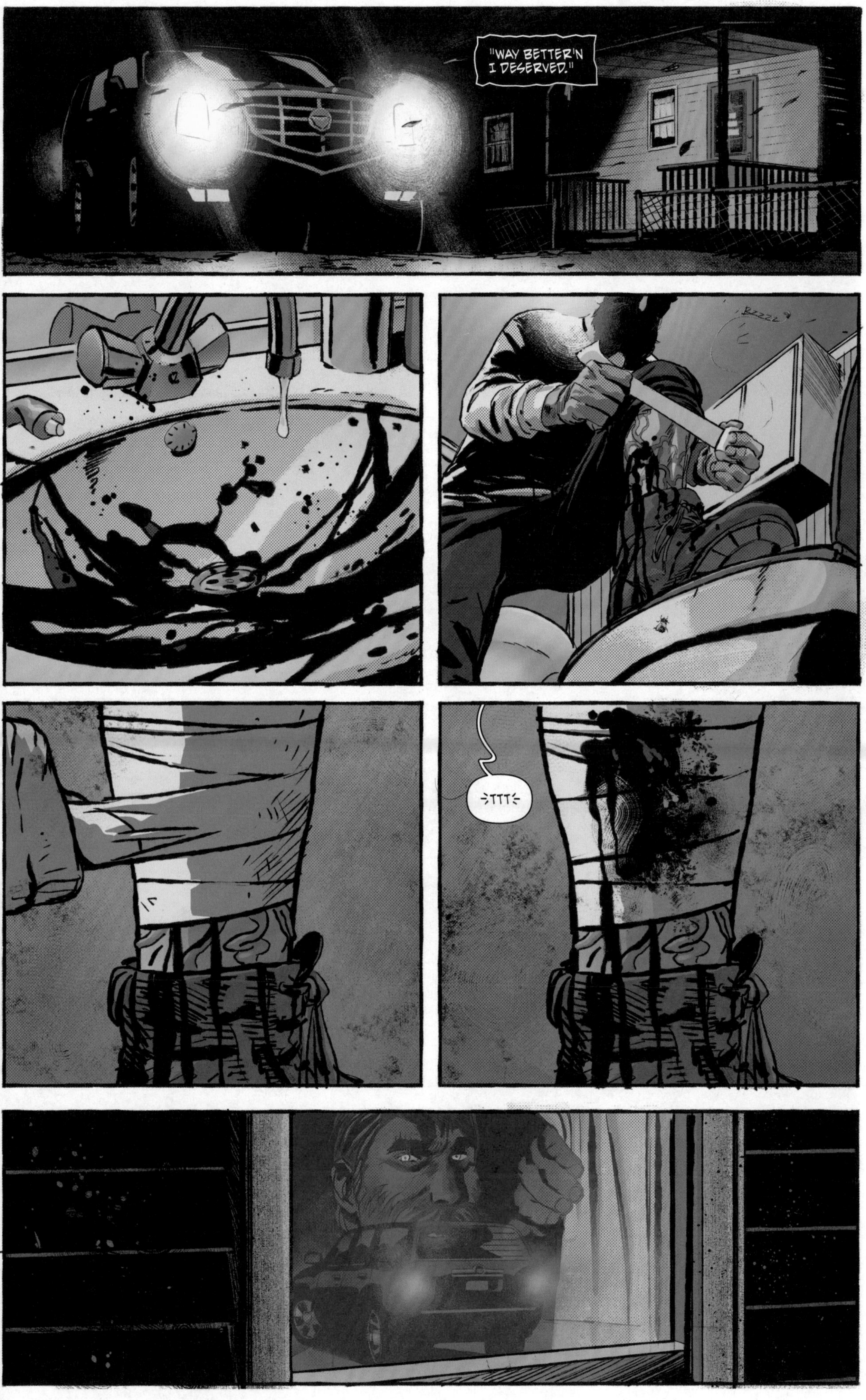
"WAY BETTER'N I DESERVED."
BZZZZ
TTT

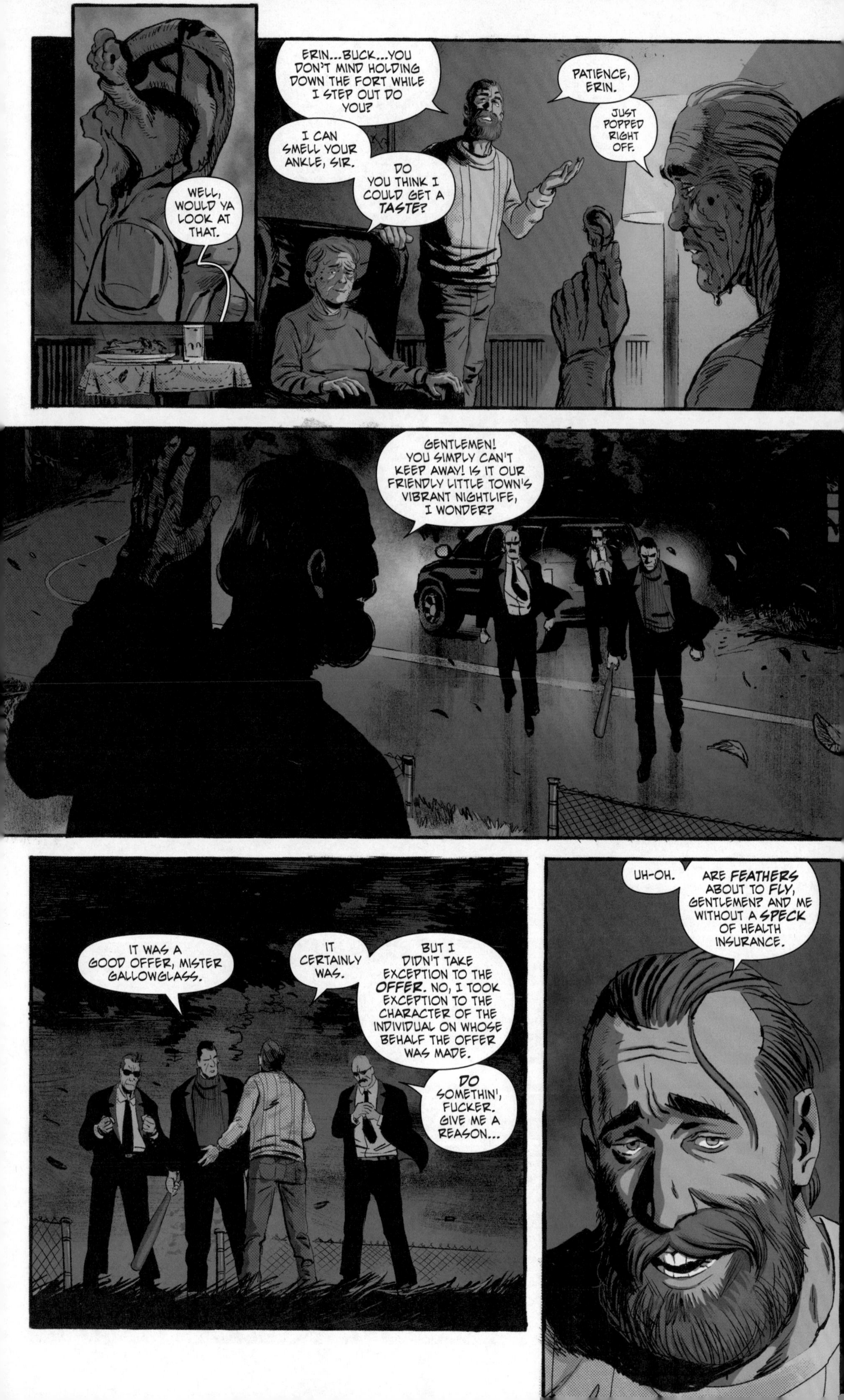
ERIN...BUCK...YOU DON'T MIND HOLDING DOWN THE FORT WHILE I STEP OUT DO YOU?
WELL, WOULD YA LOOK AT THAT.
I CAN SMELL YOUR ANKLE, SIR.
DO YOU THINK I COULD GET A TASTE?
PATIENCE, ERIN.
JUST POPPED RIGHT OFF.
GENTLEMEN! YOU SIMPLY CAN'T KEEP AWAY! IS IT OUR FRIENDLY LITTLE TOWN'S VIBRANT NIGHTLIFE, I WONDER?
IT WAS A GOOD OFFER, MISTER GALLOWGLASS.
IT CERTAINLY WAS.
BUT I DIDN'T TAKE EXCEPTION TO THE OFFER. NO, I TOOK EXCEPTION TO THE CHARACTER OF THE INDIVIDUAL ON WHOSE BEHALF THE OFFER WAS MADE.
DO SOMETHIN', FUCKER. GIVE ME A REASON...
UH-OH.
ARE FEATHERS ABOUT TO FLY, GENTLEMEN? AND ME WITHOUT A SPECK OF HEALTH INSURANCE.

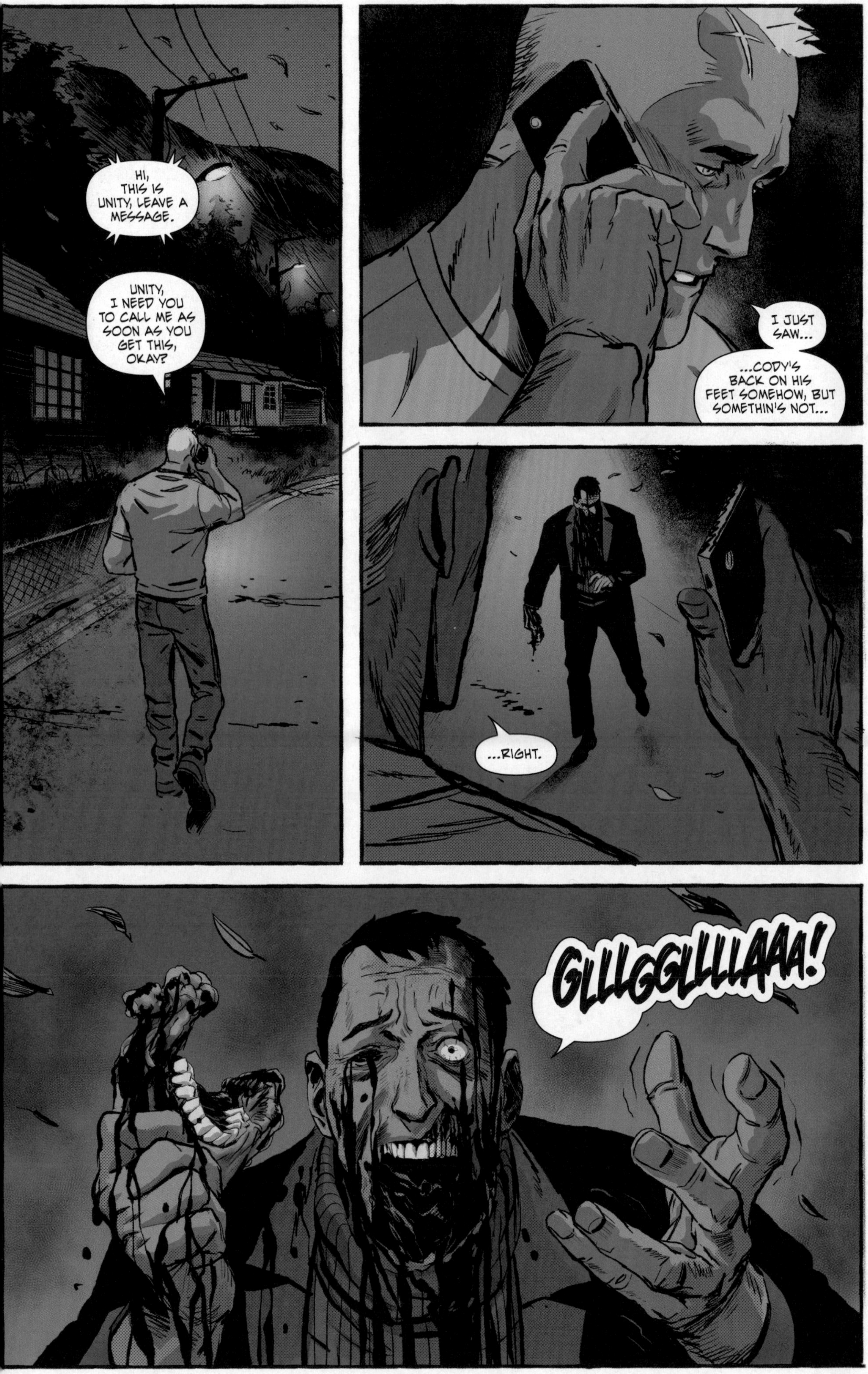
HI, THIS IS UNITY, LEAVE A MESSAGE.
UNITY, I NEED YOU TO CALL ME AS SOON AS YOU GET THIS, OKAY?
I JUST SAW...
...CODY'S BACK ON HIS FEET SOMEHOW, BUT SOMETHIN'S NOT...
...RIGHT.
GLLLGGLLLLAAA!

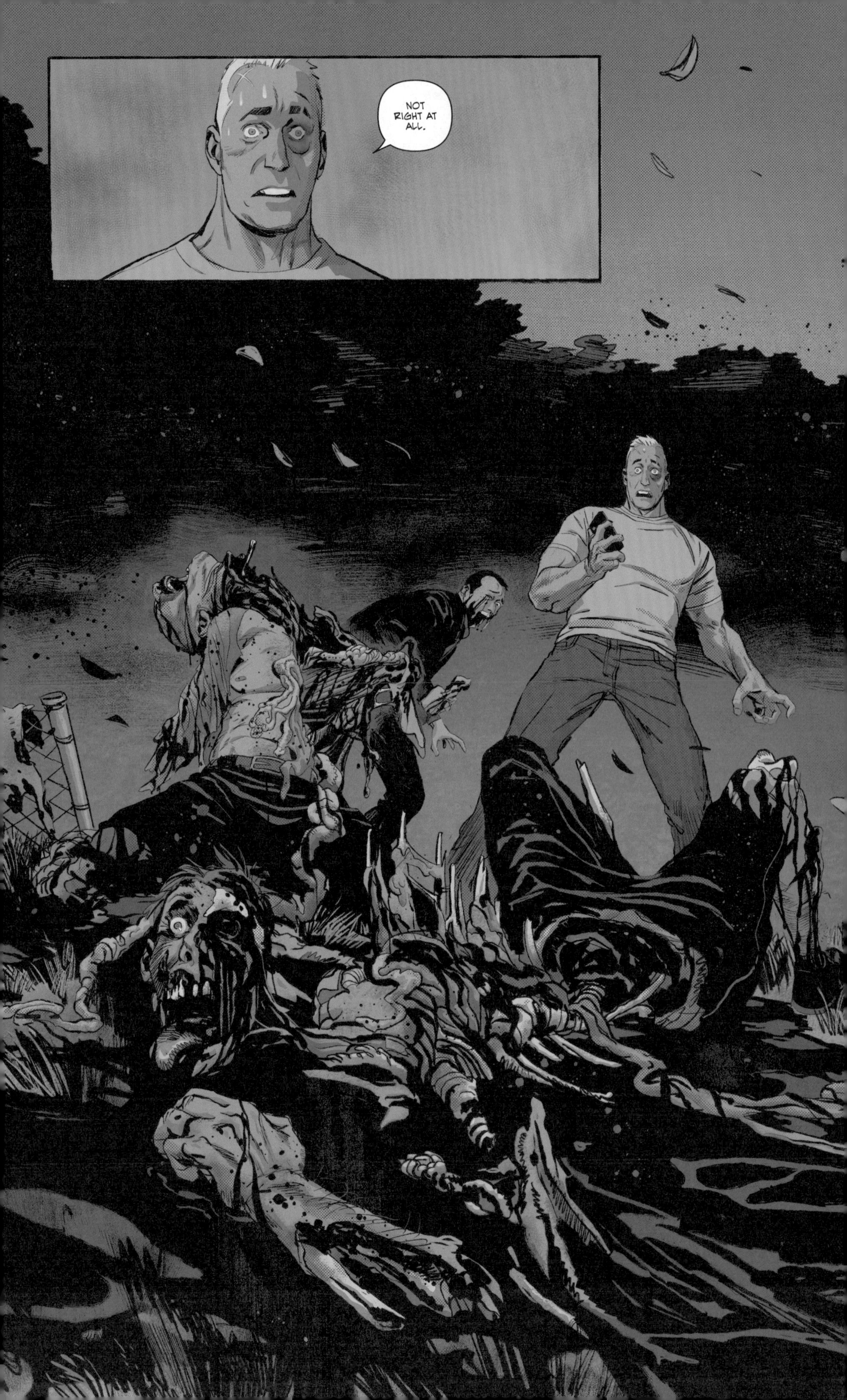
NOT RIGHT AT ALL.

CHAPTER 5

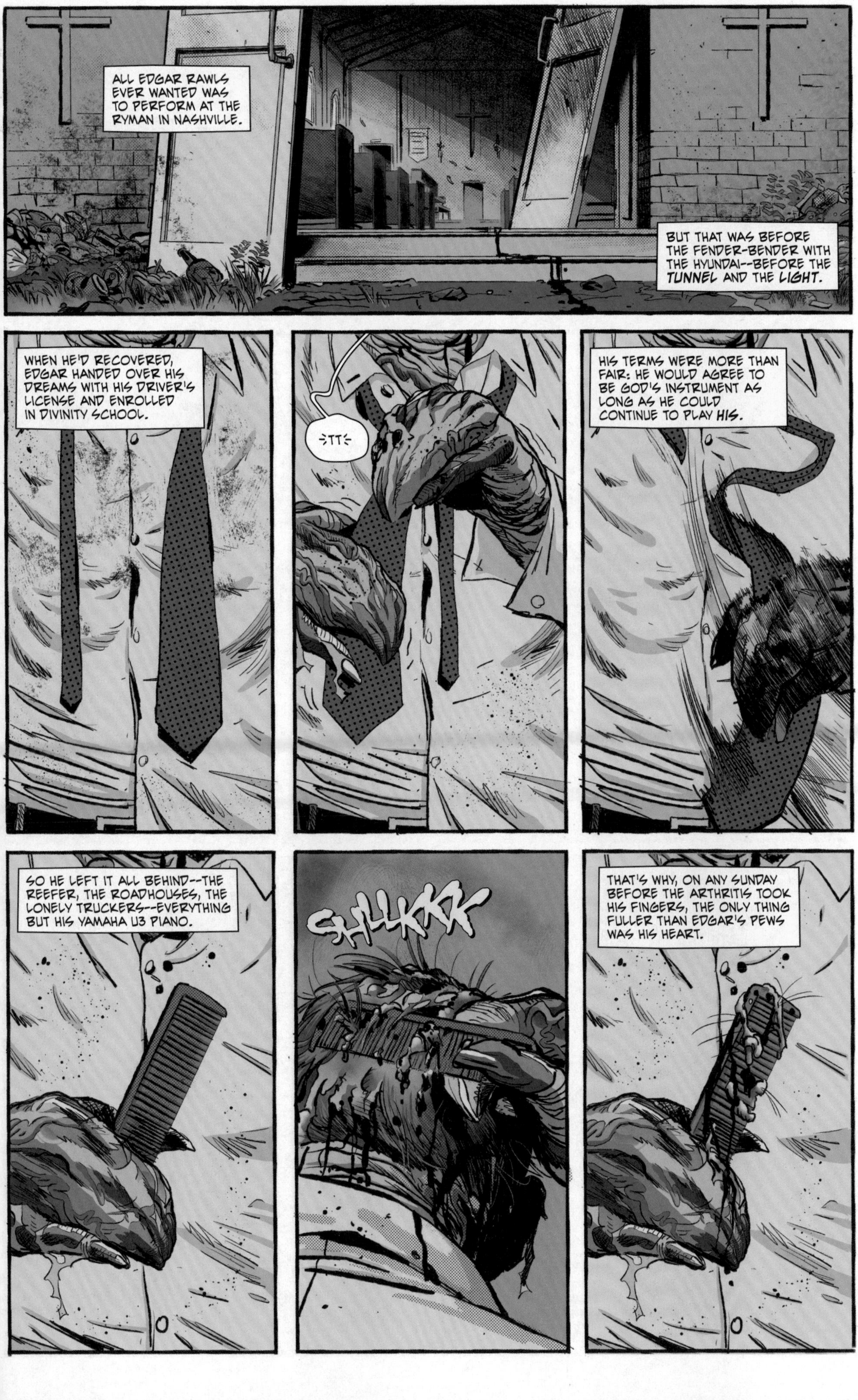
ALL EDGAR RAWLS EVER WANTED WAS TO PERFORM AT THE RYMAN IN NASHVILLE.
BUT THAT WAS BEFORE THE FENDER-BENDER WITH THE HYUNDAI--BEFORE THE TUNNEL AND THE LIGHT.
WHEN HE'D RECOVERED, EDGAR HANDED OVER HIS DREAMS WITH HIS DRIVER'S LICENSE AND ENROLLED IN DIVINITY SCHOOL.
TT
HIS TERMS WERE MORE THAN FAIR: HE WOULD AGREE TO BE GOD'S INSTRUMENT AS LONG AS HE COULD CONTINUE TO PLAY HIS.
SO HE LEFT IT ALL BEHIND--THE REEFER, THE ROADHOUSES, THE LONELY TRUCKERS--EVERYTHING BUT HIS YAMAHA U3 PIANO.
SHLLKKK
THAT'S WHY, ON ANY SUNDAY BEFORE THE ARTHRITIS TOOK HIS FINGERS, THE ONLY THING FULLER THAN EDGAR'S PEWS WAS HIS HEART.

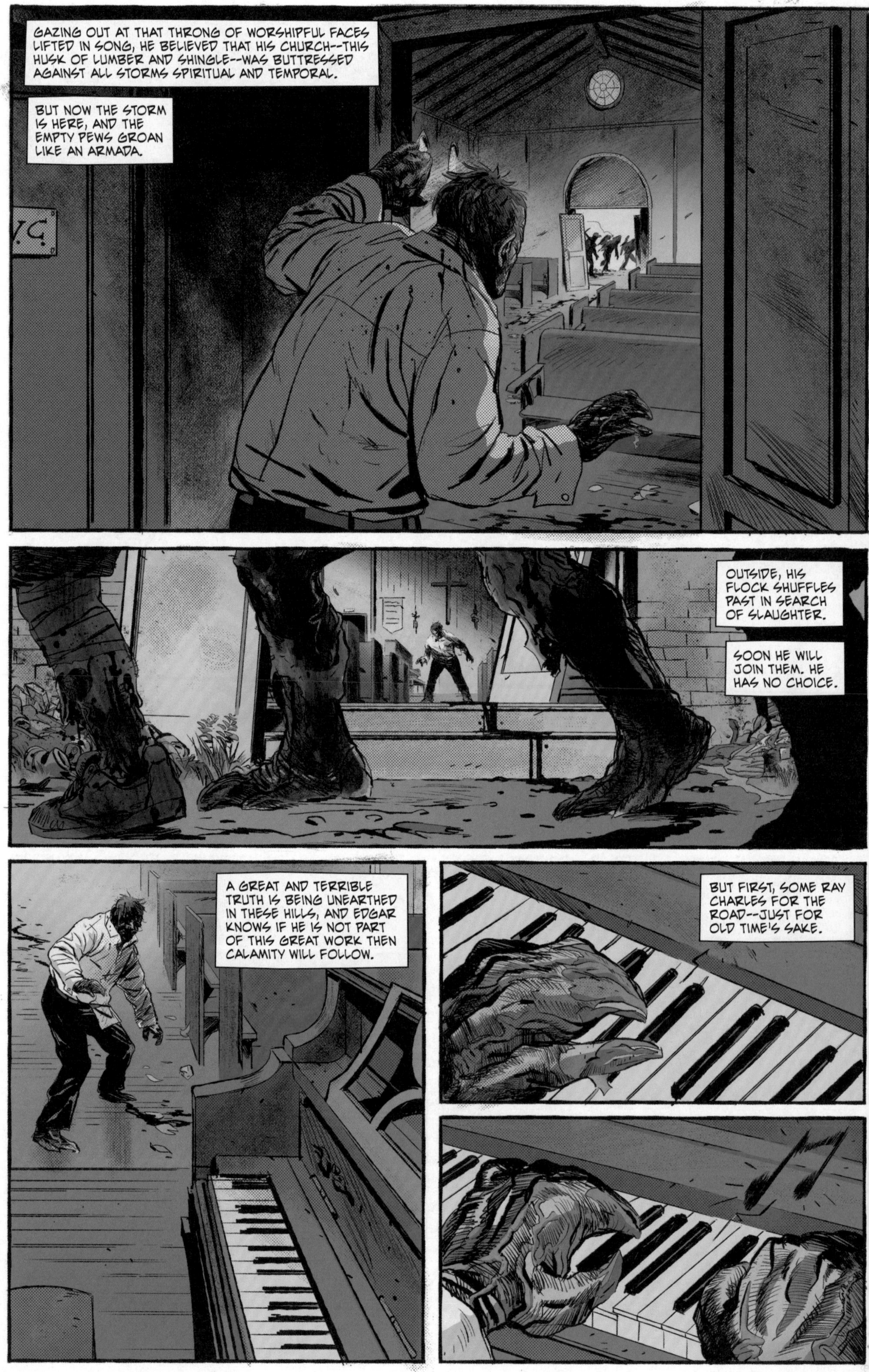
GAZING OUT AT THAT THRONG OF WORSHIPFUL FACES LIFTED IN SONG, HE BELIEVED THAT HIS CHURCH--THIS HUSK OF LUMBER AND SHINGLE--WAS BUTTRESSED AGAINST ALL STORMS SPIRITUAL AND TEMPORAL.
BUT NOW THE STORM IS HERE, AND THE EMPTY PEWS GROAN LIKE AN ARMADA.
V.G.
OUTSIDE, HIS FLOCK SHUFFLES PAST IN SEARCH OF SLAUGHTER.
SOON HE WILL JOIN THEM. HE HAS NO CHOICE.
A GREAT AND TERRIBLE TRUTH IS BEING UNEARTHED IN THESE HILLS, AND EDGAR KNOWS IF HE IS NOT PART OF THIS GREAT WORK THEN CALAMITY WILL FOLLOW.
BUT FIRST, SOME RAY CHARLES FOR THE ROAD--JUST FOR OLD TIME'S SAKE.

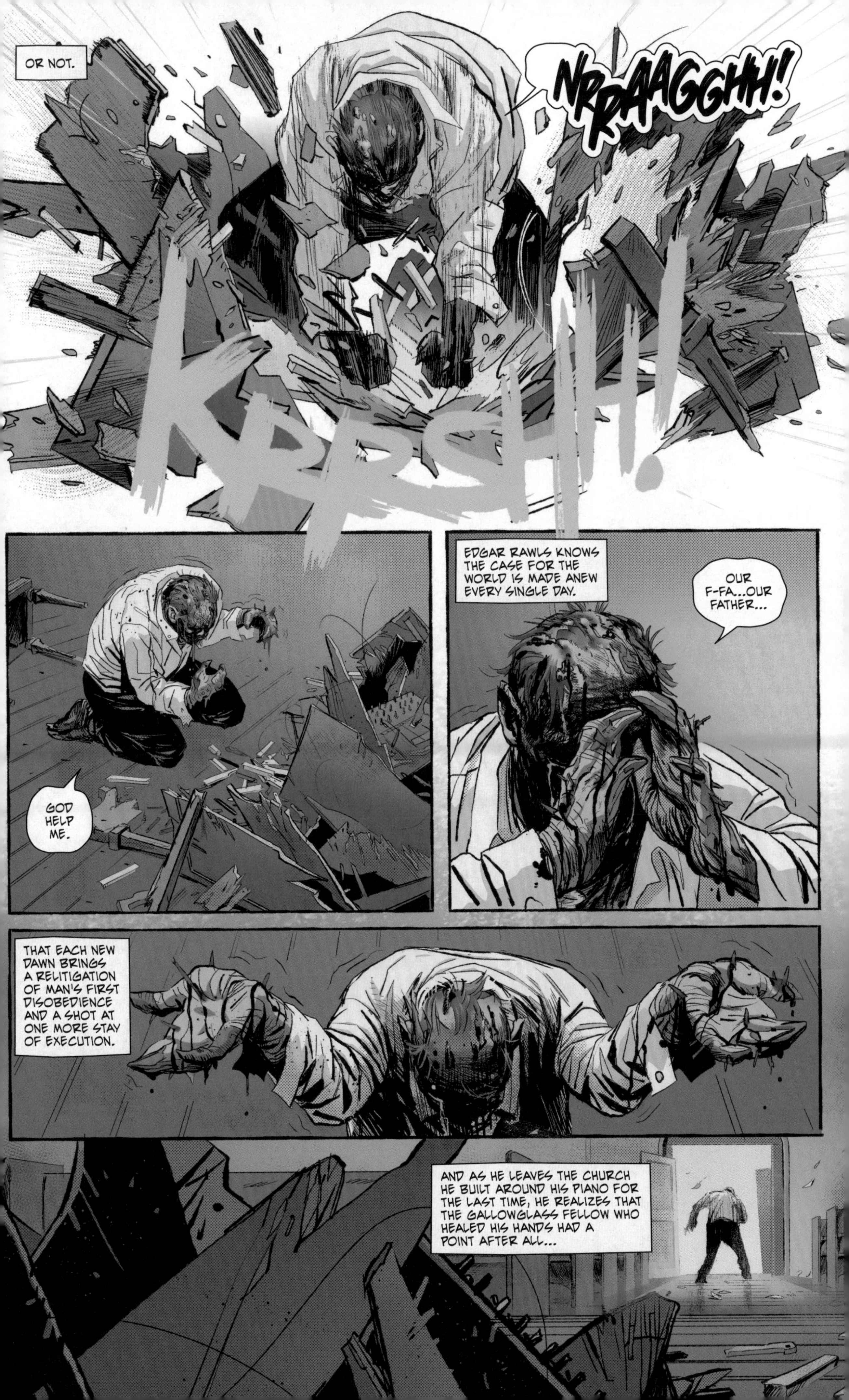
OR NOT.
NRRAAGGHH!
KRSH!!
EDGAR RAWLS KNOWS THE CASE FOR THE WORLD IS MADE ANEW EVERY SINGLE DAY.
GOD HELP ME.
OUR F-FA...OUR FATHER...
THAT EACH NEW DAWN BRINGS A RELITIGATION OF MAN'S FIRST DISOBEDIENCE AND A SHOT AT ONE MORE STAY OF EXECUTION.
AND AS HE LEAVES THE CHURCH HE BUILT AROUND HIS PIANO FOR THE LAST TIME, HE REALIZES THAT THE GALLOWGLASS FELLOW WHO HEALED HIS HANDS HAD A POINT AFTER ALL...

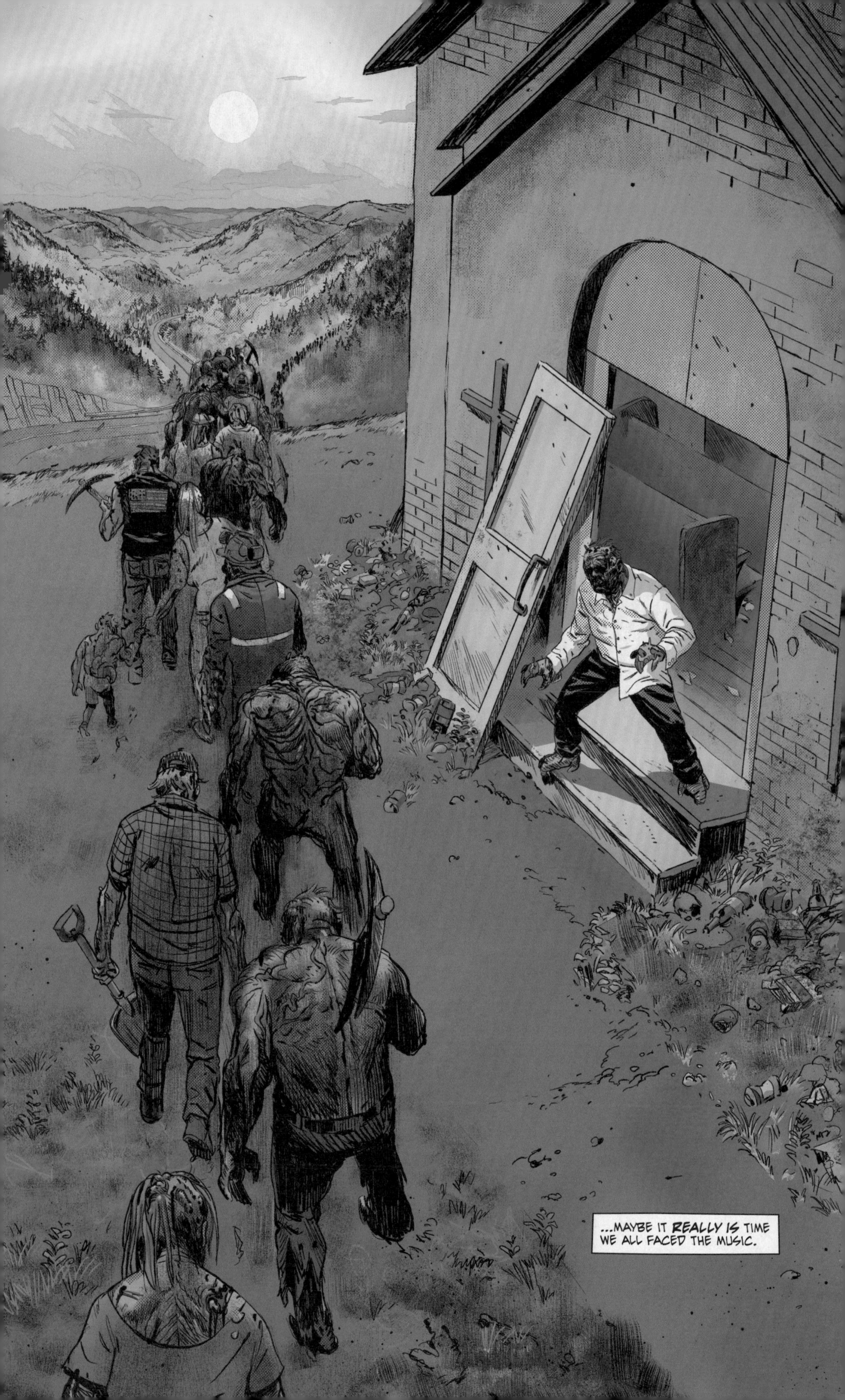
...MAYBE IT REALLY IS TIME
WE ALL FACED THE MUSIC.

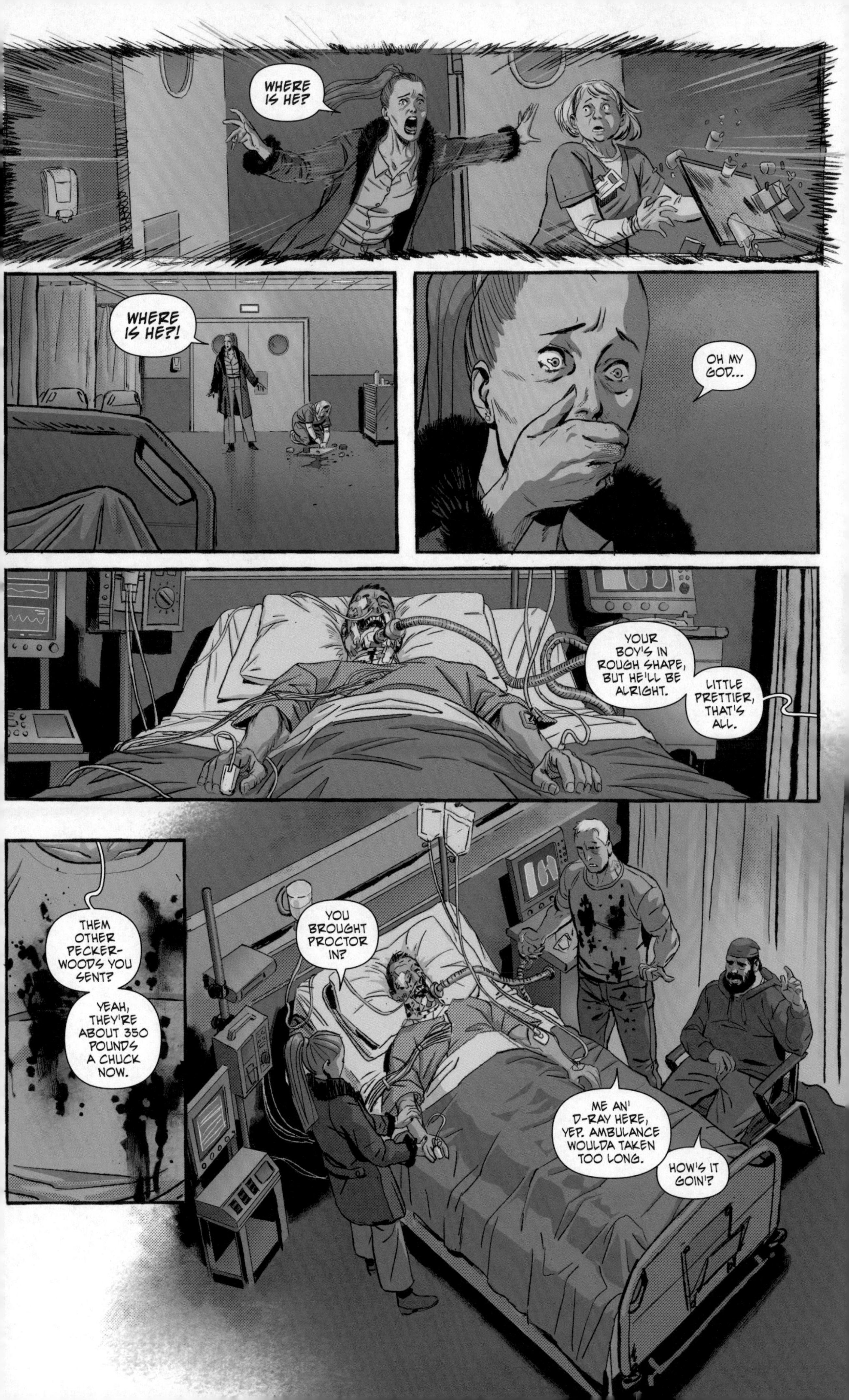
WHERE IS HE?
WHERE IS HE?!
OH MY GOD...
YOUR BOY'S IN ROUGH SHAPE, BUT HE'LL BE ALRIGHT.
LITTLE PRETTIER, THAT'S ALL.
THEM OTHER PECKER-WOODS YOU SENT?
YEAH, THEY'RE ABOUT 350 POUNDS A CHUCK NOW.
YOU BROUGHT PROCTOR IN?
ME AN' D-RAY HERE, YEP. AMBULANCE WOULDA TAKEN TOO LONG.
HOW'S IT GOIN'?

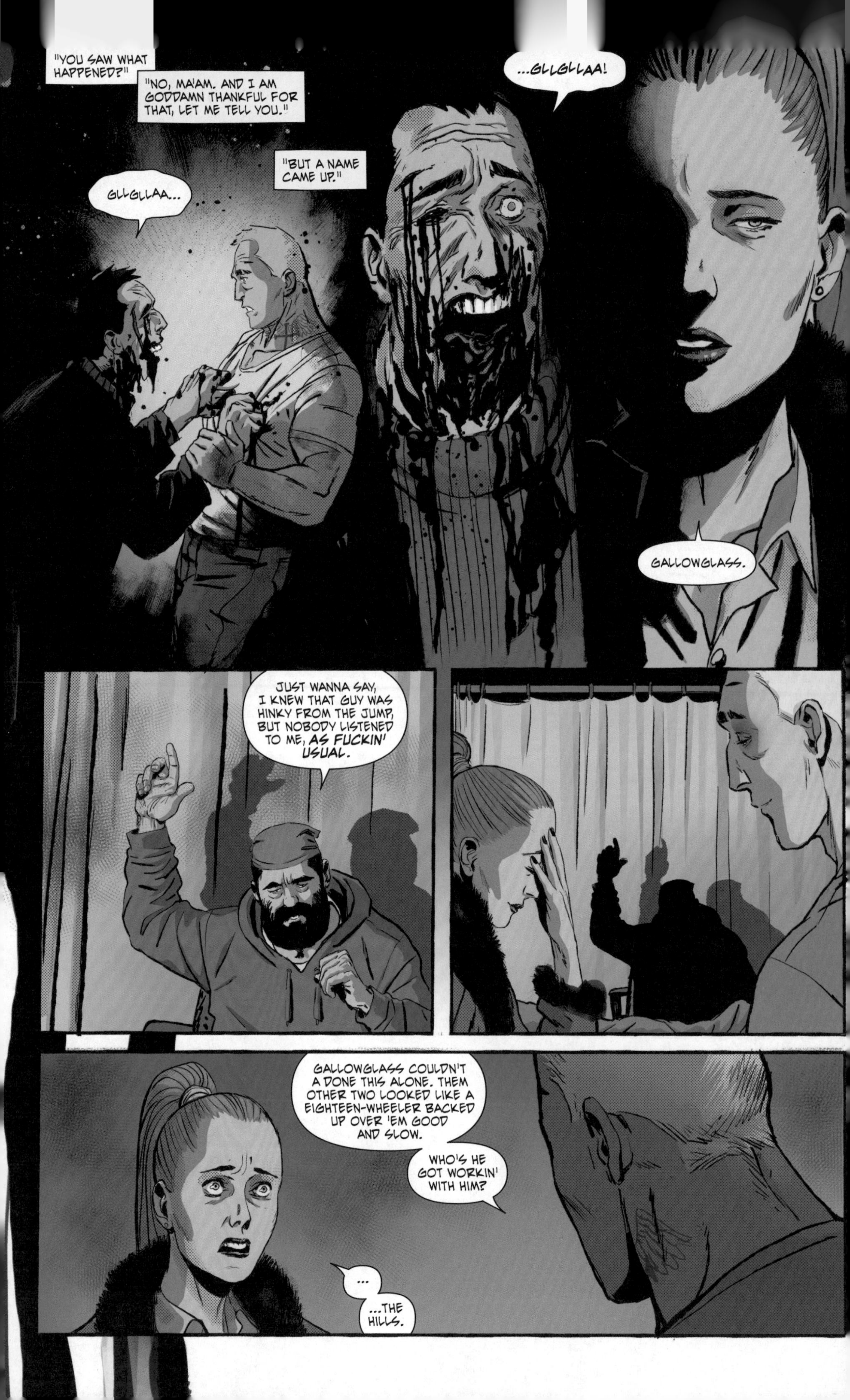
"YOU SAW WHAT HAPPENED?"
"NO, MA'AM. AND I AM GODDAMN THANKFUL FOR THAT, LET ME TELL YOU."
"BUT A NAME CAME UP."
GLLGLLAA...
...GLLGLLAA!
GALLOWGLASS.
JUST WANNA SAY, I KNEW THAT GUY WAS HINKY FROM THE JUMP, BUT NOBODY LISTENED TO ME, AS FUCKIN' USUAL.
GALLOWGLASS COULDN'T A DONE THIS ALONE. THEM OTHER TWO LOOKED LIKE A EIGHTEEN-WHEELER BACKED UP OVER 'EM GOOD AND SLOW.
WHO'S HE GOT WORKIN' WITH HIM?
...
...THE HILLS.

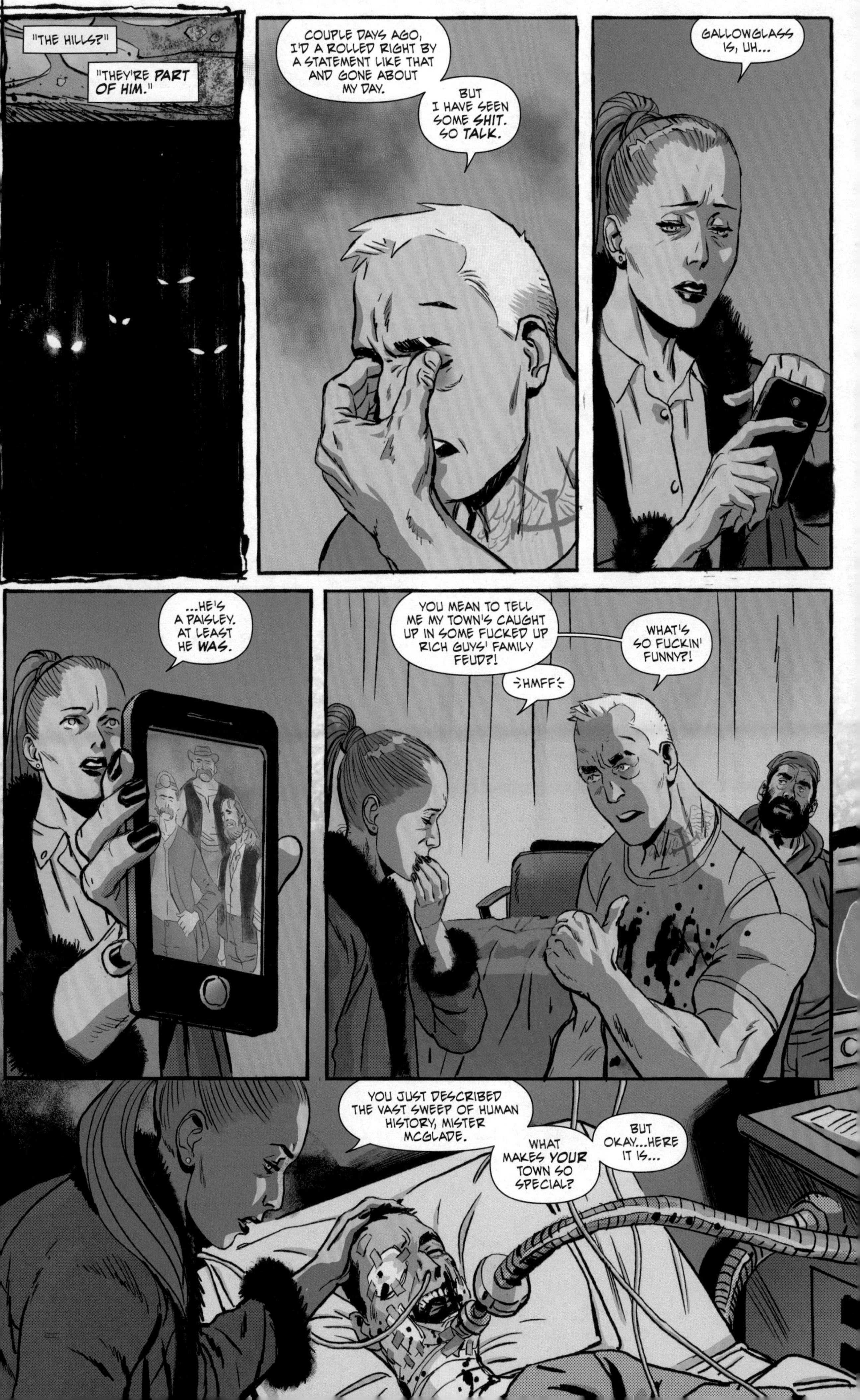
"THE HILLS?"
"THEY'RE PART OF HIM."
COUPLE DAYS AGO, I'D A ROLLED RIGHT BY A STATEMENT LIKE THAT AND GONE ABOUT MY DAY.
BUT I HAVE SEEN SOME SHIT. SO TALK.
GALLOWGLASS IS, UH...
...HE'S A PAISLEY. AT LEAST HE WAS.
YOU MEAN TO TELL ME MY TOWN'S CAUGHT UP IN SOME FUCKED UP RICH GUYS' FAMILY FEUD?!
WHAT'S SO FUCKIN' FUNNY?!
HMFF
YOU JUST DESCRIBED THE VAST SWEEP OF HUMAN HISTORY, MISTER MCGLADE.
WHAT MAKES YOUR TOWN SO SPECIAL?
BUT OKAY...HERE IT IS...

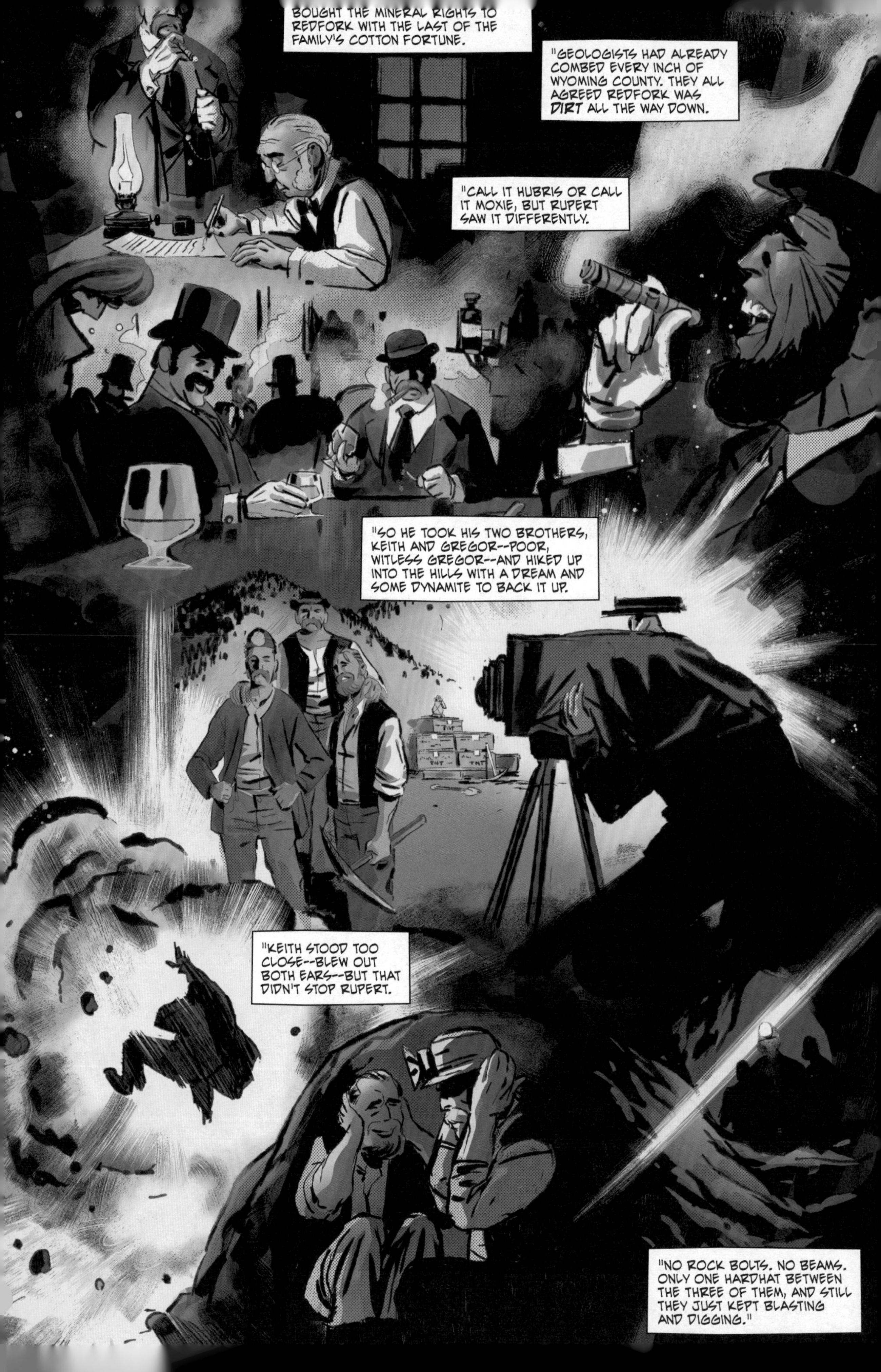
BOUGHT THE MINERAL RIGHTS TO REDFORK WITH THE LAST OF THE FAMILY'S COTTON FORTUNE.
"GEOLOGISTS HAD ALREADY COMBED EVERY INCH OF WYOMING COUNTY. THEY ALL AGREED REDFORK WAS DIRT ALL THE WAY DOWN.
"CALL IT HUBRIS OR CALL IT MOXIE, BUT RUPERT SAW IT DIFFERENTLY.
"SO HE TOOK HIS TWO BROTHERS, KEITH AND GREGOR--POOR, WITLESS GREGOR--AND HIKED UP INTO THE HILLS WITH A DREAM AND SOME DYNAMITE TO BACK IT UP.
"KEITH STOOD TOO CLOSE--BLEW OUT BOTH EARS--BUT THAT DIDN'T STOP RUPERT.
"NO ROCK BOLTS. NO BEAMS. ONLY ONE HARDHAT BETWEEN THE THREE OF THEM, AND STILL THEY JUST KEPT BLASTING AND DIGGING."

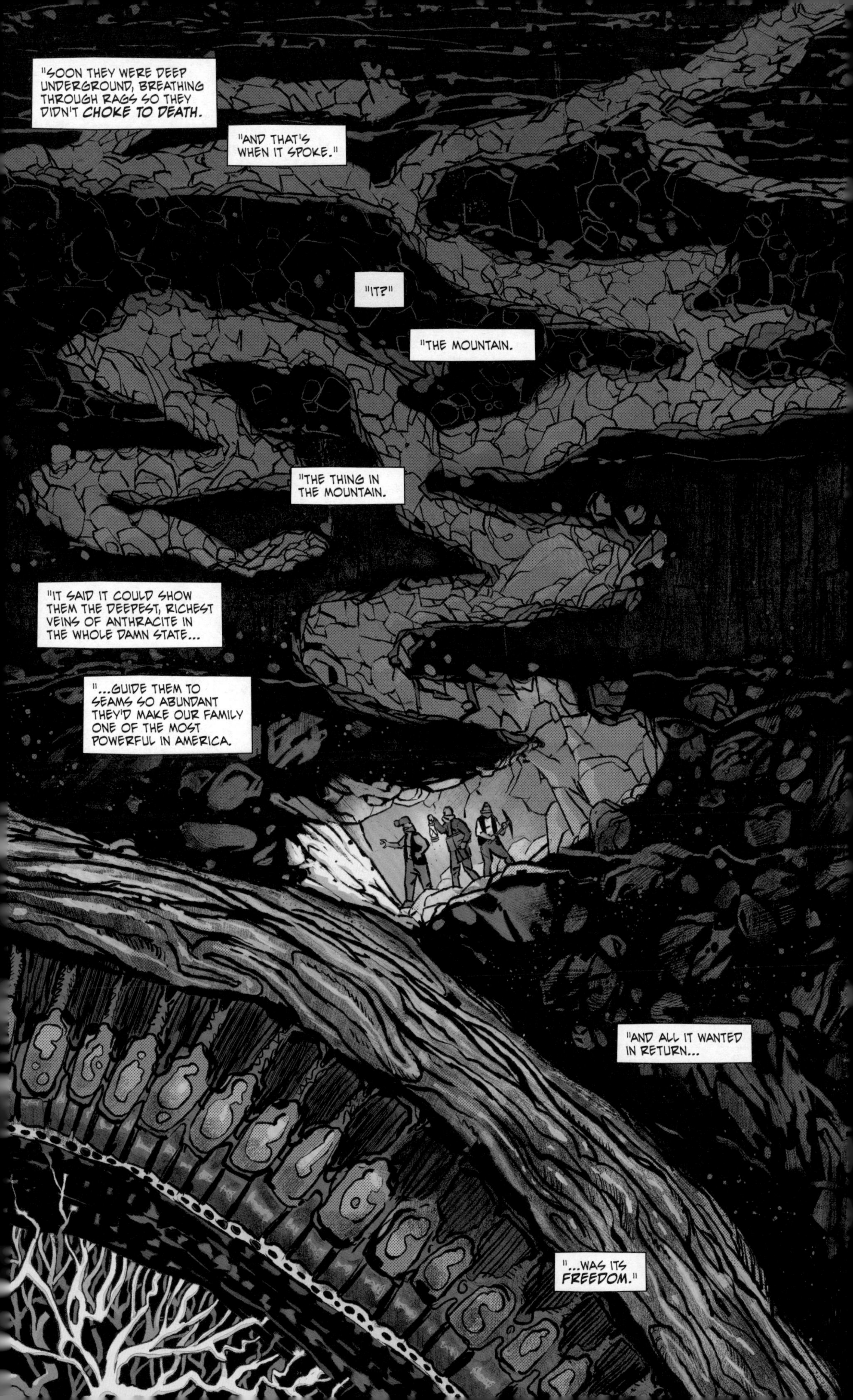
"SOON THEY WERE DEEP UNDERGROUND, BREATHING THROUGH RAGS SO THEY DIDN'T CHOKE TO DEATH.
"AND THAT'S WHEN IT SPOKE."
"IT?"
"THE MOUNTAIN.
"THE THING IN THE MOUNTAIN.
"IT SAID IT COULD SHOW THEM THE DEEPEST, RICHEST VEINS OF ANTHRACITE IN THE WHOLE DAMN STATE...
"...GUIDE THEM TO SEAMS SO ABUNDANT THEY'D MAKE OUR FAMILY ONE OF THE MOST POWERFUL IN AMERICA.
"AND ALL IT WANTED IN RETURN...
"...WAS ITS FREEDOM."

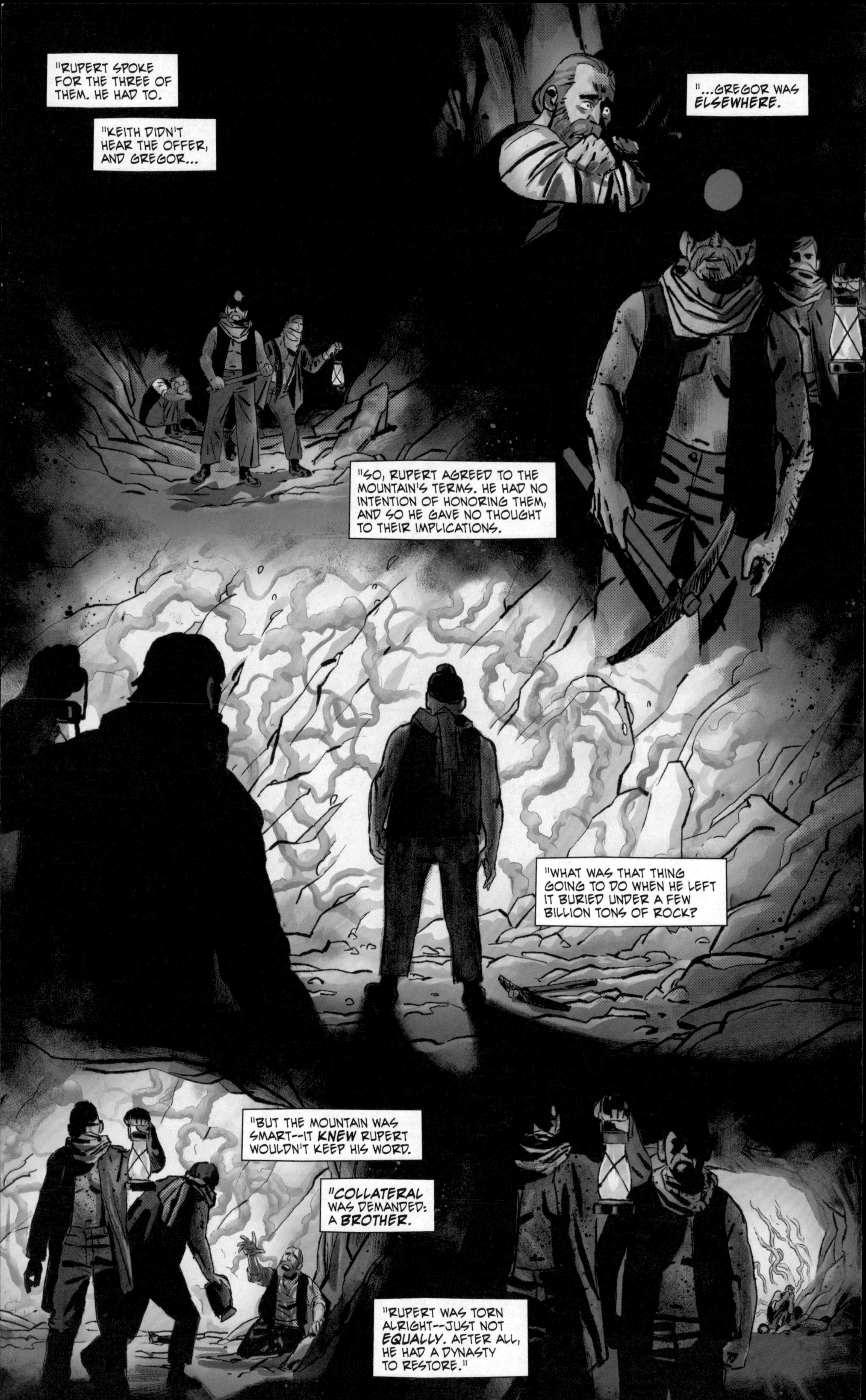
"RUPERT SPOKE FOR THE THREE OF THEM. HE HAD TO.
"KEITH DIDN'T HEAR THE OFFER, AND GREGOR...
"...GREGOR WAS ELSEWHERE.
"SO, RUPERT AGREED TO THE MOUNTAIN'S TERMS. HE HAD NO INTENTION OF HONORING THEM, AND SO HE GAVE NO THOUGHT TO THEIR IMPLICATIONS.
"WHAT WAS THAT THING GOING TO DO WHEN HE LEFT IT BURIED UNDER A FEW BILLION TONS OF ROCK?
"BUT THE MOUNTAIN WAS SMART--IT KNEW RUPERT WOULDN'T KEEP HIS WORD.
"COLLATERAL WAS DEMANDED: A BROTHER.
"RUPERT WAS TORN ALRIGHT--JUST NOT EQUALLY. AFTER ALL, HE HAD A DYNASTY TO RESTORE."

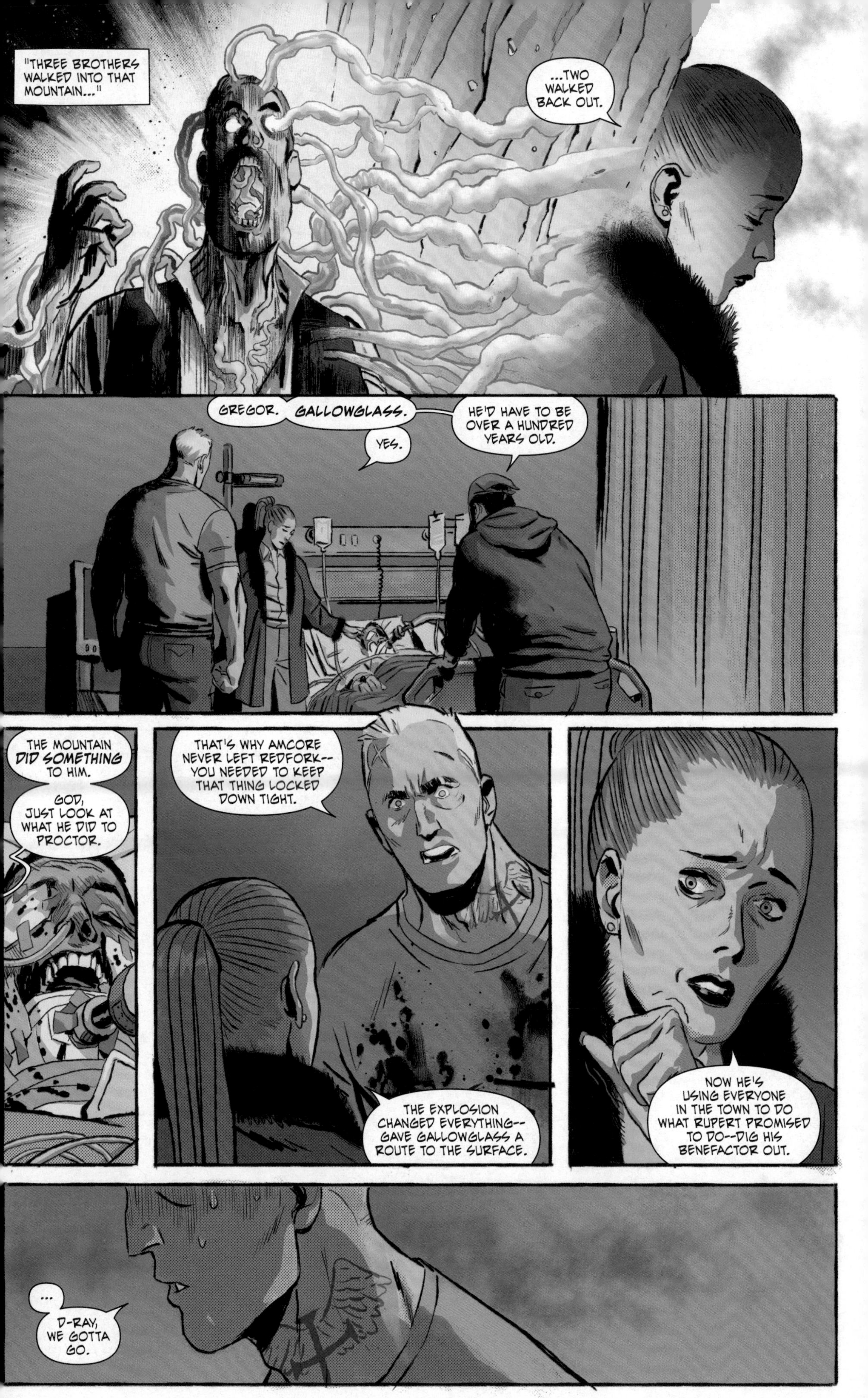
"THREE BROTHERS WALKED INTO THAT MOUNTAIN..."
...TWO WALKED BACK OUT.
GREGOR.
GALLOWGLASS.
YES.
HE'D HAVE TO BE OVER A HUNDRED YEARS OLD.
THE MOUNTAIN DID SOMETHING TO HIM.
GOD, JUST LOOK AT WHAT HE DID TO PROCTOR.
THAT'S WHY AMCORE NEVER LEFT REDFORK-- YOU NEEDED TO KEEP THAT THING LOCKED DOWN TIGHT.
THE EXPLOSION CHANGED EVERYTHING-- GAVE GALLOWGLASS A ROUTE TO THE SURFACE.
NOW HE'S USING EVERYONE IN THE TOWN TO DO WHAT RUPERT PROMISED TO DO--DIG HIS BENEFACTOR OUT.
...
D-RAY, WE GOTTA GO.

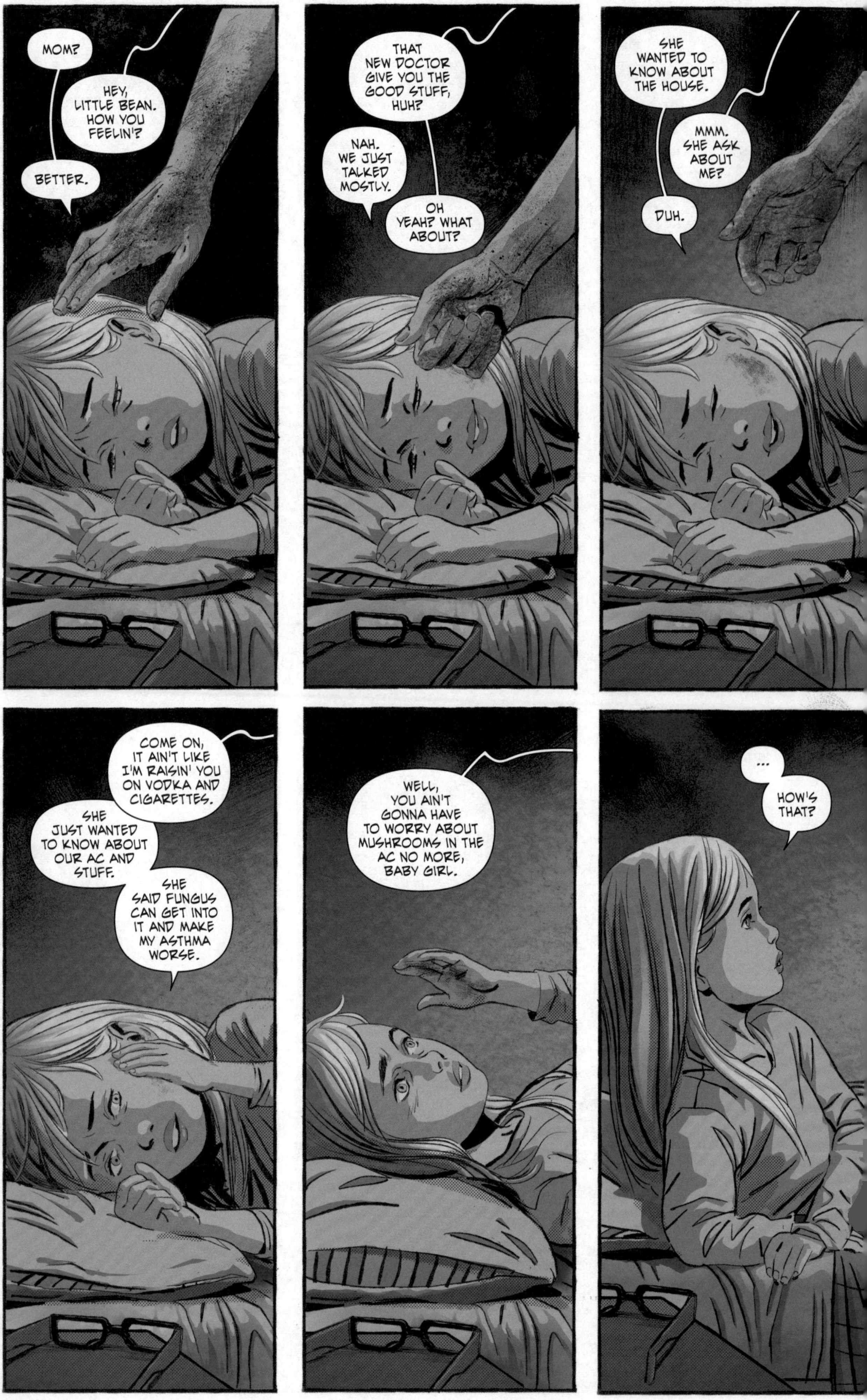
MOM?
HEY, LITTLE BEAN. HOW YOU FEELIN'?
BETTER.
THAT NEW DOCTOR GIVE YOU THE GOOD STUFF, HUH?
NAH. WE JUST TALKED MOSTLY.
OH YEAH? WHAT ABOUT?
SHE WANTED TO KNOW ABOUT THE HOUSE.
MMM. SHE ASK ABOUT ME?
DUH.
COME ON, IT AIN'T LIKE I'M RAISIN' YOU ON VODKA AND CIGARETTES.
SHE JUST WANTED TO KNOW ABOUT OUR AC AND STUFF.
SHE SAID FUNGUS CAN GET INTO IT AND MAKE MY ASTHMA WORSE.
WELL, YOU AIN'T GONNA HAVE TO WORRY ABOUT MUSHROOMS IN THE AC NO MORE, BABY GIRL.
...
HOW'S THAT?

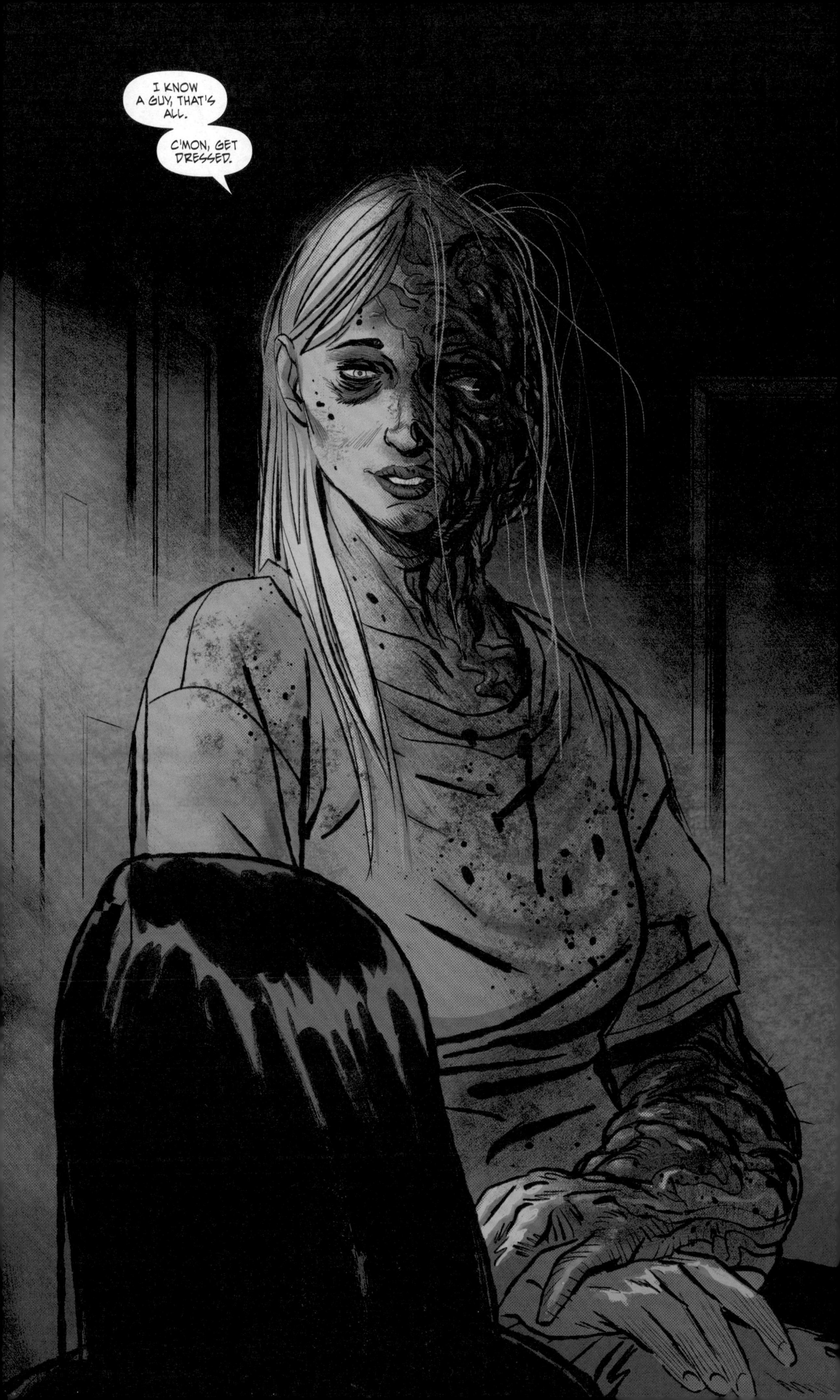
I KNOW A GUY, THAT'S ALL.
C'MON, GET DRESSED.

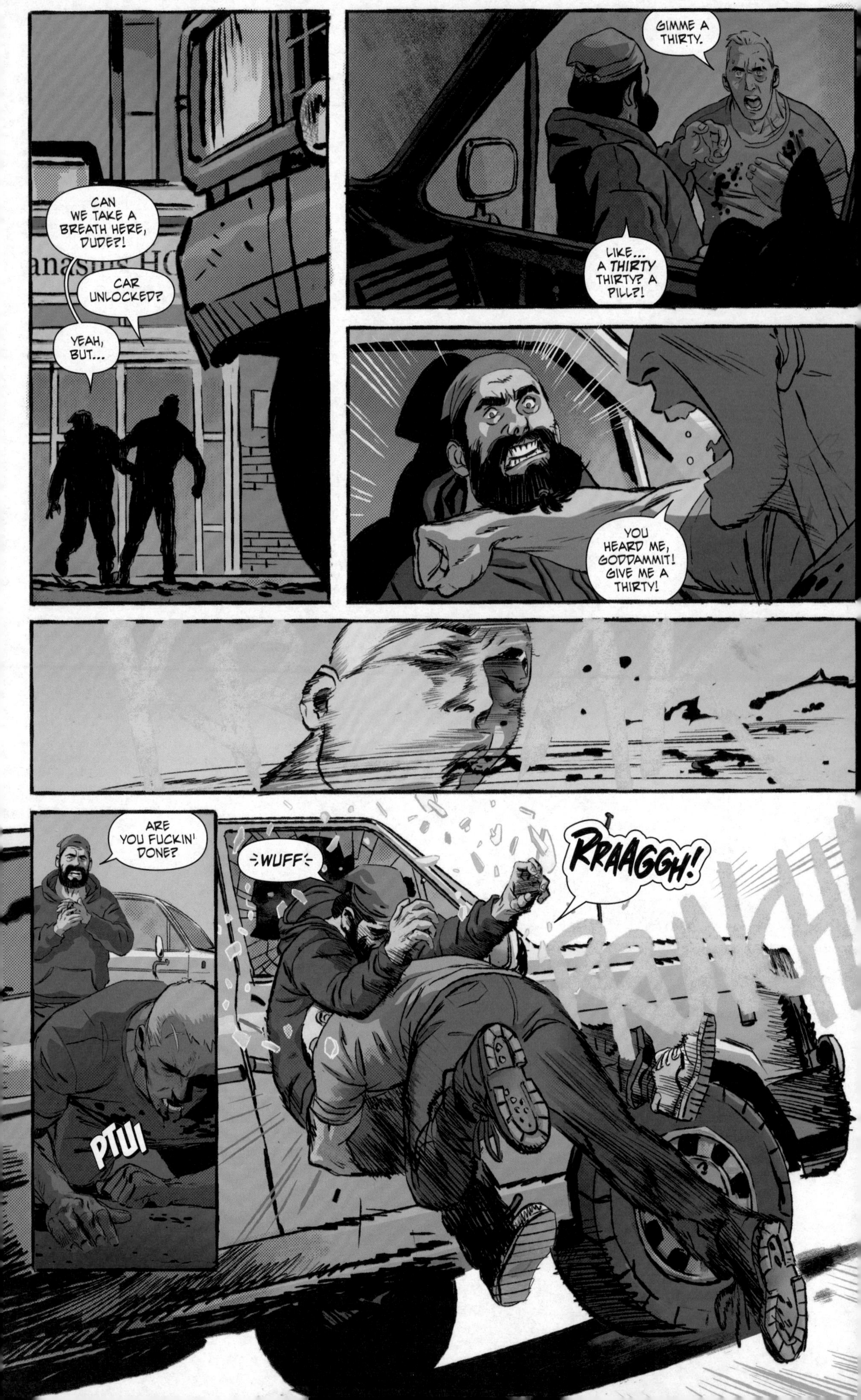

CAN WE TAKE A BREATH HERE, DUDE?!
CAR UNLOCKED?
YEAH, BUT...
GIMME A THIRTY.
LIKE... A THIRTY THIRTY? A PILL?!
YOU HEARD ME, GODDAMMIT! GIVE ME A THIRTY!
ARE YOU FUCKIN' DONE?
WUFF
RRAAGGH!
PTUI

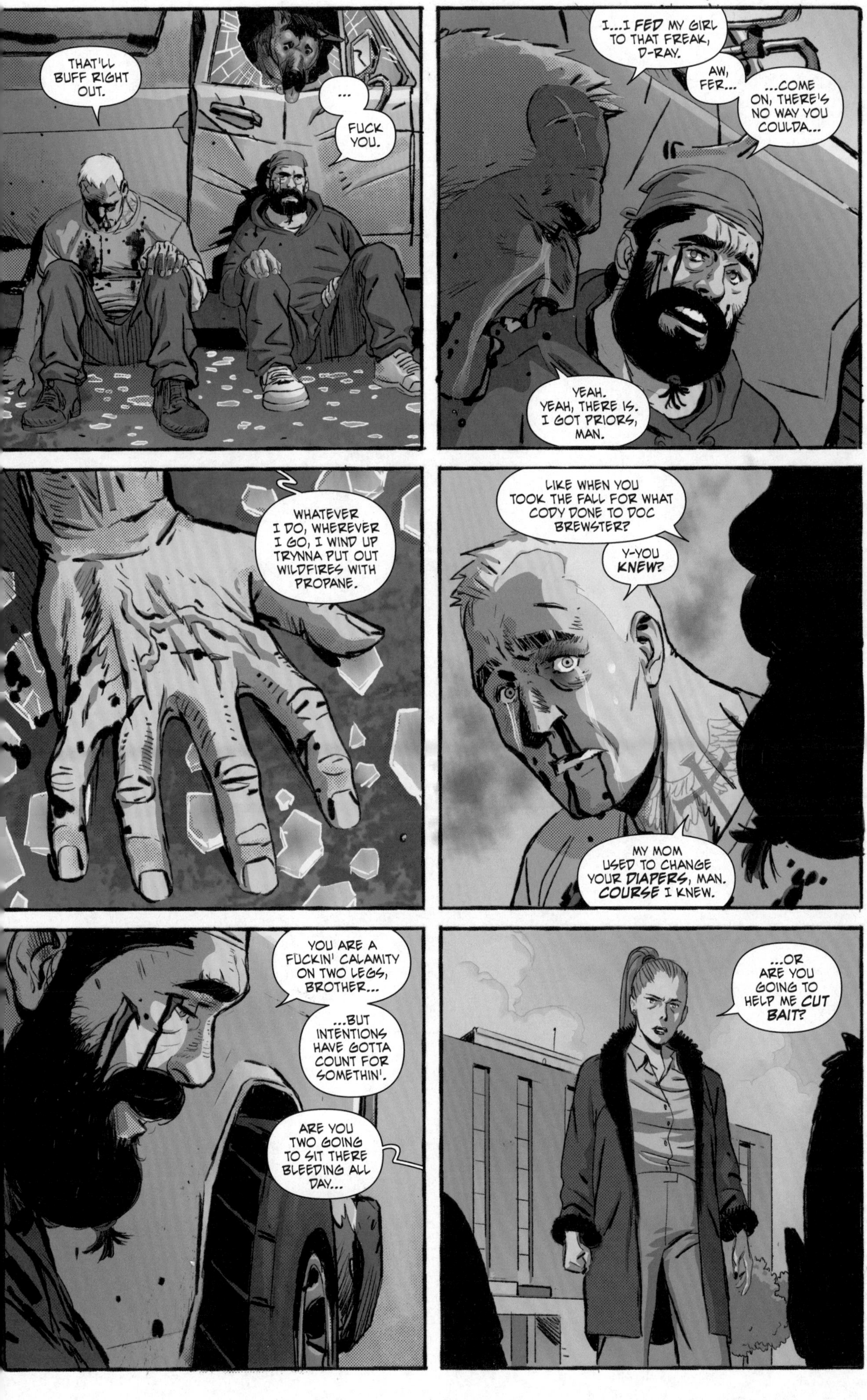
THAT'LL BUFF RIGHT OUT.
...
FUCK YOU.
I...I **FED** MY GIRL TO THAT FREAK, D-RAY.
AW, FER...
...COME ON, THERE'S NO WAY YOU COULDA...
YEAH. YEAH, THERE IS. I GOT PRIORS, MAN.
WHATEVER I DO, WHEREVER I GO, I WIND UP TRYNNA PUT OUT WILDFIRES WITH PROPANE.
LIKE WHEN YOU TOOK THE FALL FOR WHAT CODY DONE TO DOC BREWSTER?
Y-YOU **KNEW?**
MY MOM USED TO CHANGE YOUR **DIAPERS**, MAN. **COURSE** I KNEW.
YOU ARE A FUCKIN' CALAMITY ON TWO LEGS, BROTHER...
...BUT INTENTIONS HAVE GOTTA COUNT FOR SOMETHIN'.
ARE YOU TWO GOING TO SIT THERE BLEEDING ALL DAY...
...OR ARE YOU GOING TO HELP ME **CUT BAIT?**

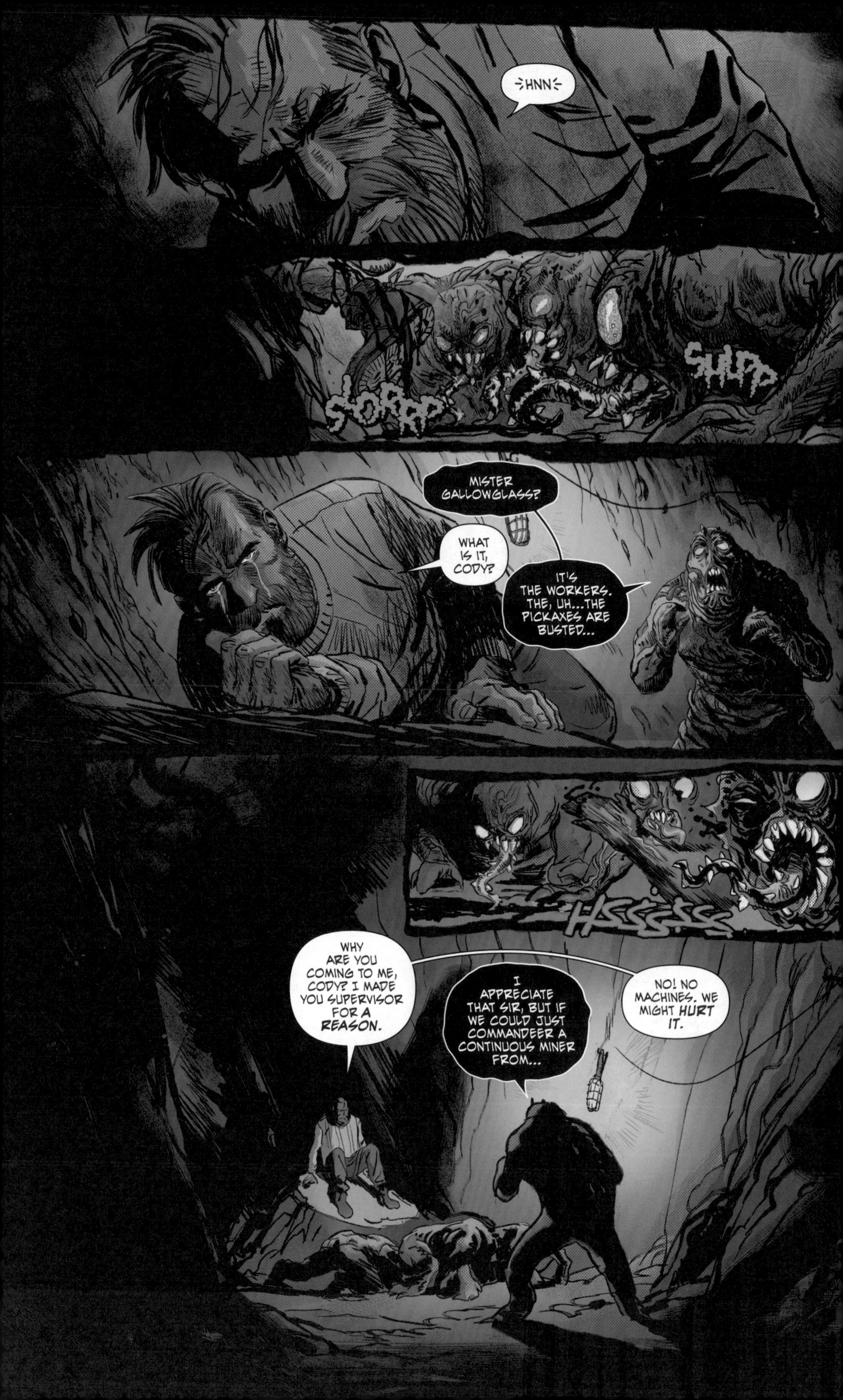

HNN
SHLPP
SLORRP
MISTER GALLOWGLASS?
WHAT IS IT, CODY?
IT'S THE WORKERS. THE, UH...THE PICKAXES ARE BUSTED...
HSSSSS
WHY ARE YOU COMING TO ME, CODY? I MADE YOU SUPERVISOR FOR A REASON.
I APPRECIATE THAT SIR, BUT IF WE COULD JUST COMMANDEER A CONTINUOUS MINER FROM...
NO! NO MACHINES. WE MIGHT HURT IT.

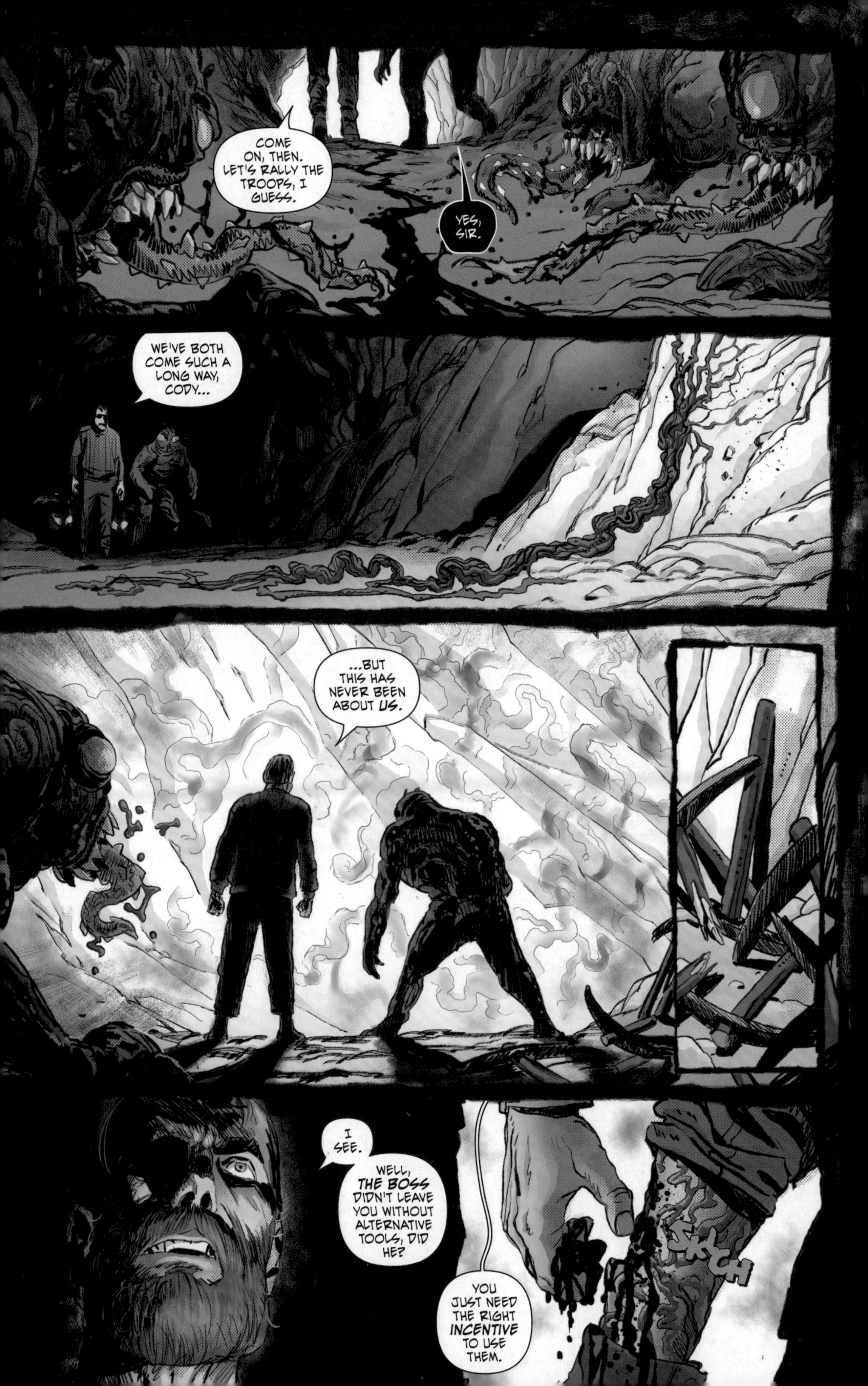

COME ON, THEN. LET'S RALLY THE TROOPS, I GUESS.
YES, SIR.
WE'VE BOTH COME SUCH A LONG WAY, CODY...
...BUT THIS HAS NEVER BEEN ABOUT US.
I SEE.
WELL, THE BOSS DIDN'T LEAVE YOU WITHOUT ALTERNATIVE TOOLS, DID HE?
SKCH
YOU JUST NEED THE RIGHT INCENTIVE TO USE THEM.

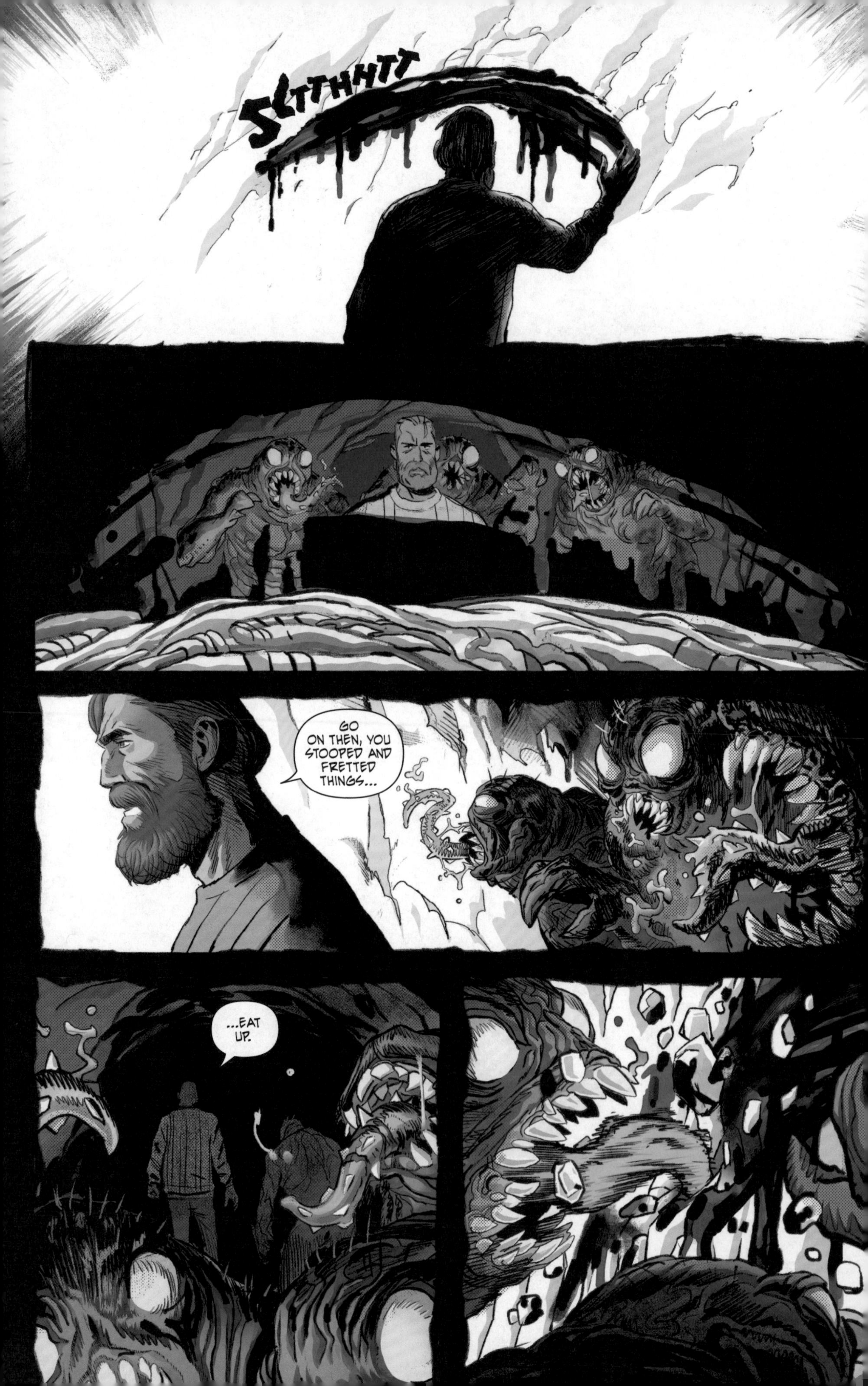
SLTTHHTT
GO ON THEN, YOU STOOPED AND FRETTED THINGS...
...EAT UP.

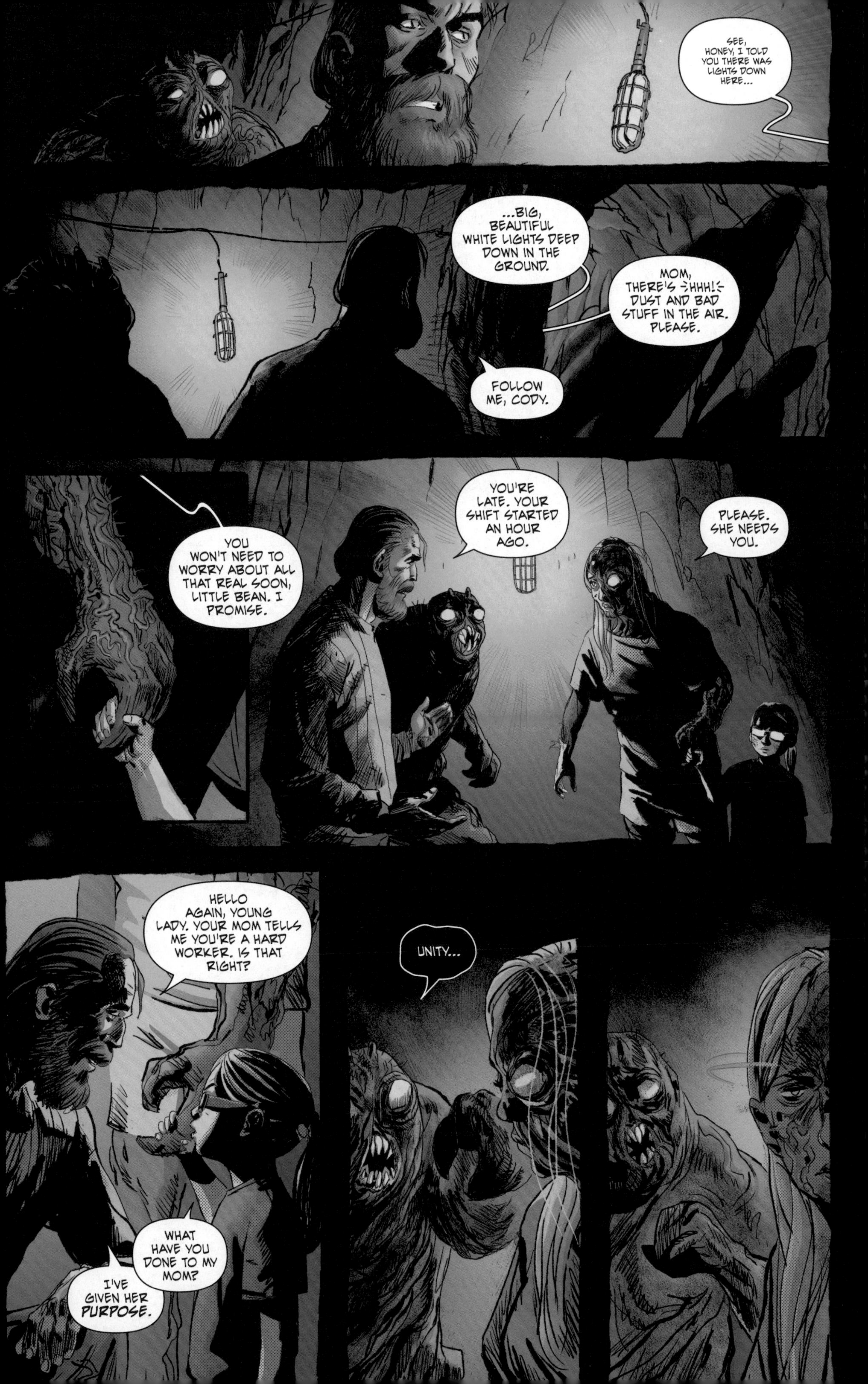
SEE, HONEY, I TOLD YOU THERE WAS LIGHTS DOWN HERE...
...BIG, BEAUTIFUL WHITE LIGHTS DEEP DOWN IN THE GROUND.
MOM, THERE'S -HHH!- DUST AND BAD STUFF IN THE AIR. PLEASE.
FOLLOW ME, CODY.
YOU WON'T NEED TO WORRY ABOUT ALL THAT REAL SOON, LITTLE BEAN. I PROMISE.
YOU'RE LATE. YOUR SHIFT STARTED AN HOUR AGO.
PLEASE. SHE NEEDS YOU.
HELLO AGAIN, YOUNG LADY. YOUR MOM TELLS ME YOU'RE A HARD WORKER. IS THAT RIGHT?
WHAT HAVE YOU DONE TO MY MOM?
I'VE GIVEN HER PURPOSE.
UNITY...

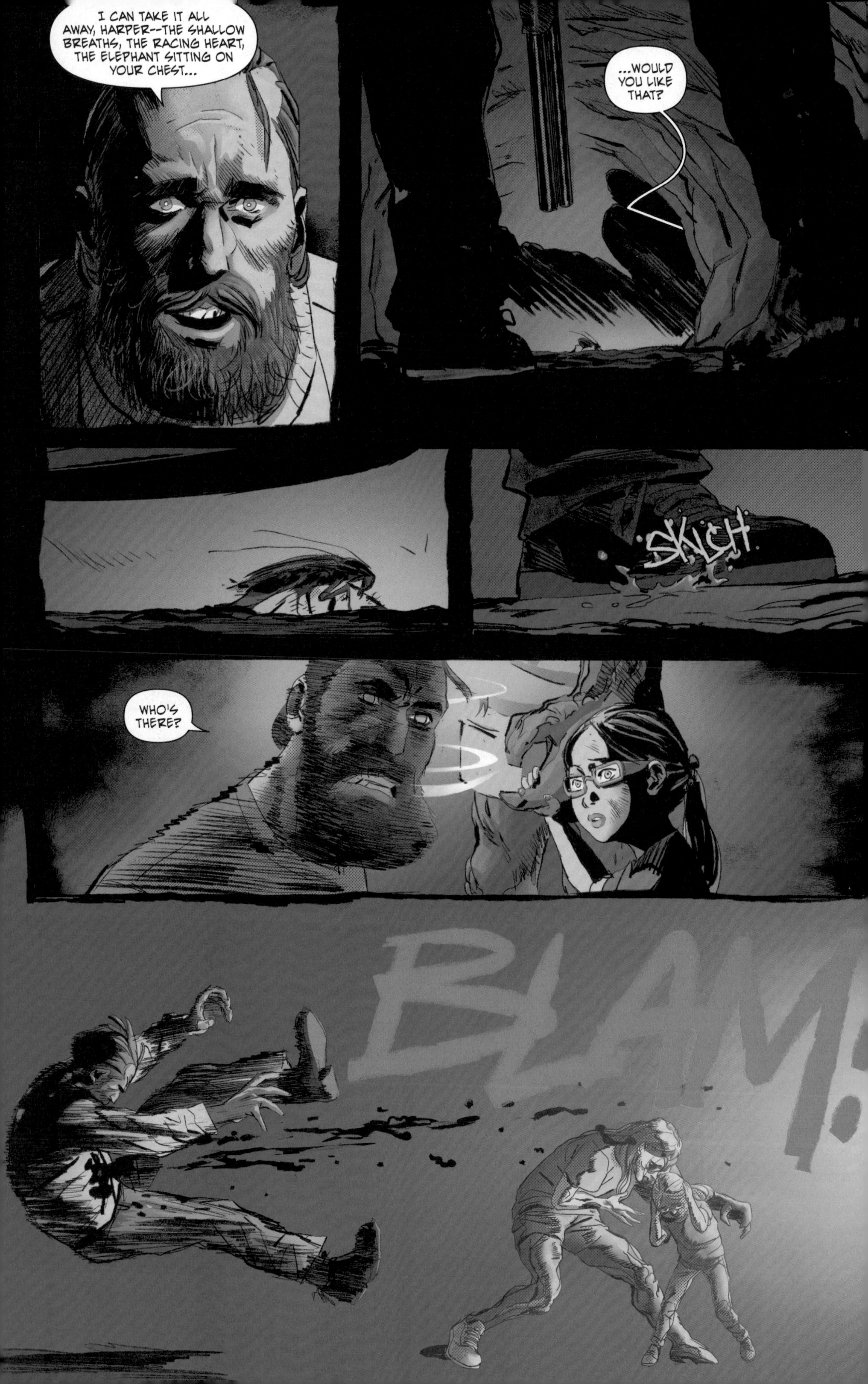
I CAN TAKE IT ALL AWAY, HARPER--THE SHALLOW BREATHS, THE RACING HEART, THE ELEPHANT SITTING ON YOUR CHEST...
...WOULD YOU LIKE THAT?
SKLCH
WHO'S THERE?
BLAM!

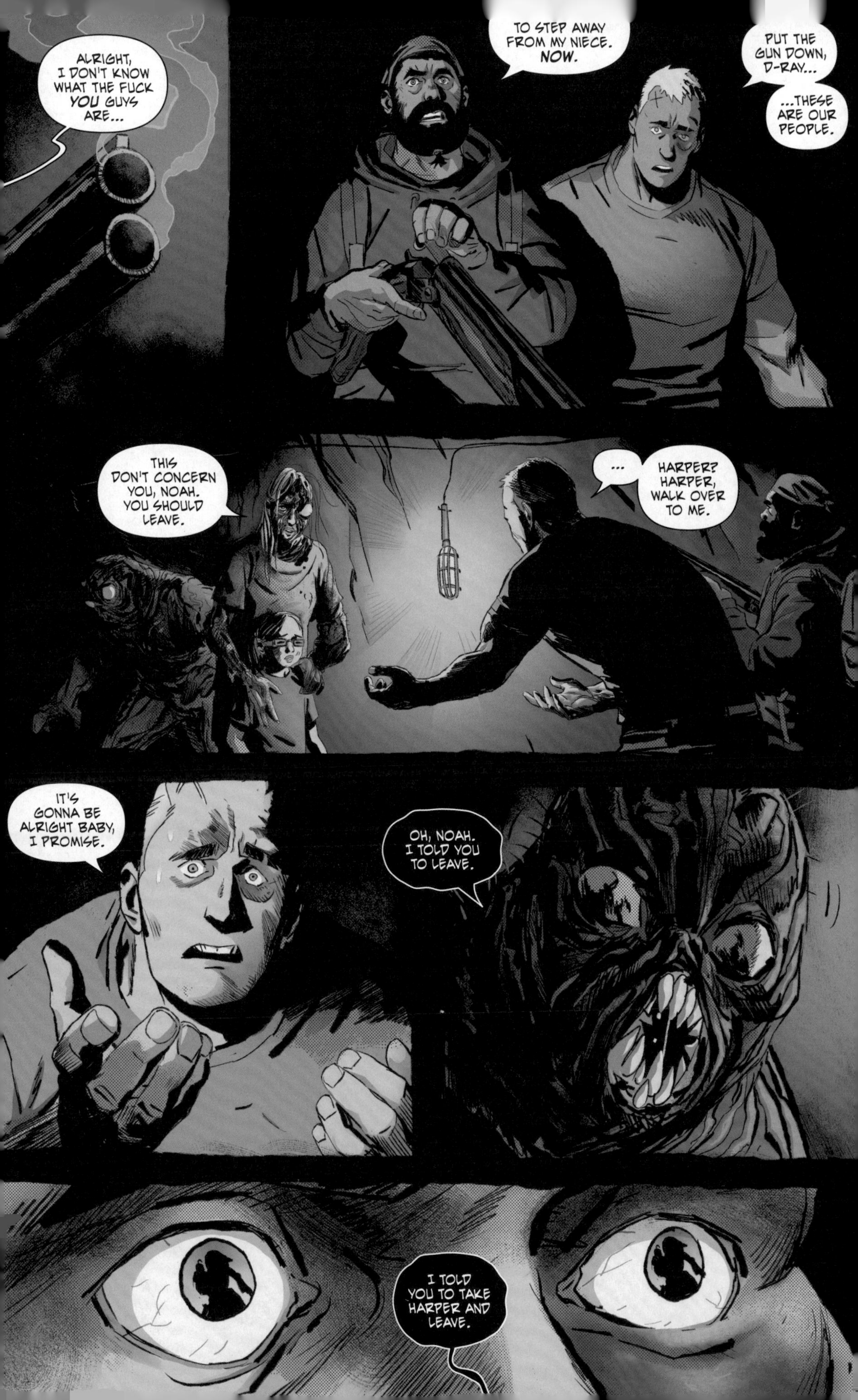
ALRIGHT, I DON'T KNOW WHAT THE FUCK YOU GUYS ARE...
TO STEP AWAY FROM MY NIECE. NOW.
PUT THE GUN DOWN, D-RAY...
...THESE ARE OUR PEOPLE.
THIS DON'T CONCERN YOU, NOAH. YOU SHOULD LEAVE.
...
HARPER? HARPER, WALK OVER TO ME.
IT'S GONNA BE ALRIGHT BABY, I PROMISE.
OH, NOAH. I TOLD YOU TO LEAVE.
I TOLD YOU TO TAKE HARPER AND LEAVE.

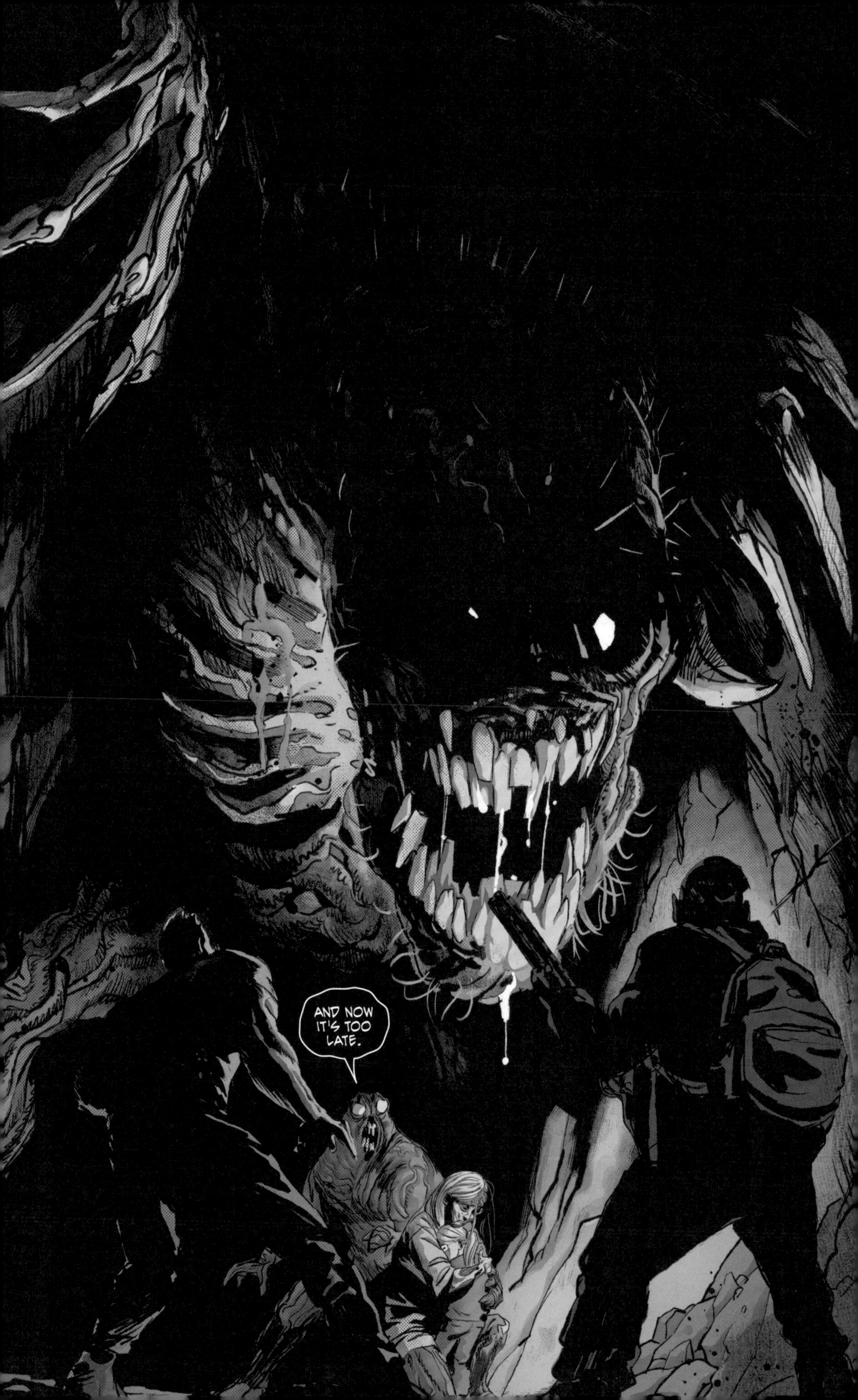
AND NOW IT'S TOO LATE.

CHAPTER 6

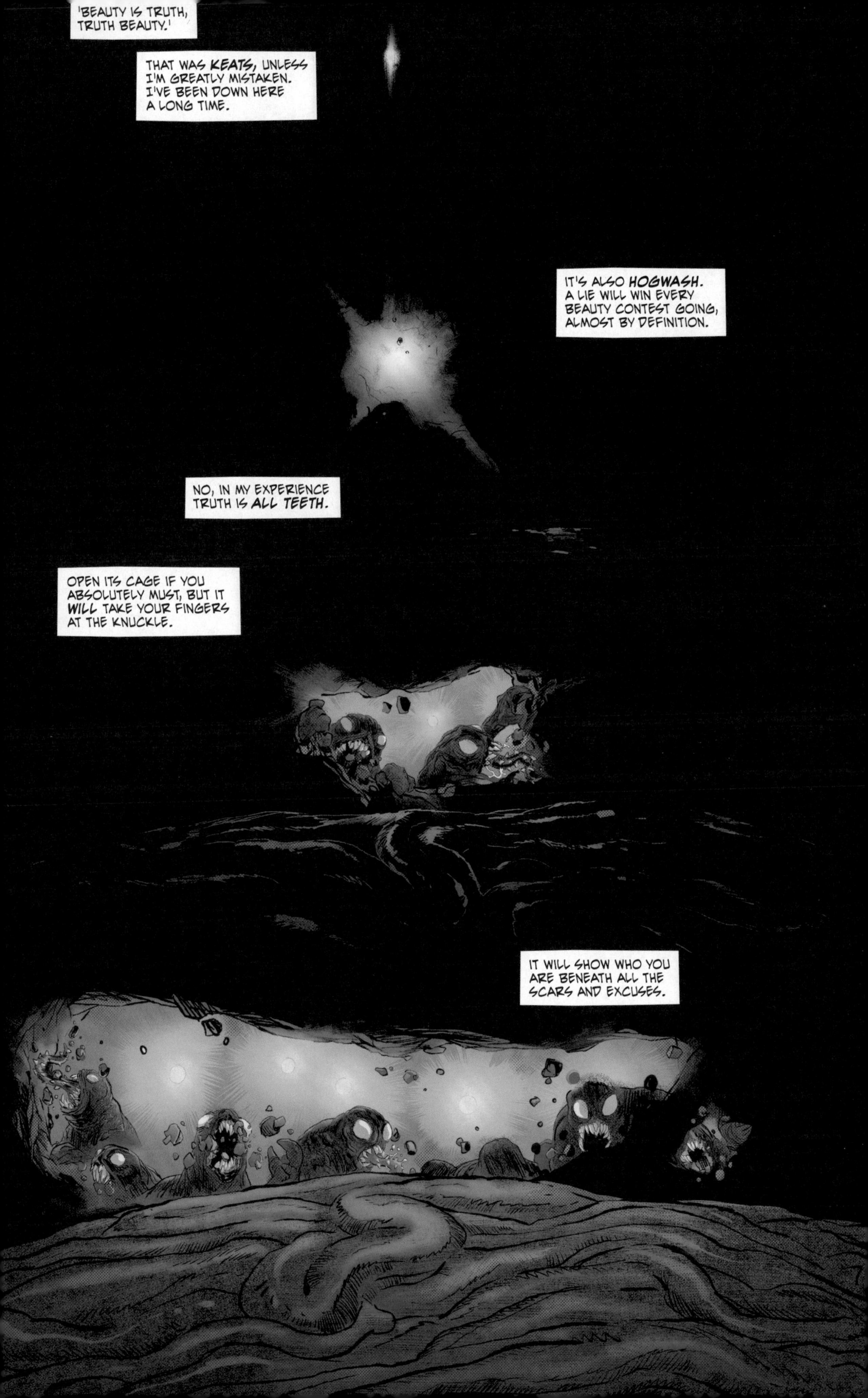
'BEAUTY IS TRUTH, TRUTH BEAUTY.'
THAT WAS KEATS, UNLESS I'M GREATLY MISTAKEN. I'VE BEEN DOWN HERE A LONG TIME.
IT'S ALSO HOGWASH. A LIE WILL WIN EVERY BEAUTY CONTEST GOING, ALMOST BY DEFINITION.
NO, IN MY EXPERIENCE TRUTH IS ALL TEETH.
OPEN ITS CAGE IF YOU ABSOLUTELY MUST, BUT IT WILL TAKE YOUR FINGERS AT THE KNUCKLE.
IT WILL SHOW WHO YOU ARE BENEATH ALL THE SCARS AND EXCUSES.

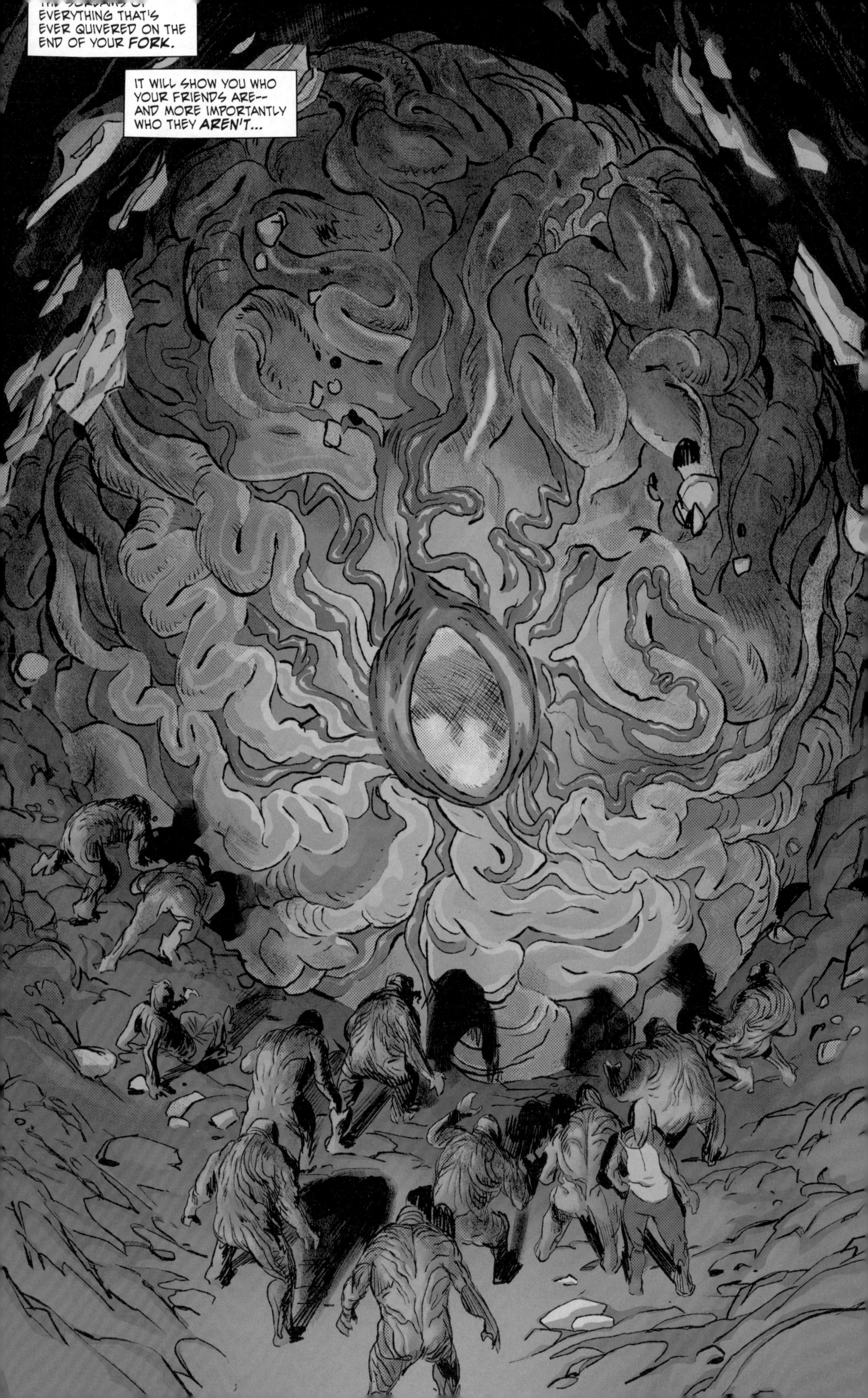
EVERYTHING THAT'S EVER QUIVERED ON THE END OF YOUR **FORK**.
IT WILL SHOW YOU WHO YOUR FRIENDS ARE-- AND MORE IMPORTANTLY WHO THEY **AREN'T**...

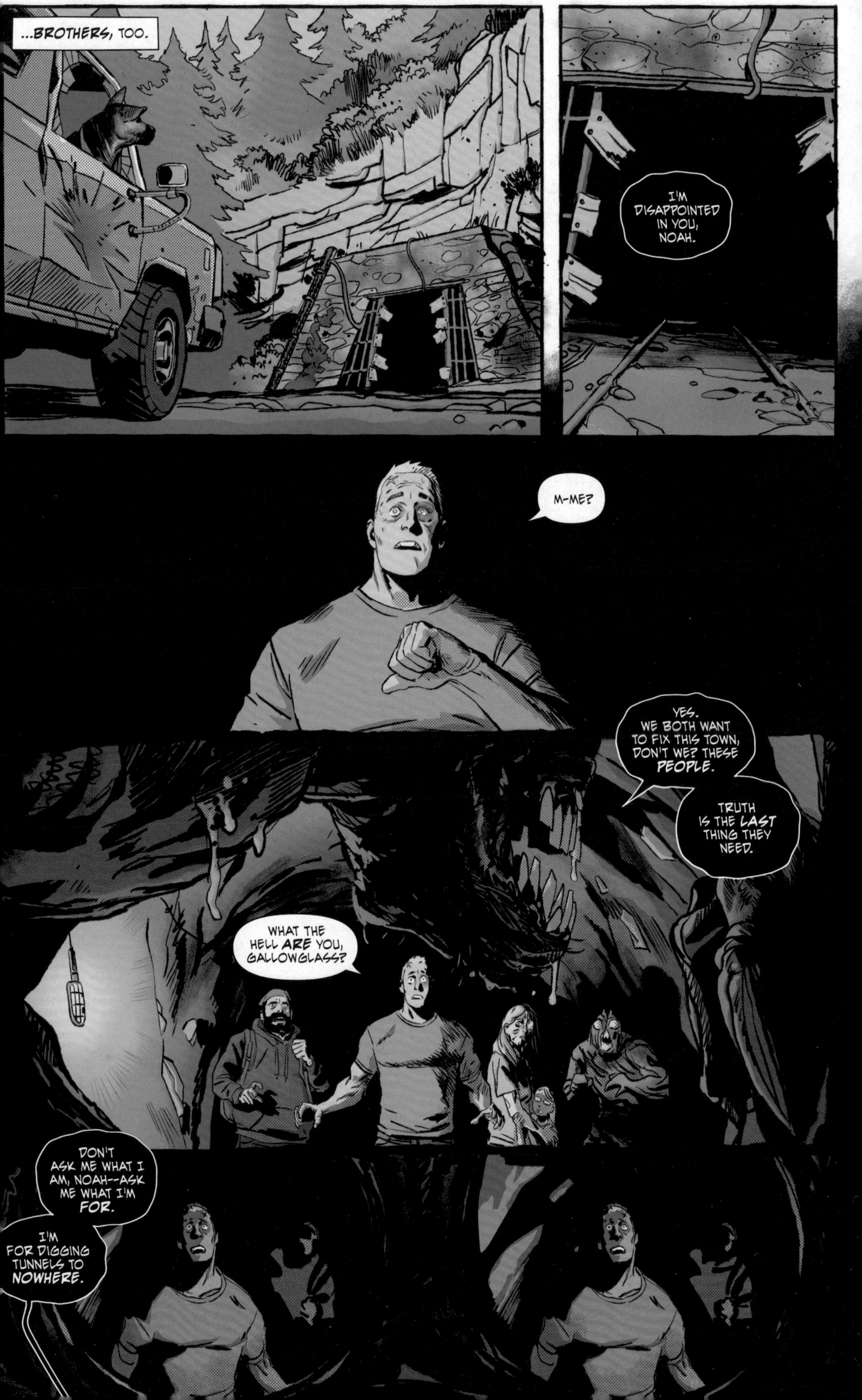
...BROTHERS, TOO.
I'M DISAPPOINTED IN YOU, NOAH.
M-ME?
YES. WE BOTH WANT TO FIX THIS TOWN, DON'T WE? THESE PEOPLE.
TRUTH IS THE LAST THING THEY NEED.
WHAT THE HELL ARE YOU, GALLOWGLASS?
DON'T ASK ME WHAT I AM, NOAH--ASK ME WHAT I'M FOR.
I'M FOR DIGGING TUNNELS TO NOWHERE.

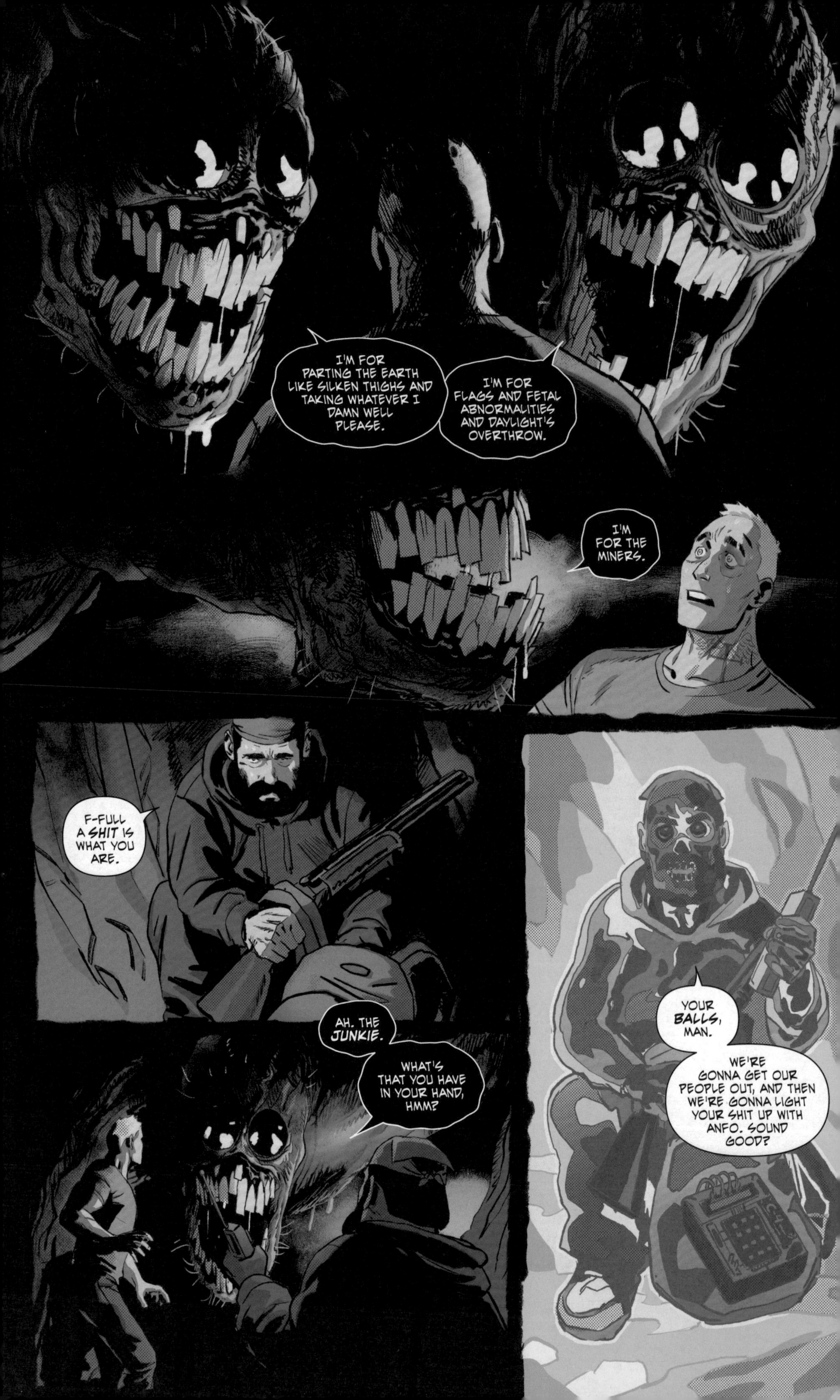

I'M FOR PARTING THE EARTH LIKE SILKEN THIGHS AND TAKING WHATEVER I DAMN WELL PLEASE.
I'M FOR FLAGS AND FETAL ABNORMALITIES AND DAYLIGHT'S OVERTHROW.
I'M FOR THE MINERS.
F-FULL A SHIT IS WHAT YOU ARE.
AH. THE JUNKIE.
WHAT'S THAT YOU HAVE IN YOUR HAND, HMM?
YOUR BALLS, MAN.
WE'RE GONNA GET OUR PEOPLE OUT, AND THEN WE'RE GONNA LIGHT YOUR SHIT UP WITH ANFO. SOUND GOOD?

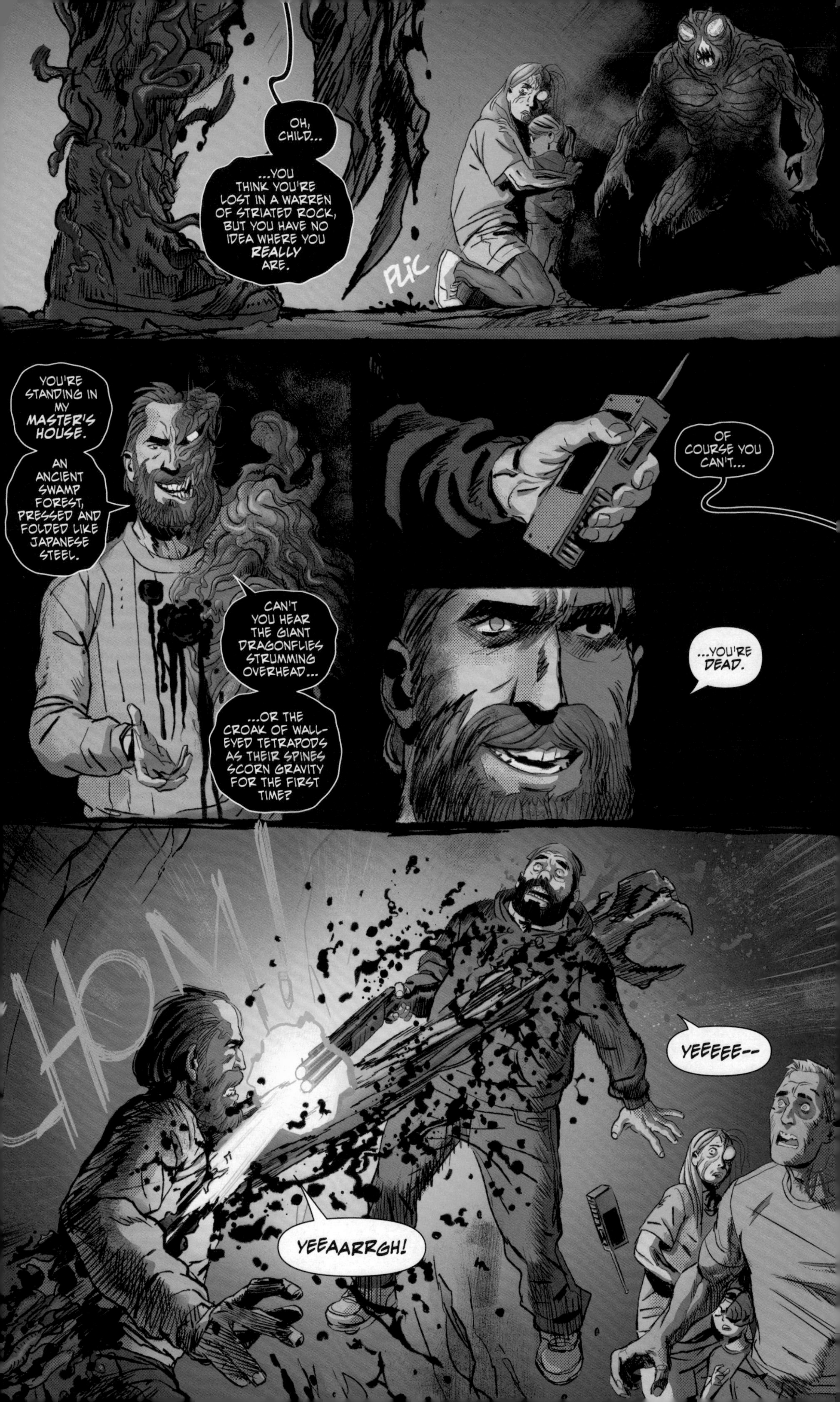

OH, CHILD...
...YOU THINK YOU'RE LOST IN A WARREN OF STRIATED ROCK, BUT YOU HAVE NO IDEA WHERE YOU REALLY ARE.
PLIC
YOU'RE STANDING IN MY MASTER'S HOUSE.
AN ANCIENT SWAMP FOREST, PRESSED AND FOLDED LIKE JAPANESE STEEL.
CAN'T YOU HEAR THE GIANT DRAGONFLIES STRUMMING OVERHEAD...
...OR THE CROAK OF WALL-EYED TETRAPODS AS THEIR SPINES SCORN GRAVITY FOR THE FIRST TIME?
OF COURSE YOU CAN'T...
...YOU'RE DEAD.
CHOM!
YEEEEE--
YEEAARRGH!

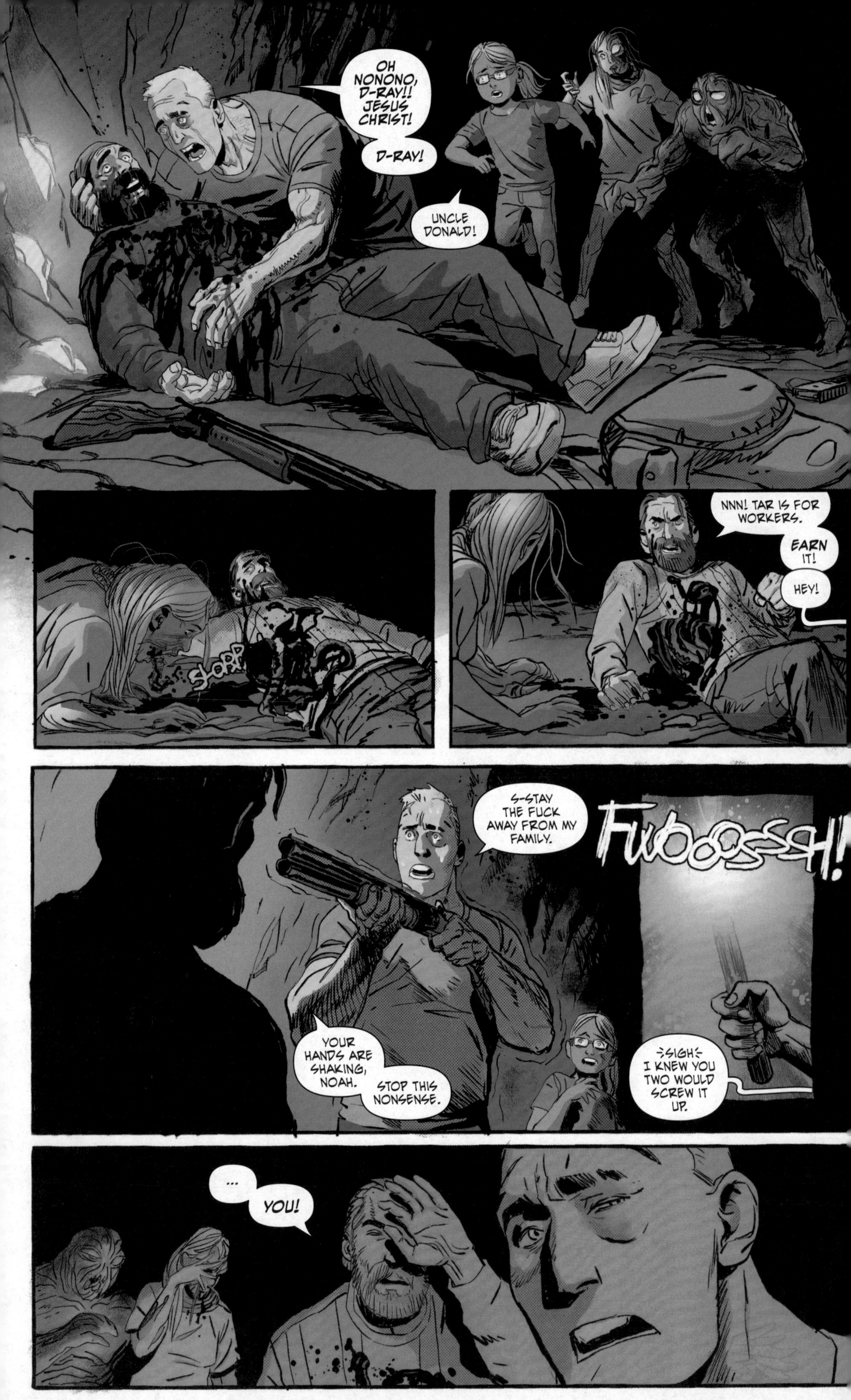
OH NONONO, D-RAY!! JESUS CHRIST!
D-RAY!
UNCLE DONALD!
SLORP
NNN! TAR IS FOR WORKERS.
EARN IT!
HEY!
S-STAY THE FUCK AWAY FROM MY FAMILY.
FWOOSSSH!
YOUR HANDS ARE SHAKING, NOAH.
STOP THIS NONSENSE.
÷SIGH÷ I KNEW YOU TWO WOULD SCREW IT UP.
...
YOU!

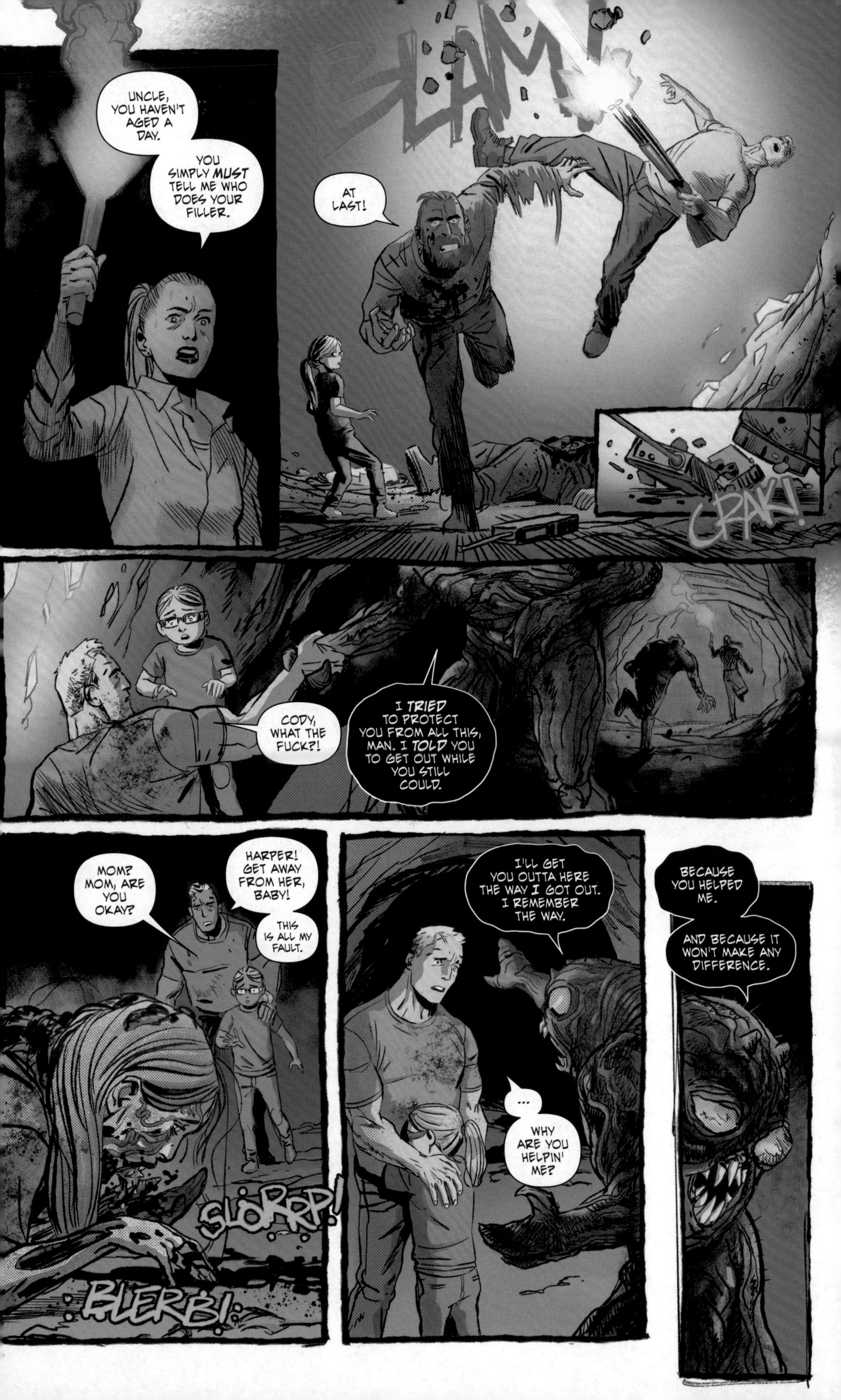
UNCLE, YOU HAVEN'T AGED A DAY.
YOU SIMPLY MUST TELL ME WHO DOES YOUR FILLER.
AT LAST!
CRAK!
CODY, WHAT THE FUCK?!
I TRIED TO PROTECT YOU FROM ALL THIS, MAN. I TOLD YOU TO GET OUT WHILE YOU STILL COULD.
MOM? MOM, ARE YOU OKAY?
HARPER! GET AWAY FROM HER, BABY!
THIS IS ALL MY FAULT.
SLORRP!
BLERB!
I'LL GET YOU OUTTA HERE THE WAY I GOT OUT. I REMEMBER THE WAY.
...
WHY ARE YOU HELPIN' ME?
BECAUSE YOU HELPED ME.
AND BECAUSE IT WON'T MAKE ANY DIFFERENCE.

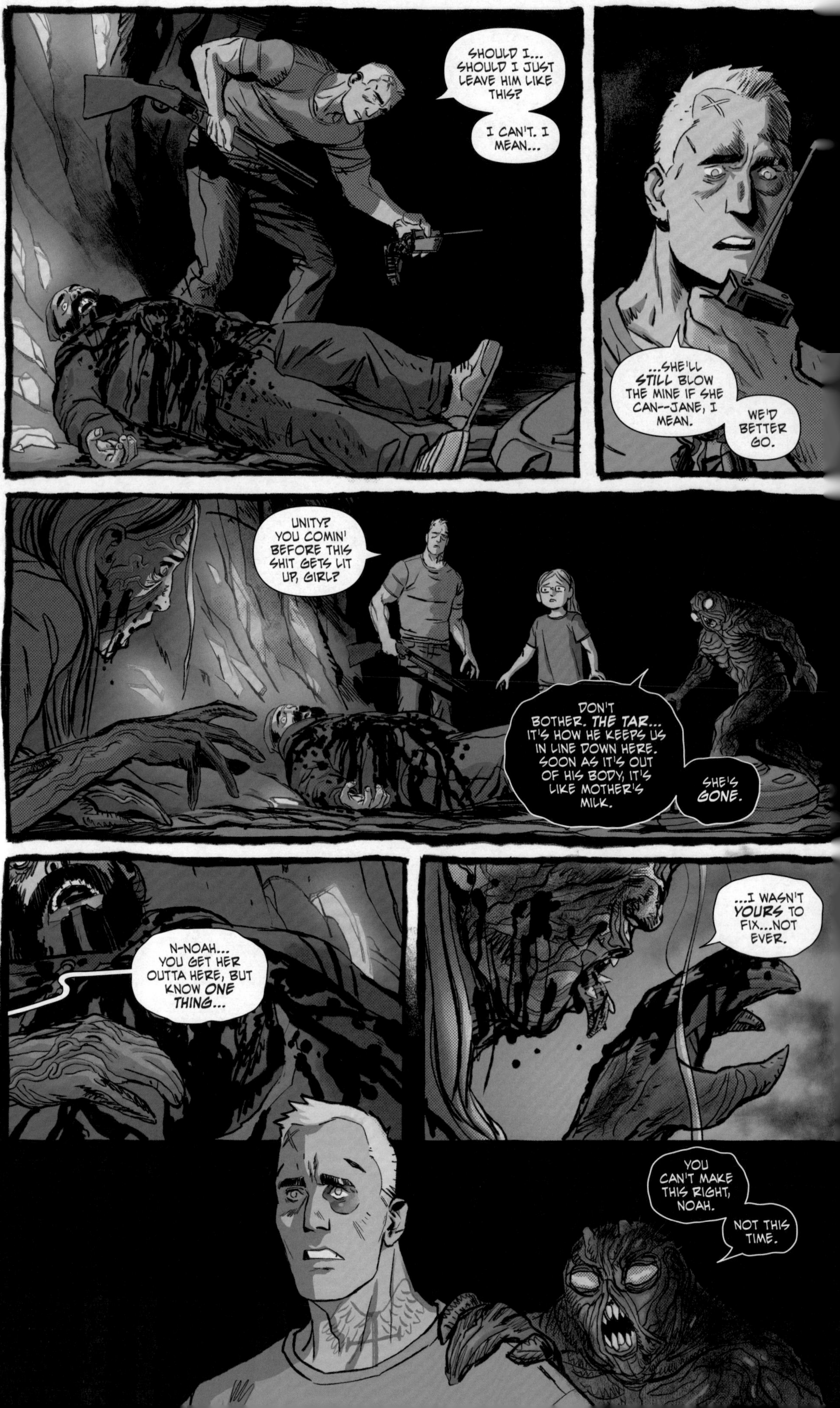
SHOULD I... SHOULD I JUST LEAVE HIM LIKE THIS?
I CAN'T. I MEAN...
...SHE'LL STILL BLOW THE MINE IF SHE CAN--JANE, I MEAN.
WE'D BETTER GO.
UNITY? YOU COMIN' BEFORE THIS SHIT GETS LIT UP, GIRL?
DON'T BOTHER. THE TAR... IT'S HOW HE KEEPS US IN LINE DOWN HERE. SOON AS IT'S OUT OF HIS BODY, IT'S LIKE MOTHER'S MILK.
SHE'S GONE.
N-NOAH... YOU GET HER OUTTA HERE, BUT KNOW ONE THING...
...I WASN'T YOURS TO FIX...NOT EVER.
YOU CAN'T MAKE THIS RIGHT, NOAH.
NOT THIS TIME.

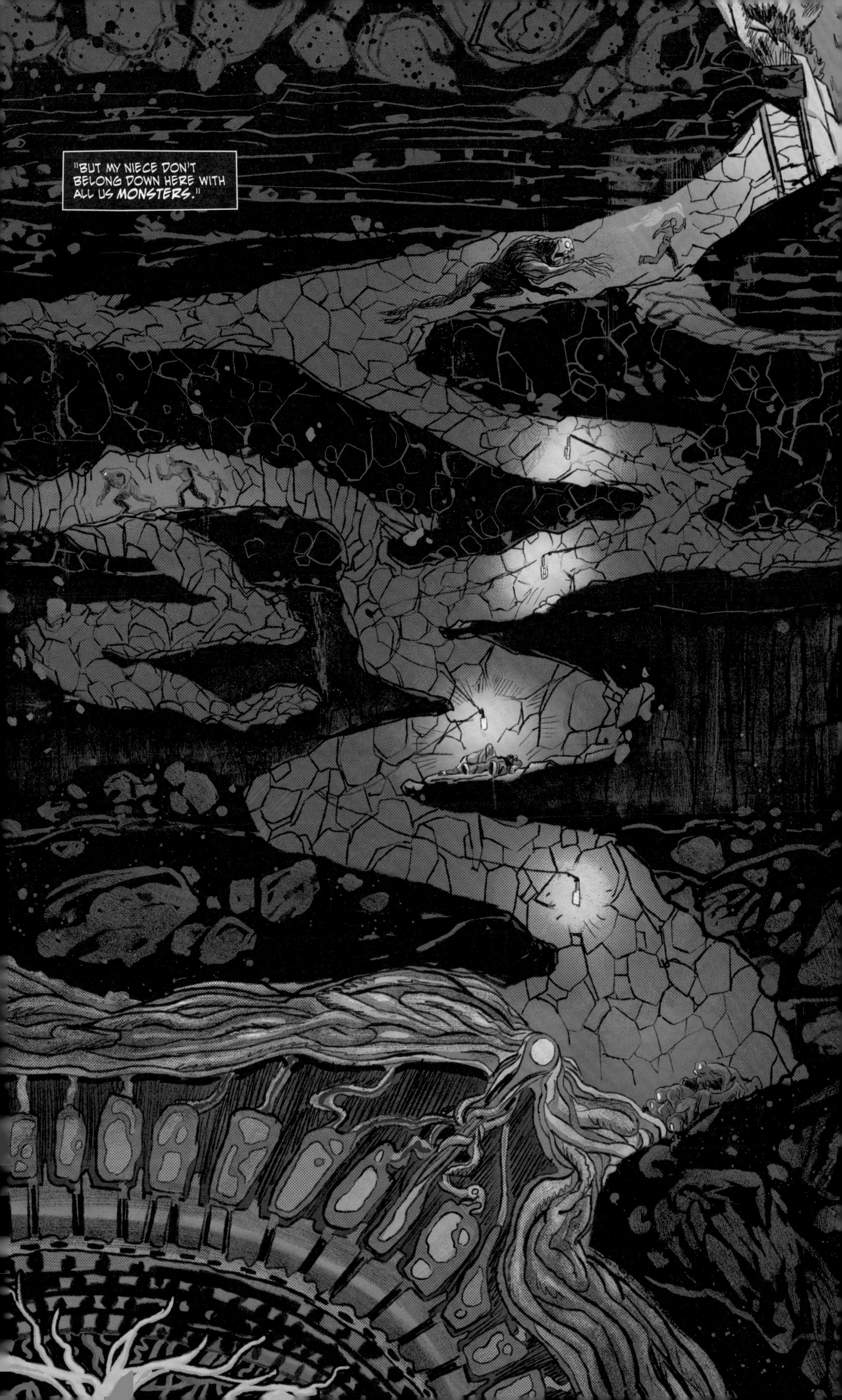
"BUT MY NIECE DON'T BELONG DOWN HERE WITH ALL US MONSTERS."

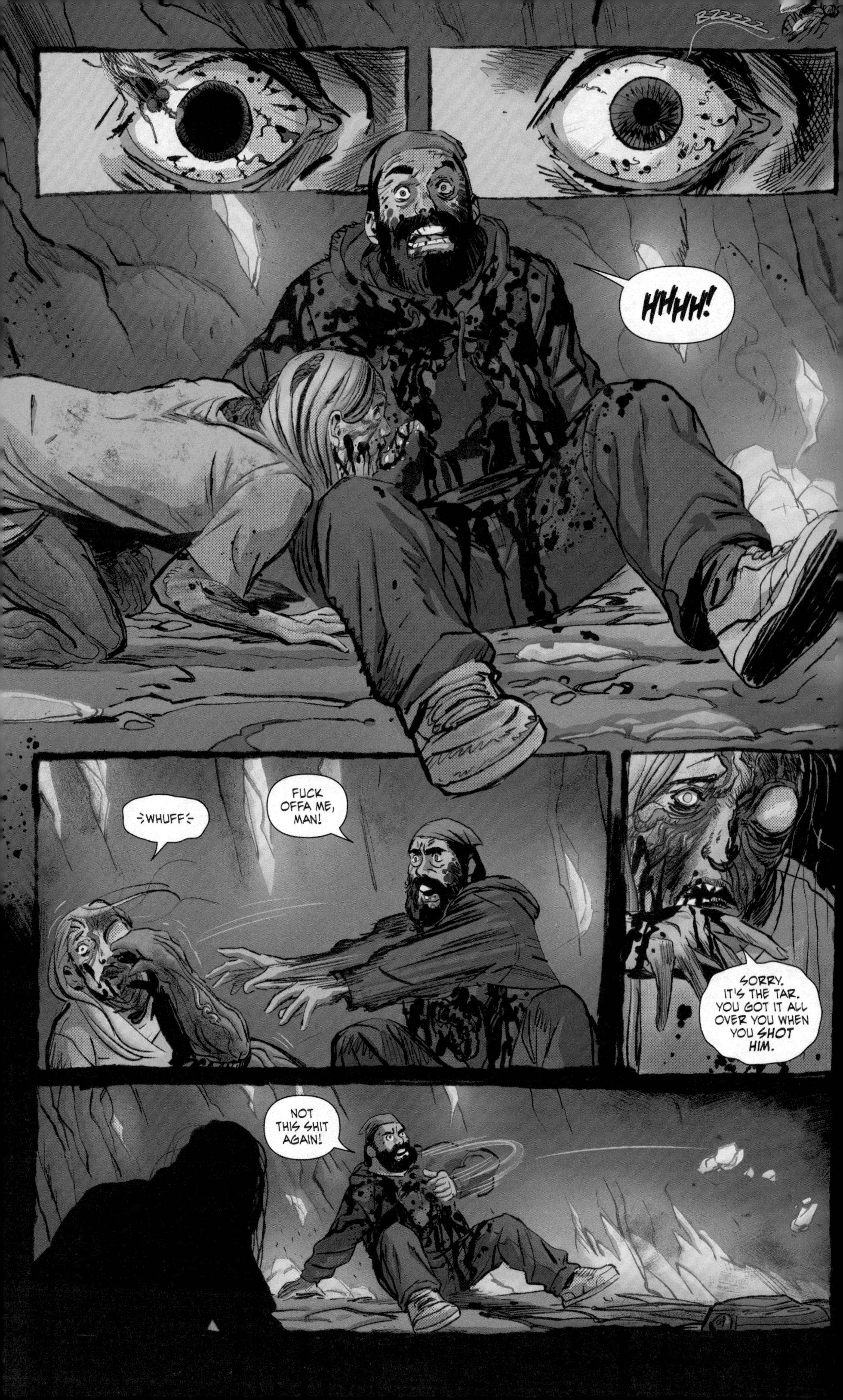
BZZZZZ
HHHH!
WHUFF
FUCK OFFA ME, MAN!
SORRY. IT'S THE TAR. YOU GOT IT ALL OVER YOU WHEN YOU SHOT HIM.
NOT THIS SHIT AGAIN!

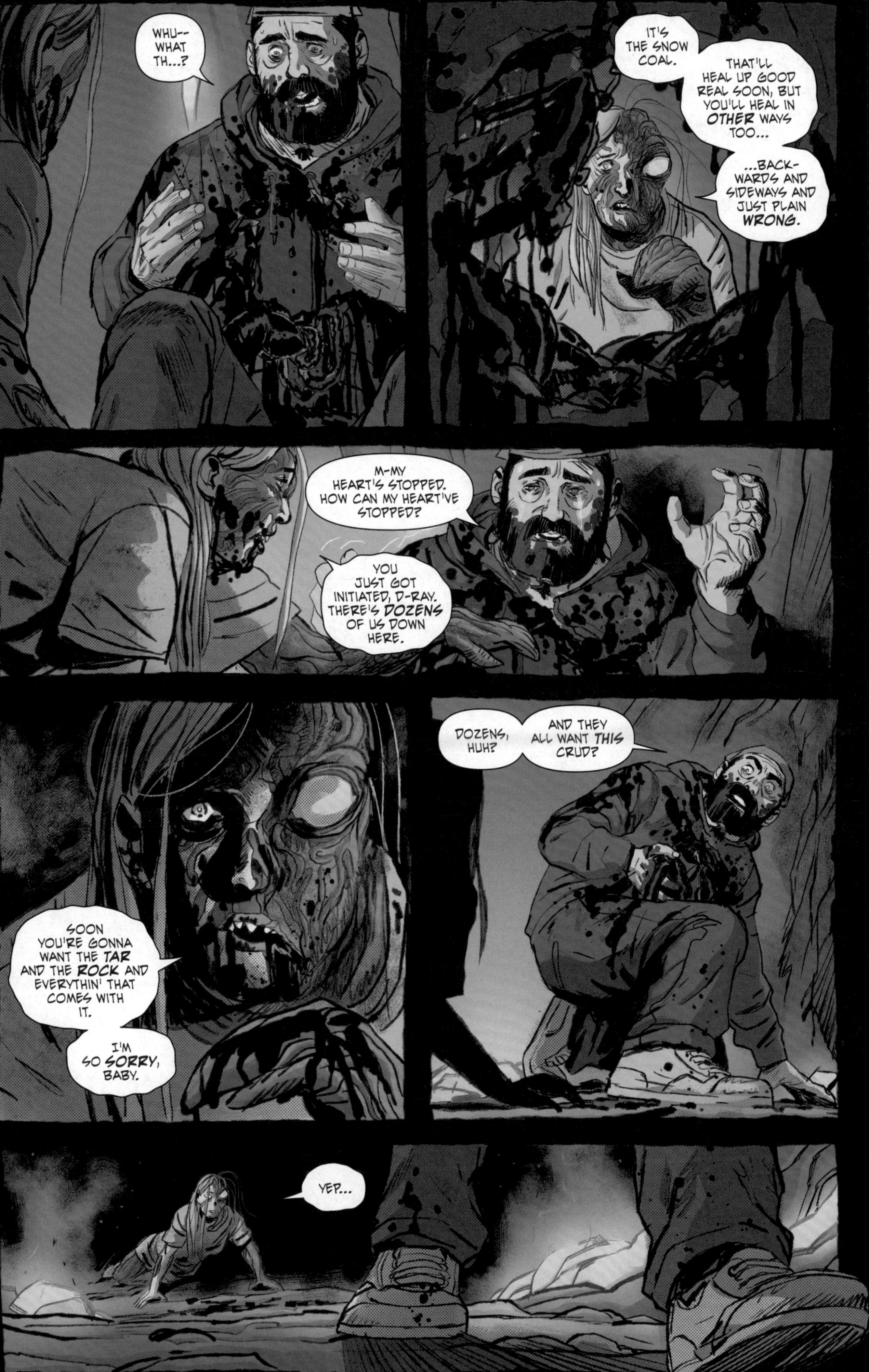
WHU-- WHAT TH...?
IT'S THE SNOW COAL.
THAT'LL HEAL UP GOOD REAL SOON, BUT YOU'LL HEAL IN OTHER WAYS TOO...
...BACK-WARDS AND SIDEWAYS AND JUST PLAIN WRONG.
M-MY HEART'S STOPPED. HOW CAN MY HEART'VE STOPPED?
YOU JUST GOT INITIATED, D-RAY. THERE'S DOZENS OF US DOWN HERE.
SOON YOU'RE GONNA WANT THE TAR AND THE ROCK AND EVERYTHIN' THAT COMES WITH IT.
I'M SO SORRY, BABY.
DOZENS, HUH?
AND THEY ALL WANT THIS CRUD?
YEP...

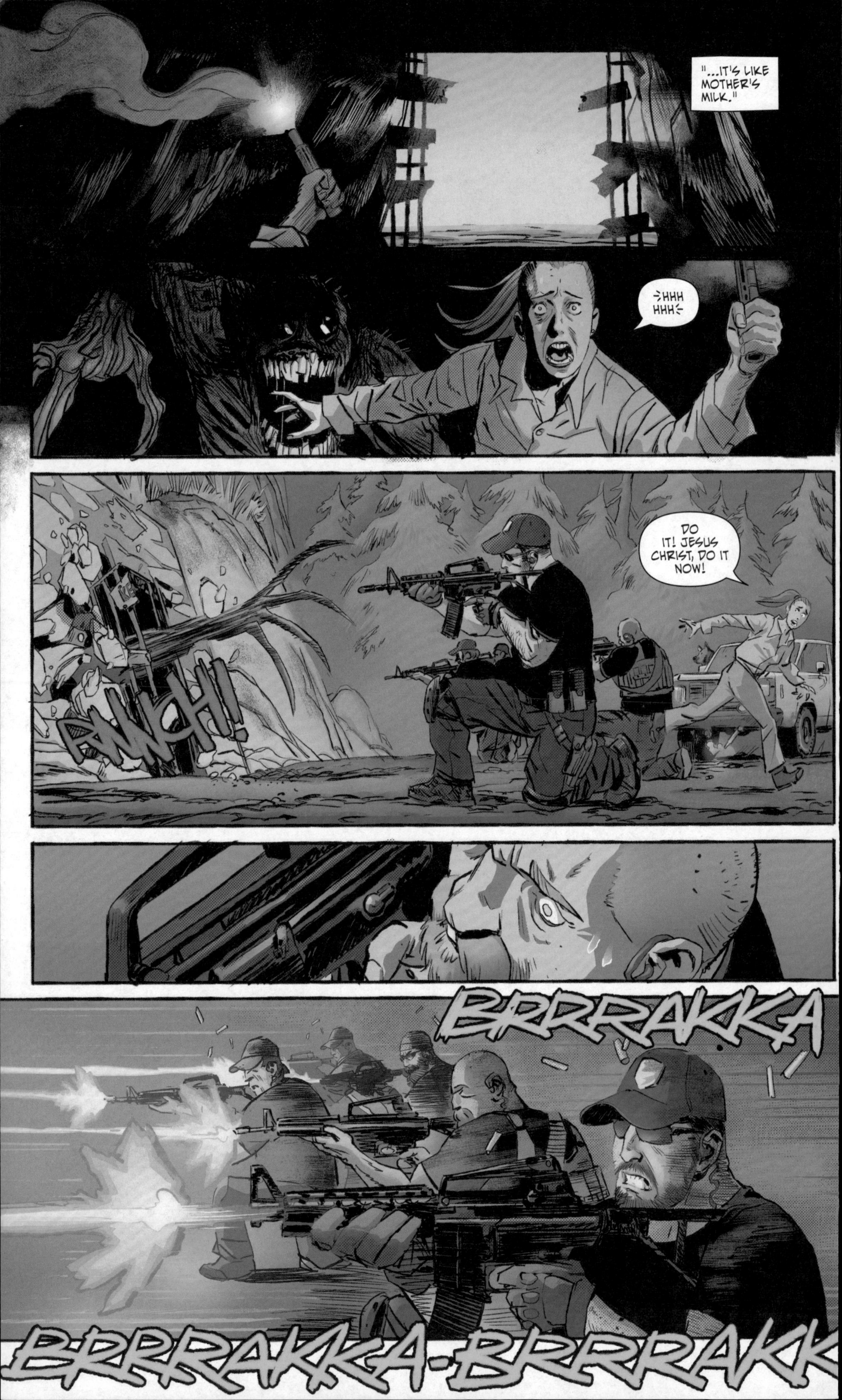
"...IT'S LIKE MOTHER'S MILK."
HHH HHH
DO IT! JESUS CHRIST, DO IT NOW!
BRRRAKKA
BRRRAKKA-BRRRRAKK

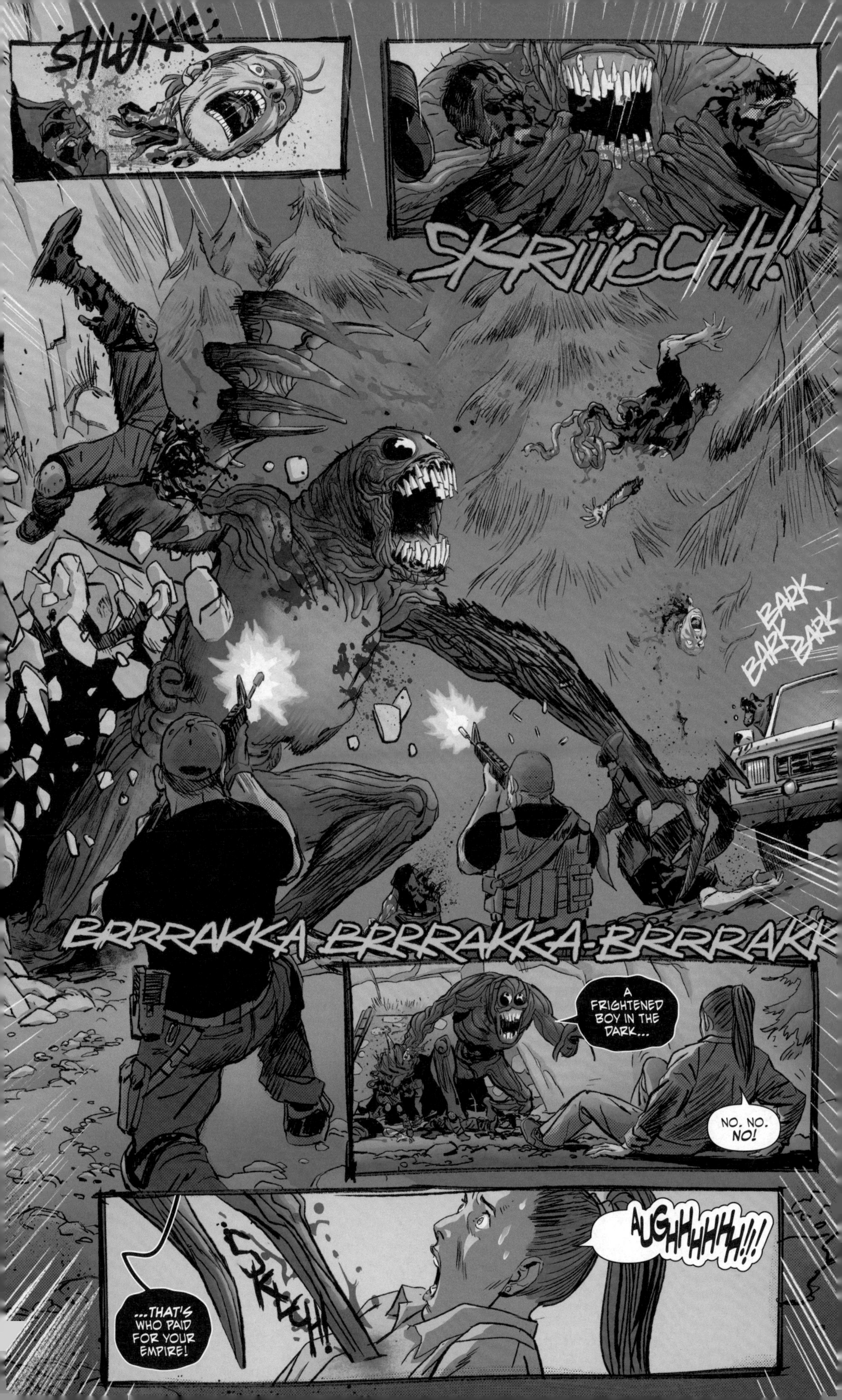
SHUKK
SKRIICCHH!
BARK BARK BARK
BRRRAKKA BRRRAKKA BRRRAKK
A FRIGHTENED BOY IN THE DARK...
NO. NO. NO!
...THAT'S WHO PAID FOR YOUR EMPIRE!
AUGHHHHHH!!!

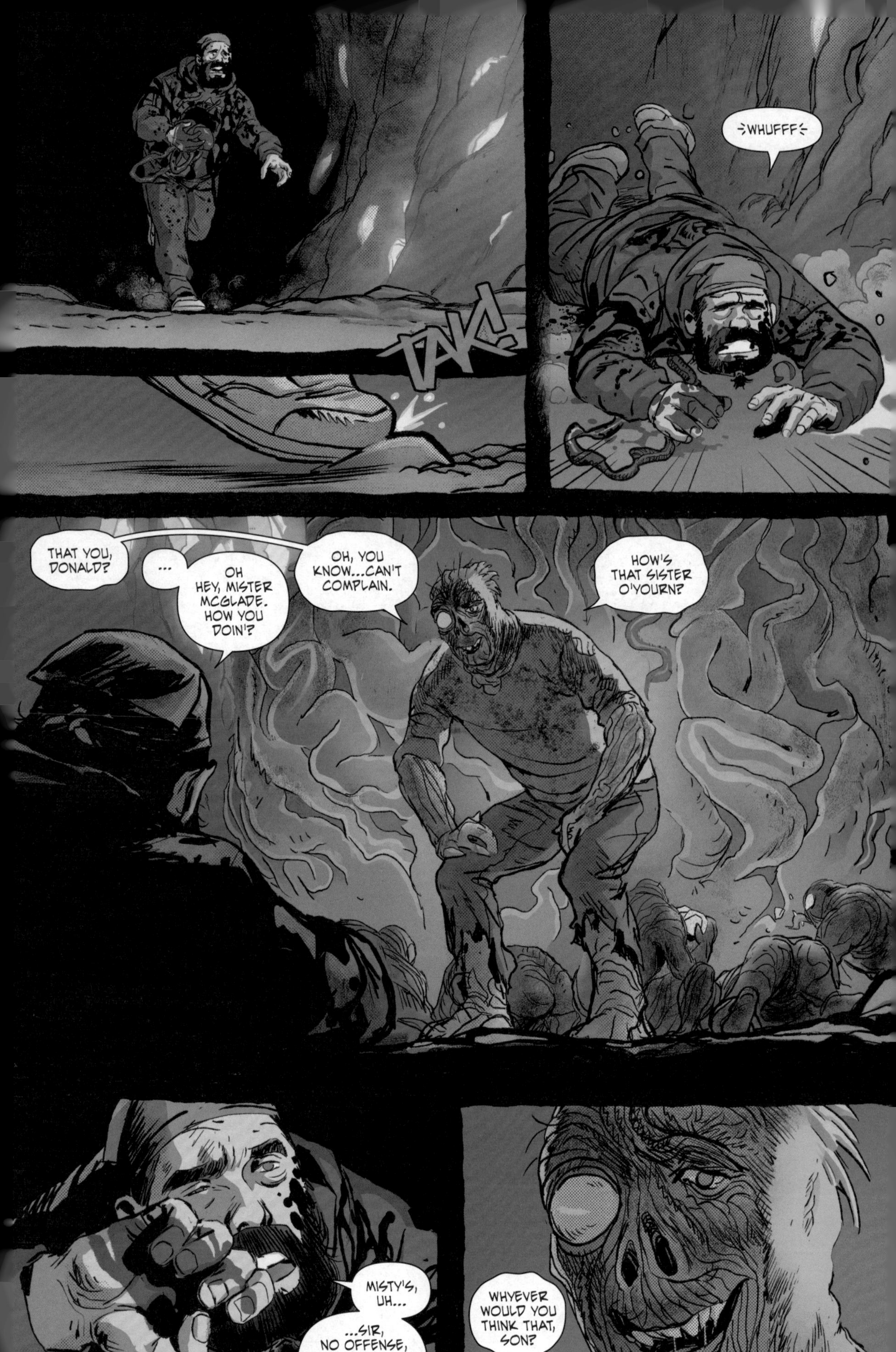

TAK!
-WHUFFF-
THAT YOU, DONALD?
...
OH HEY, MISTER MCGLADE. HOW YOU DOIN'?
OH, YOU KNOW...CAN'T COMPLAIN.
HOW'S THAT SISTER O'YOURN?
MISTY'S, UH...
...SIR, NO OFFENSE, BUT...THIS ISN'T A GOOD PLACE FOR YOU TO BE.
WHYEVER WOULD YOU THINK THAT, SON?
EVERYTHIN'S BACK ON TRACK.

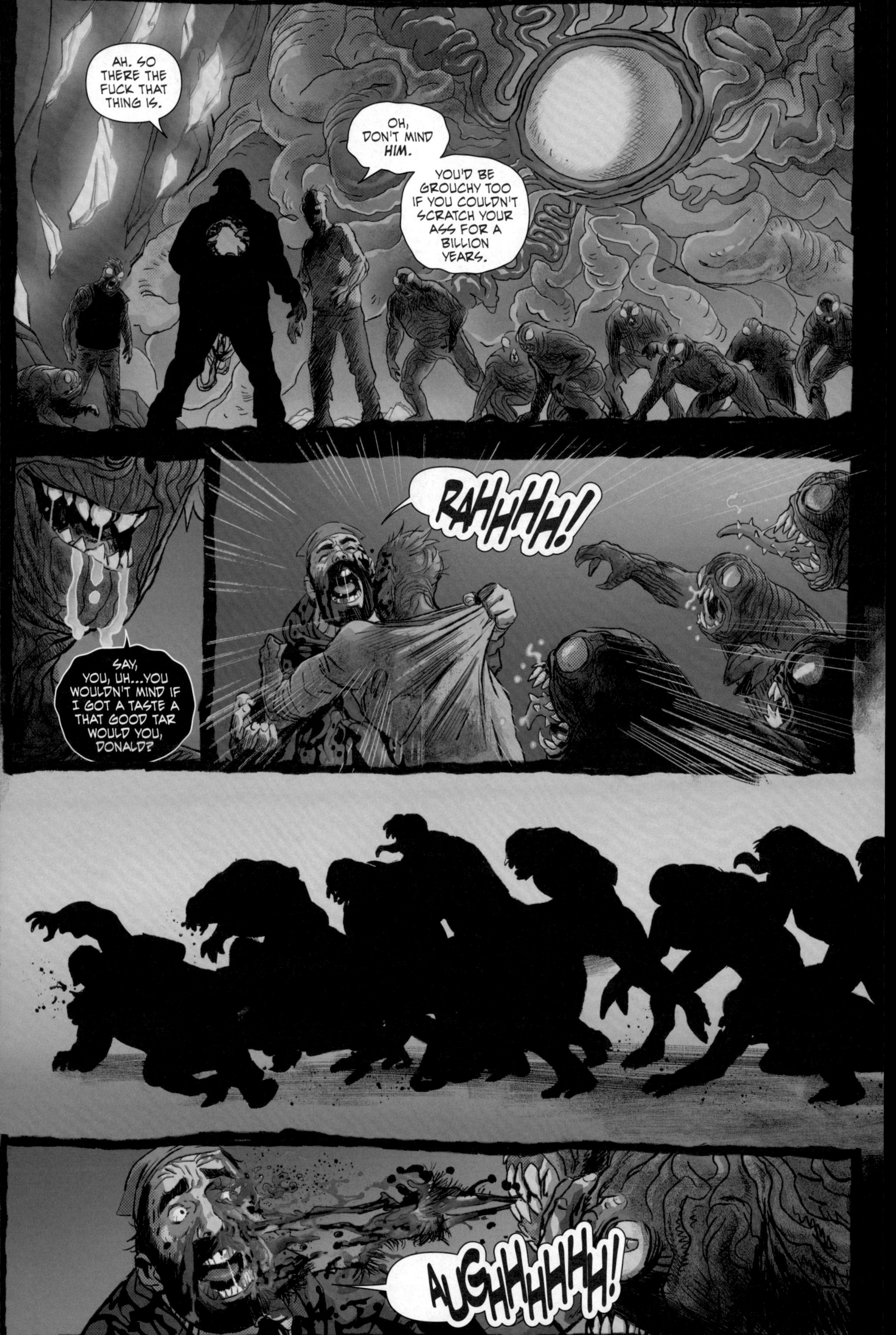
AH. SO THERE THE FUCK THAT THING IS.
OH, DON'T MIND HIM.
YOU'D BE GROUCHY TOO IF YOU COULDN'T SCRATCH YOUR ASS FOR A BILLION YEARS.
SAY, YOU, UH...YOU WOULDN'T MIND IF I GOT A TASTE A THAT GOOD TAR WOULD YOU, DONALD?
RAHHHH!
AUGHHHHHH!

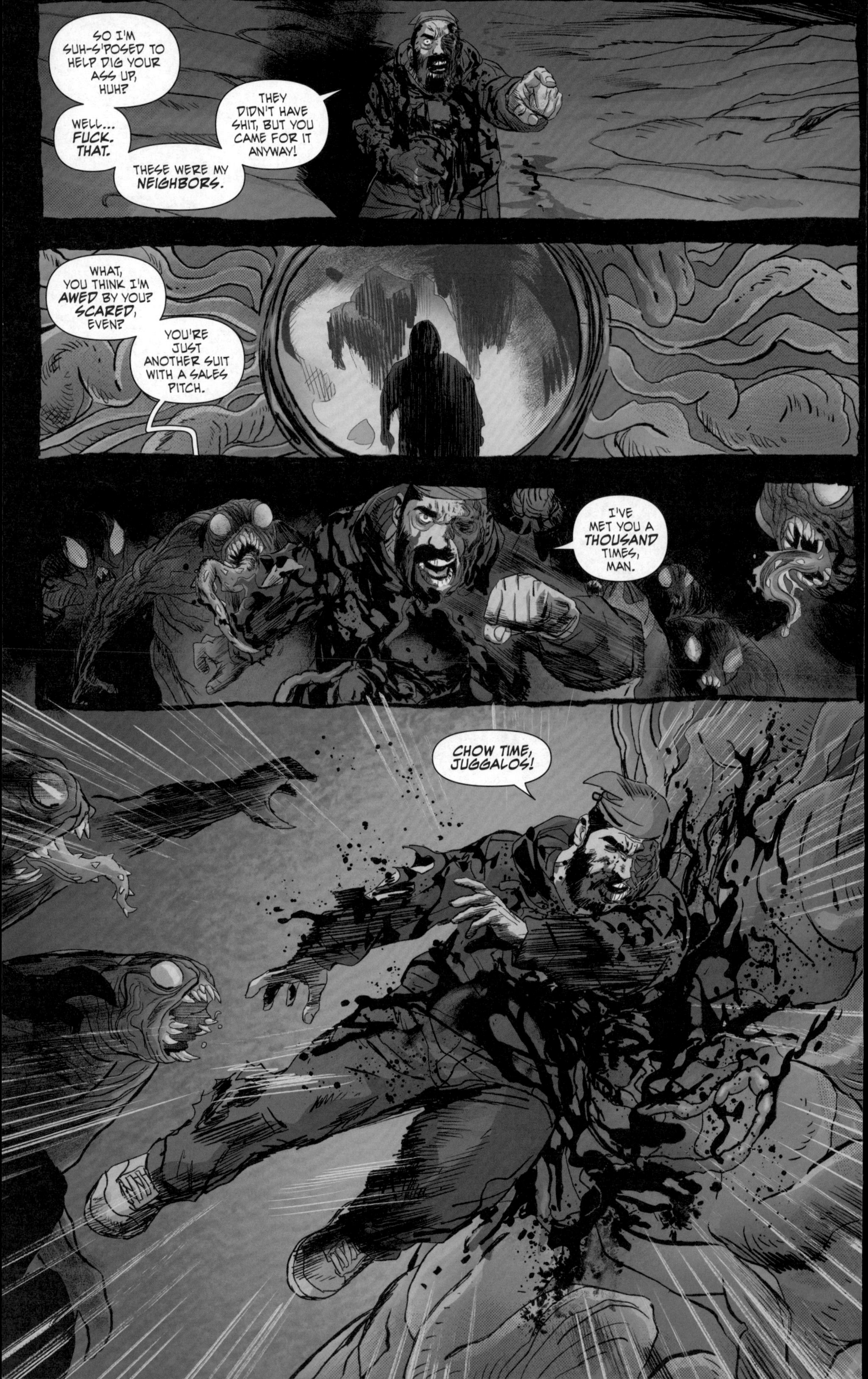
SO I'M SUH-S'POSED TO HELP DIG YOUR ASS UP, HUH?
WELL... FUCK. THAT.
THEY DIDN'T HAVE SHIT, BUT YOU CAME FOR IT ANYWAY!
THESE WERE MY NEIGHBORS.
WHAT, YOU THINK I'M AWED BY YOU? SCARED, EVEN?
YOU'RE JUST ANOTHER SUIT WITH A SALES PITCH.
I'VE MET YOU A THOUSAND TIMES, MAN.
CHOW TIME, JUGGALOS!

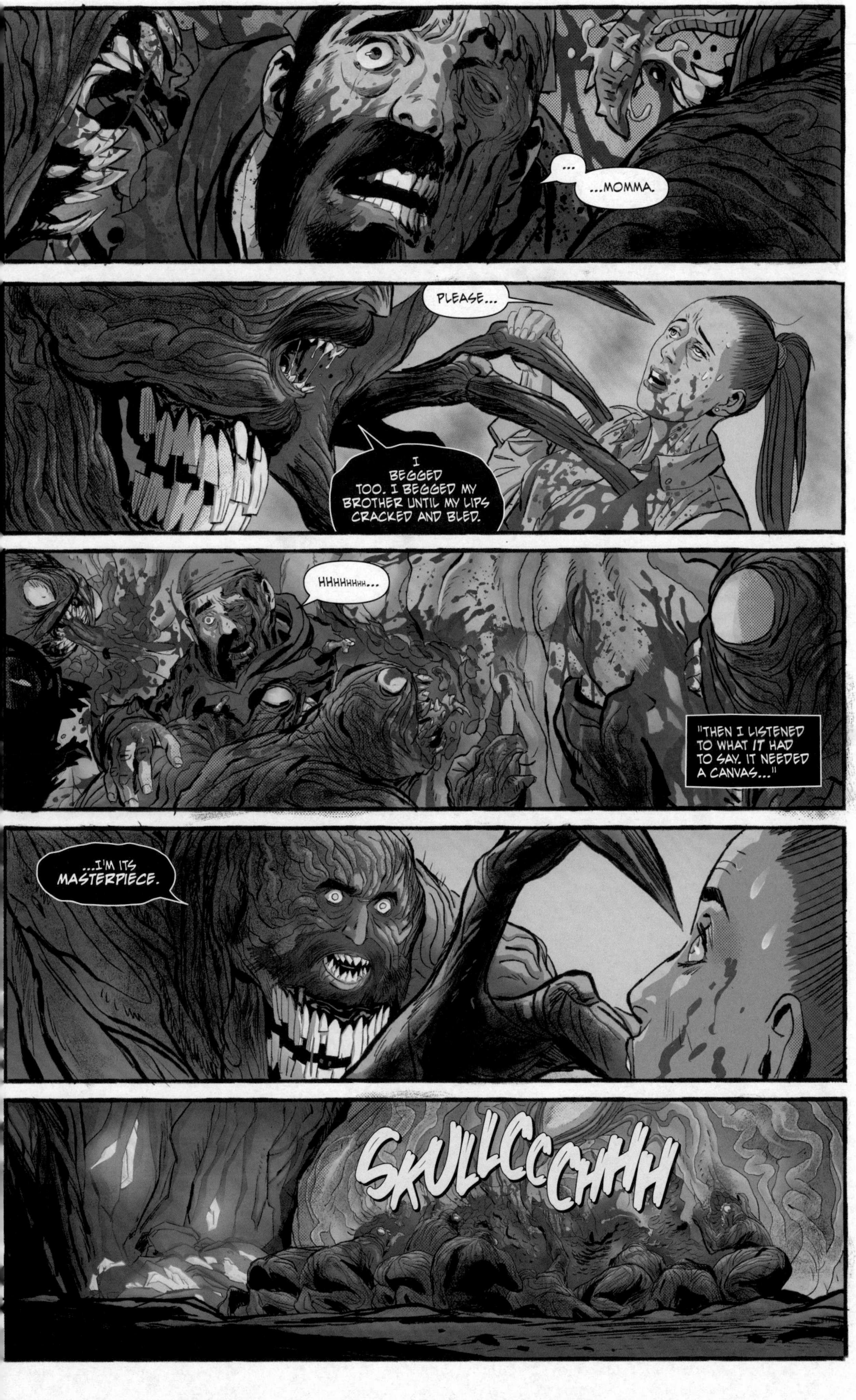
...
...MOMMA.
PLEASE...
I BEGGED TOO. I BEGGED MY BROTHER UNTIL MY LIPS CRACKED AND BLED.
HHHHHHHH...
"THEN I LISTENED TO WHAT IT HAD TO SAY. IT NEEDED A CANVAS..."
...I'M ITS MASTERPIECE.
SKULLCCCHHH

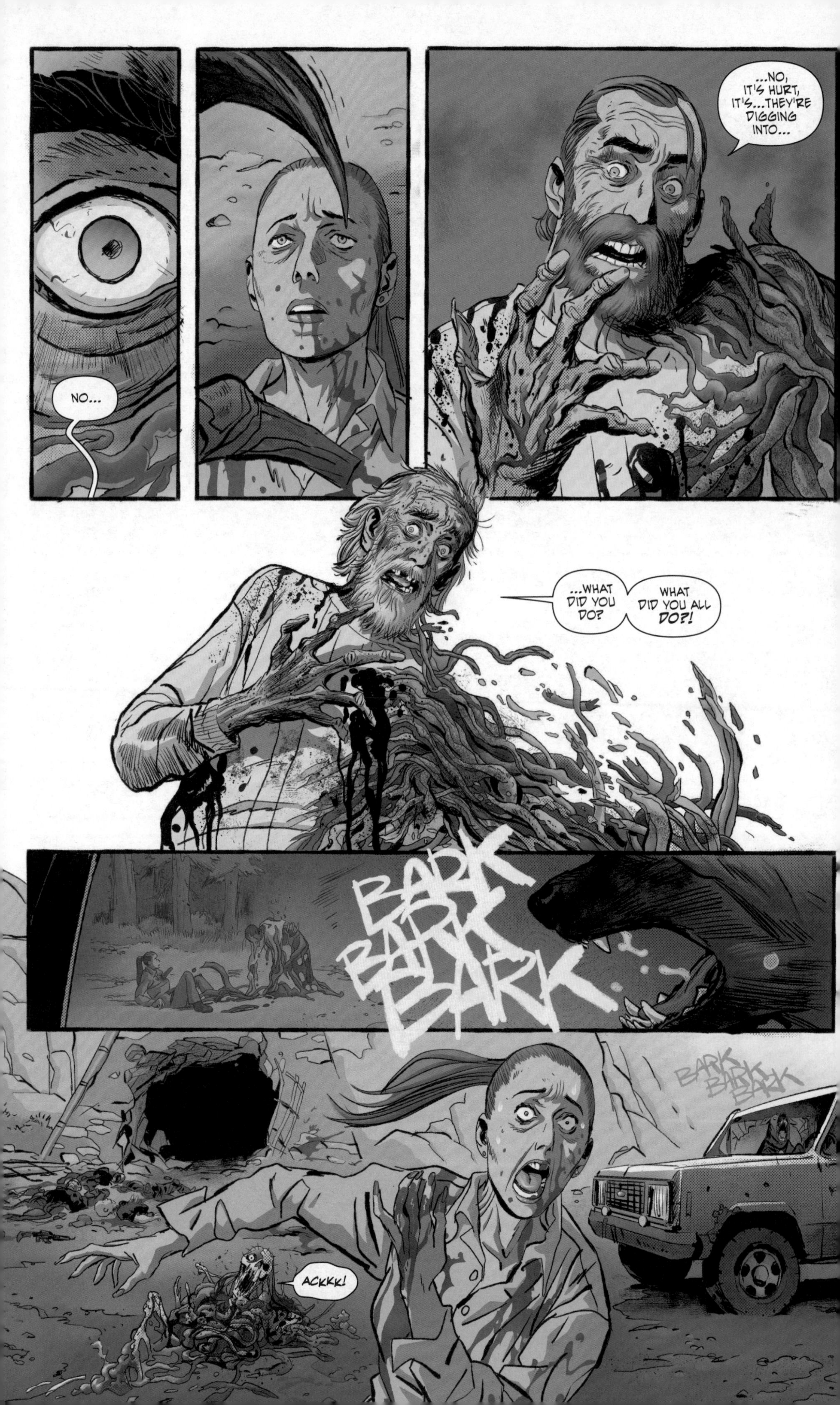

NO...
...NO, IT'S HURT, IT'S...THEY'RE DIGGING INTO...
...WHAT DID YOU DO?
WHAT DID YOU ALL DO?!
BARK BARK BARK
BARK BARK BARK
ACKKK!

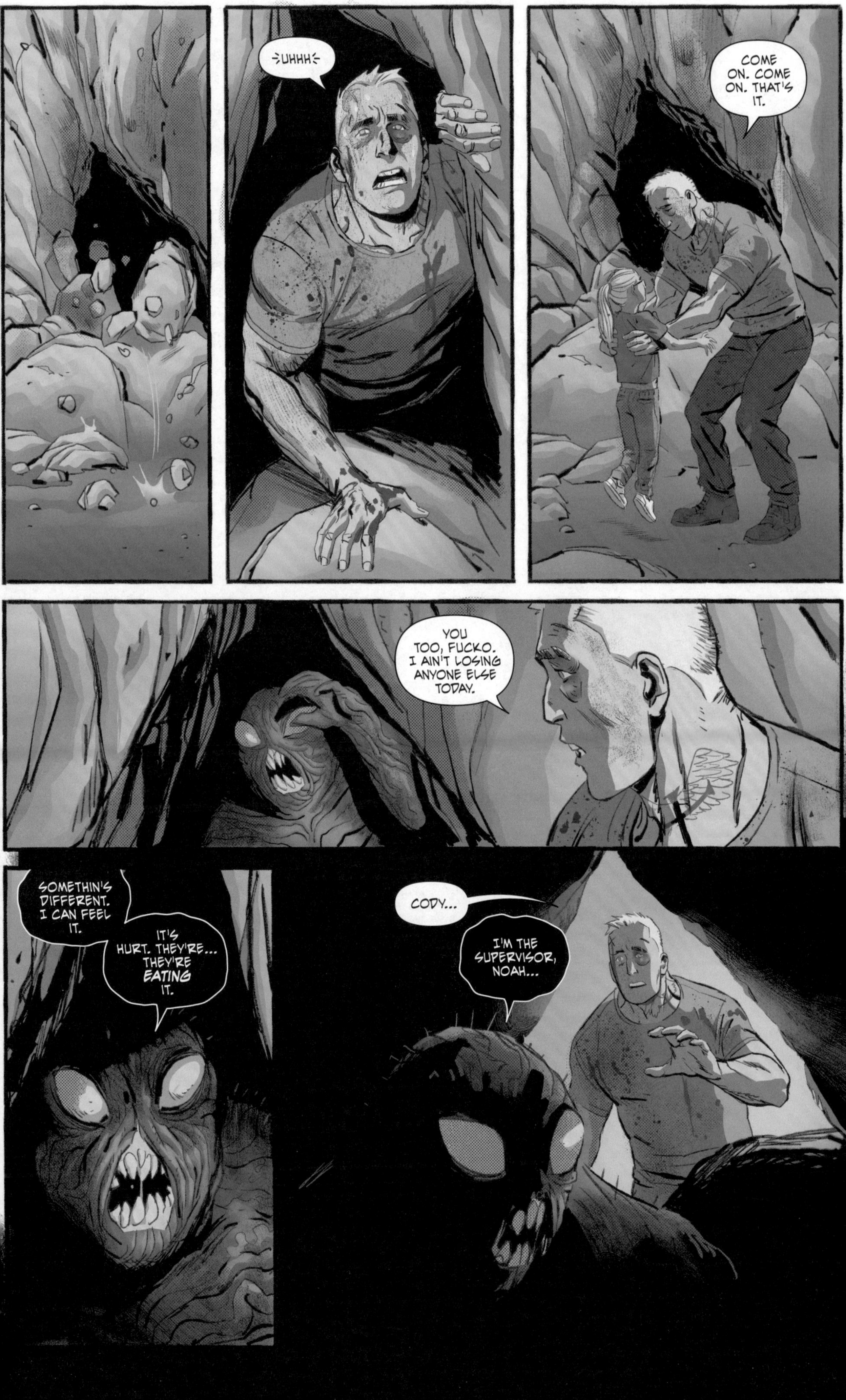

-UHHH-
COME ON. COME ON. THAT'S IT.
YOU TOO, FUCKO. I AIN'T LOSING ANYONE ELSE TODAY.
SOMETHIN'S DIFFERENT. I CAN FEEL IT.
IT'S HURT. THEY'RE... THEY'RE EATING IT.
CODY...
I'M THE SUPERVISOR, NOAH...

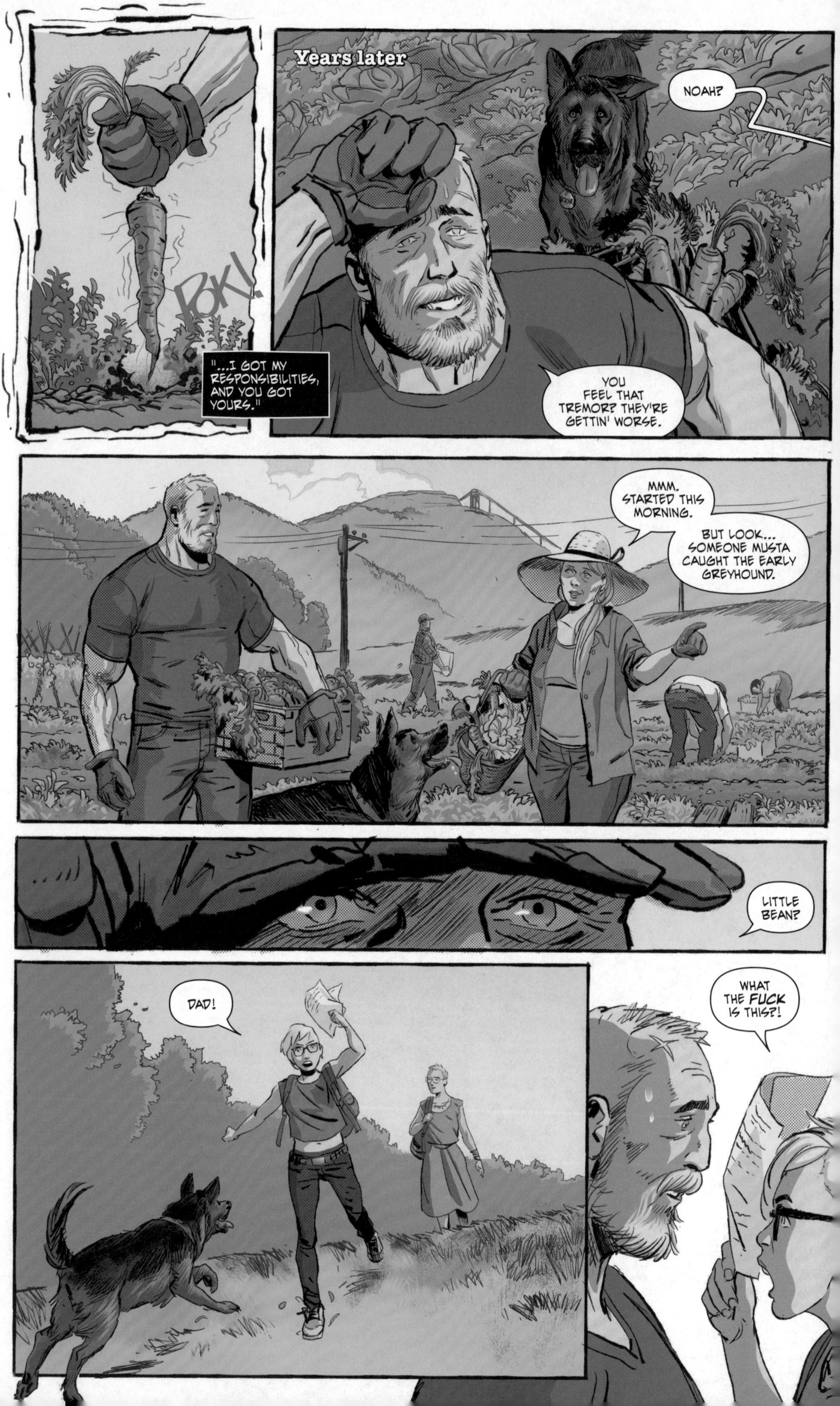
POK!
"...I GOT MY RESPONSIBILITIES, AND YOU GOT YOURS."
Years later
NOAH?
YOU FEEL THAT TREMOR? THEY'RE GETTIN' WORSE.
MMM. STARTED THIS MORNING.
BUT LOOK... SOMEONE MUSTA CAUGHT THE EARLY GREYHOUND.
LITTLE BEAN?
DAD!
WHAT THE FUCK IS THIS?!

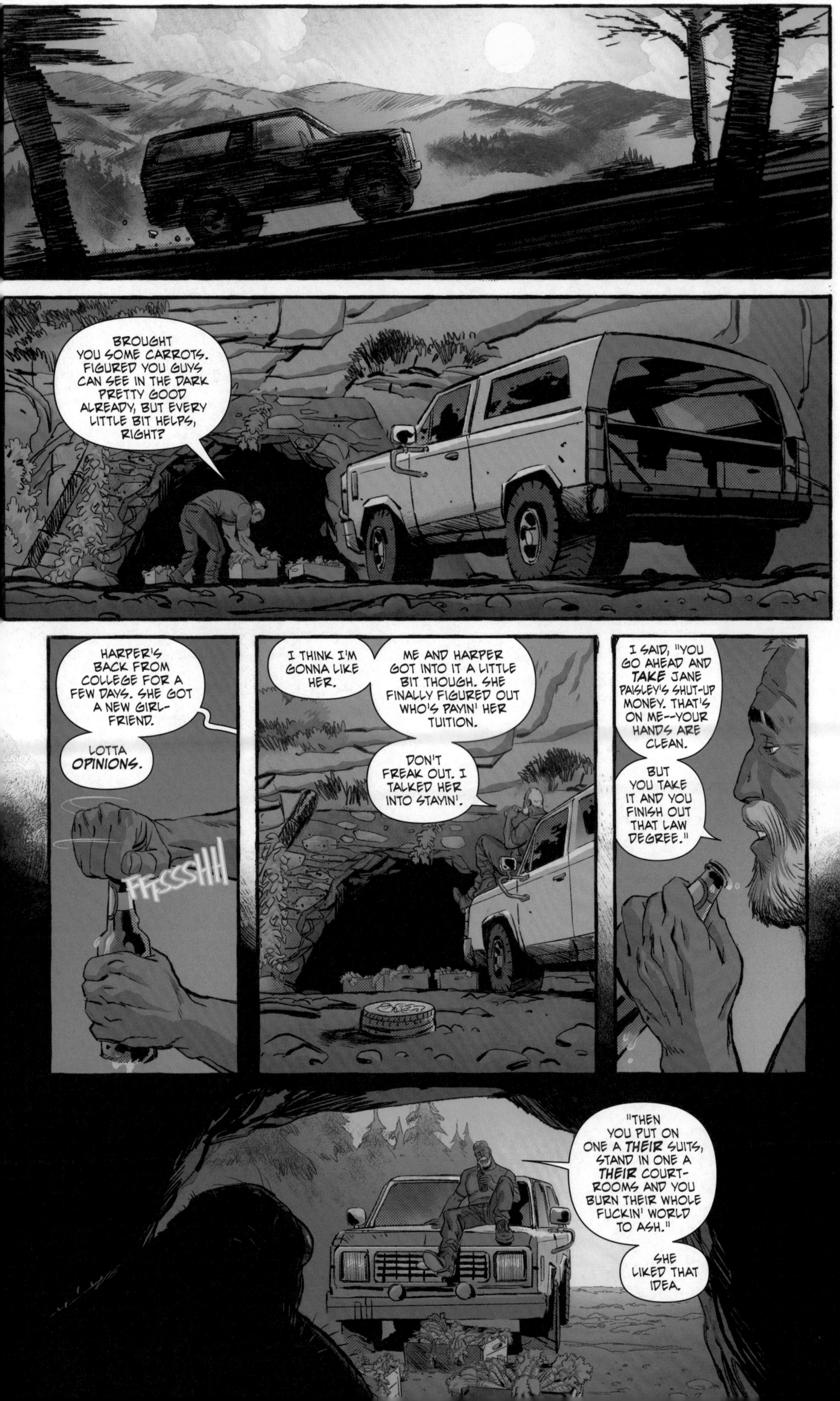
BROUGHT YOU SOME CARROTS. FIGURED YOU GUYS CAN SEE IN THE DARK PRETTY GOOD ALREADY, BUT EVERY LITTLE BIT HELPS, RIGHT?
HARPER'S BACK FROM COLLEGE FOR A FEW DAYS. SHE GOT A NEW GIRL-FRIEND.
LOTTA OPINIONS.
FFFSSSHH
I THINK I'M GONNA LIKE HER.
ME AND HARPER GOT INTO IT A LITTLE BIT THOUGH. SHE FINALLY FIGURED OUT WHO'S PAYIN' HER TUITION.
DON'T FREAK OUT. I TALKED HER INTO STAYIN'.
I SAID, "YOU GO AHEAD AND TAKE JANE PAISLEY'S SHUT-UP MONEY. THAT'S ON ME--YOUR HANDS ARE CLEAN.
BUT YOU TAKE IT AND YOU FINISH OUT THAT LAW DEGREE."
"THEN YOU PUT ON ONE A THEIR SUITS, STAND IN ONE A THEIR COURT-ROOMS AND YOU BURN THEIR WHOLE FUCKIN' WORLD TO ASH."
SHE LIKED THAT IDEA.

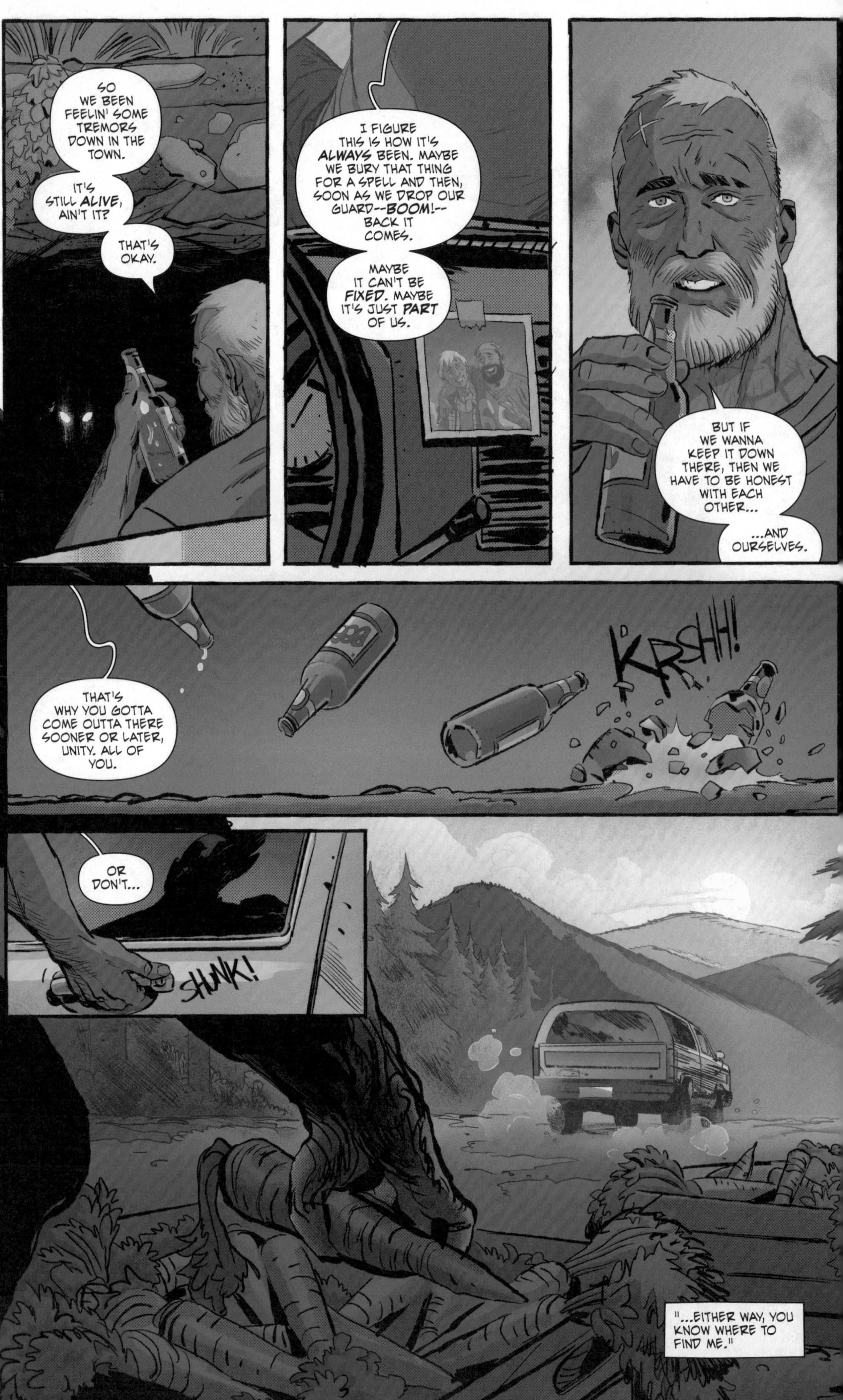
SO WE BEEN FEELIN' SOME TREMORS DOWN IN THE TOWN.
IT'S STILL ALIVE, AIN'T IT?
THAT'S OKAY.
I FIGURE THIS IS HOW IT'S ALWAYS BEEN. MAYBE WE BURY THAT THING FOR A SPELL AND THEN, SOON AS WE DROP OUR GUARD--BOOM!--BACK IT COMES.
MAYBE IT CAN'T BE FIXED. MAYBE IT'S JUST PART OF US.
BUT IF WE WANNA KEEP IT DOWN THERE, THEN WE HAVE TO BE HONEST WITH EACH OTHER...
...AND OURSELVES.
THAT'S WHY YOU GOTTA COME OUTTA THERE SOONER OR LATER, UNITY. ALL OF YOU.
KRSHH!
OR DON'T...
SHUNK!
"...EITHER WAY, YOU KNOW WHERE TO FIND ME."

ORIGINAL COVER ART BY
NIL VENDRELL

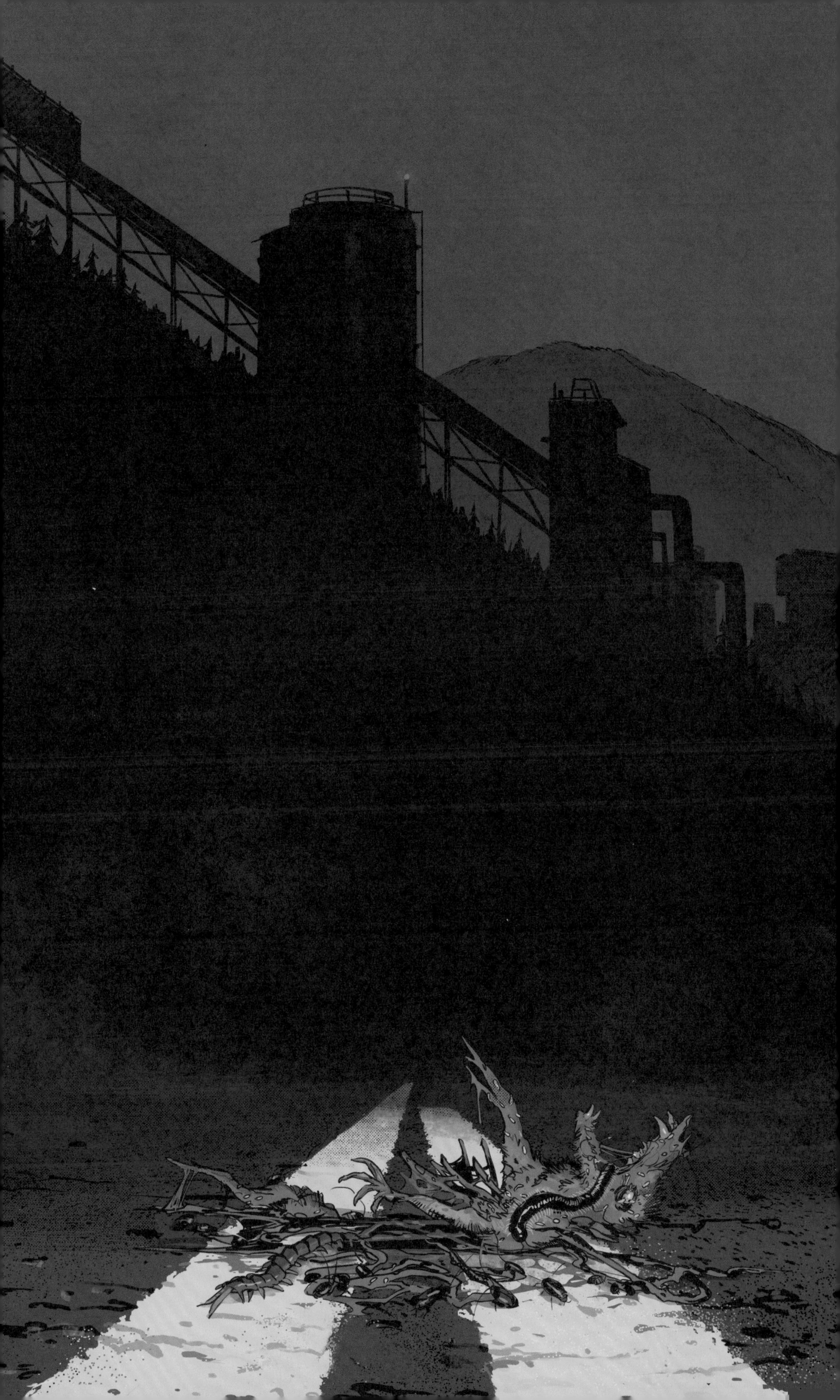

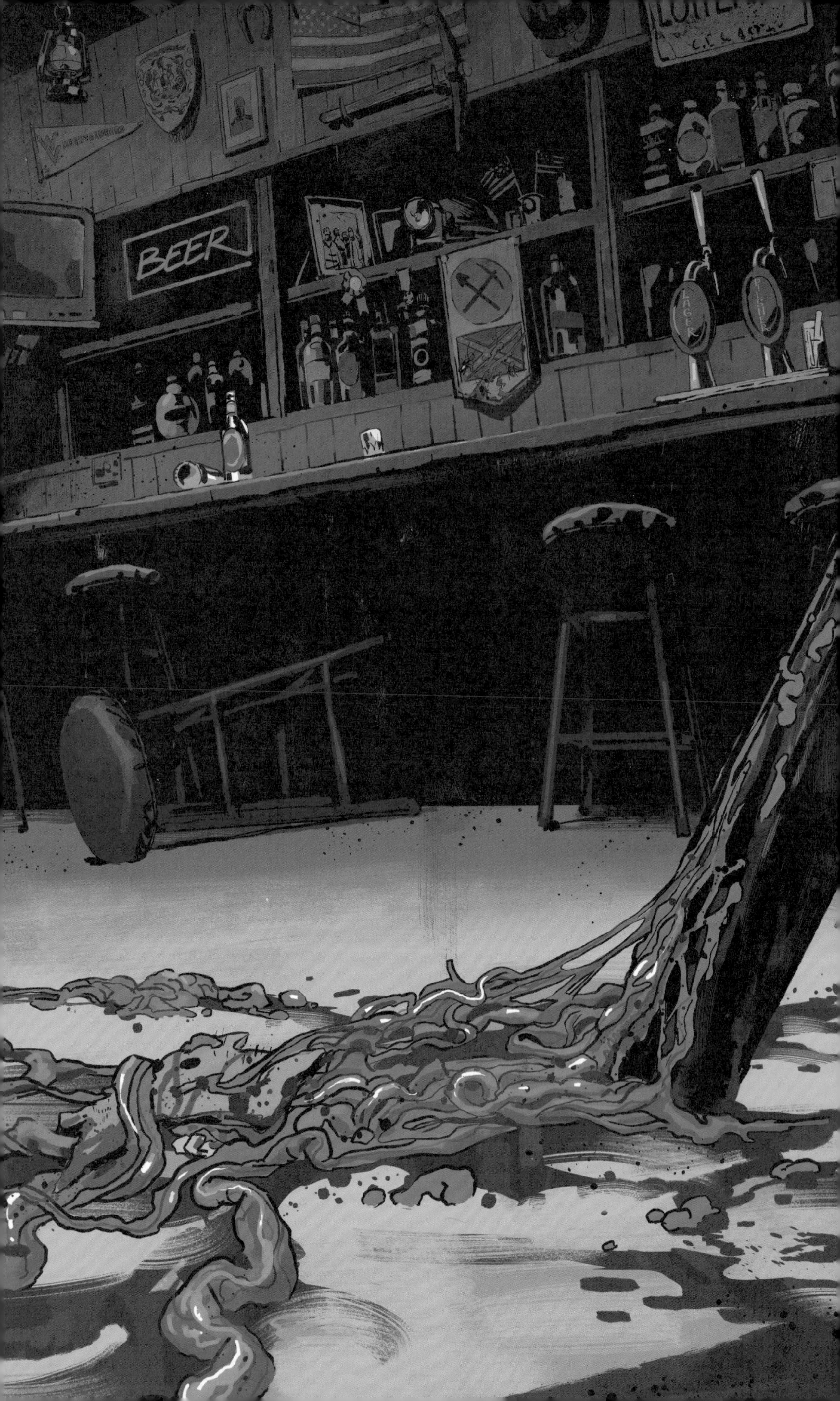
BEER
LAGER

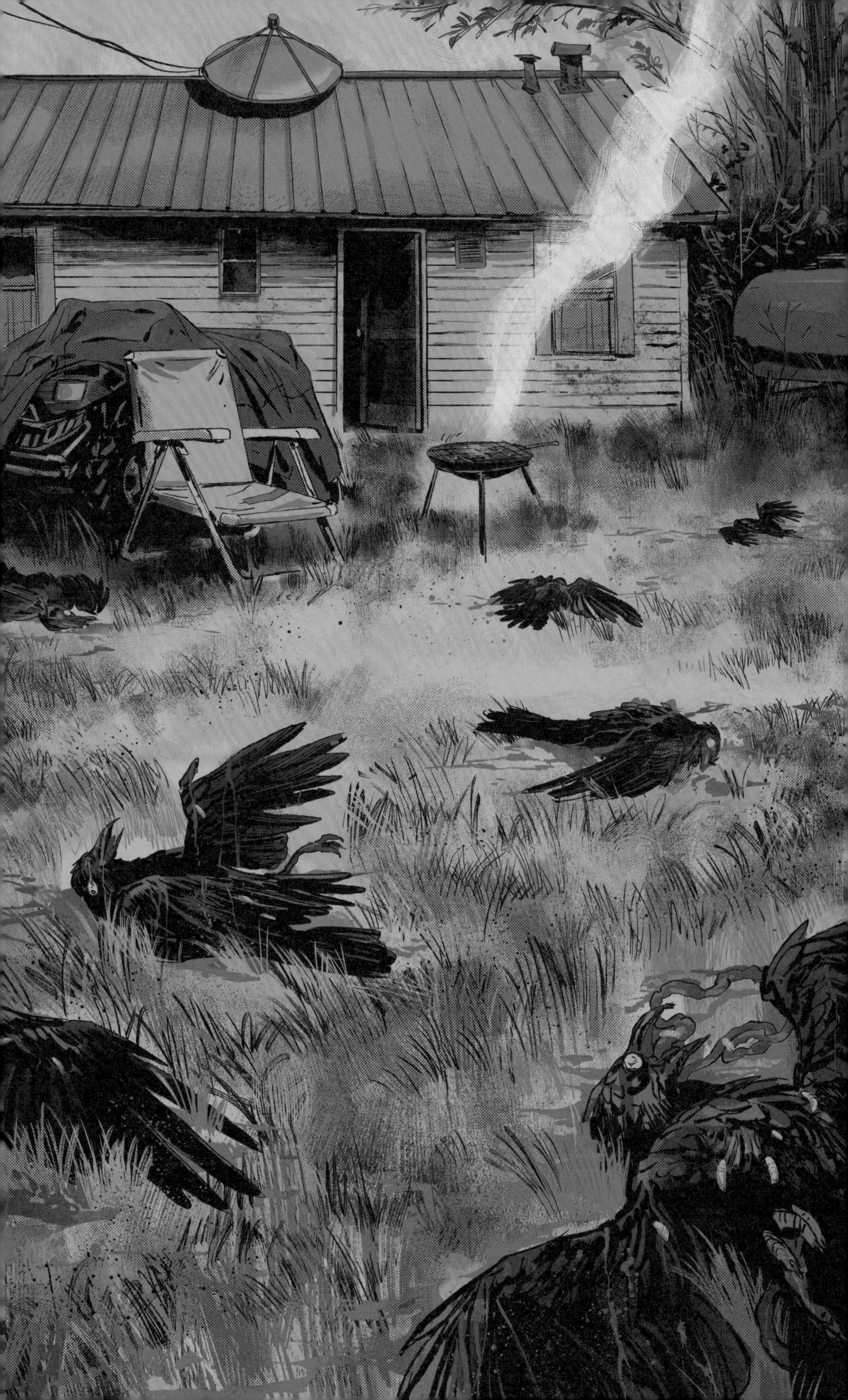

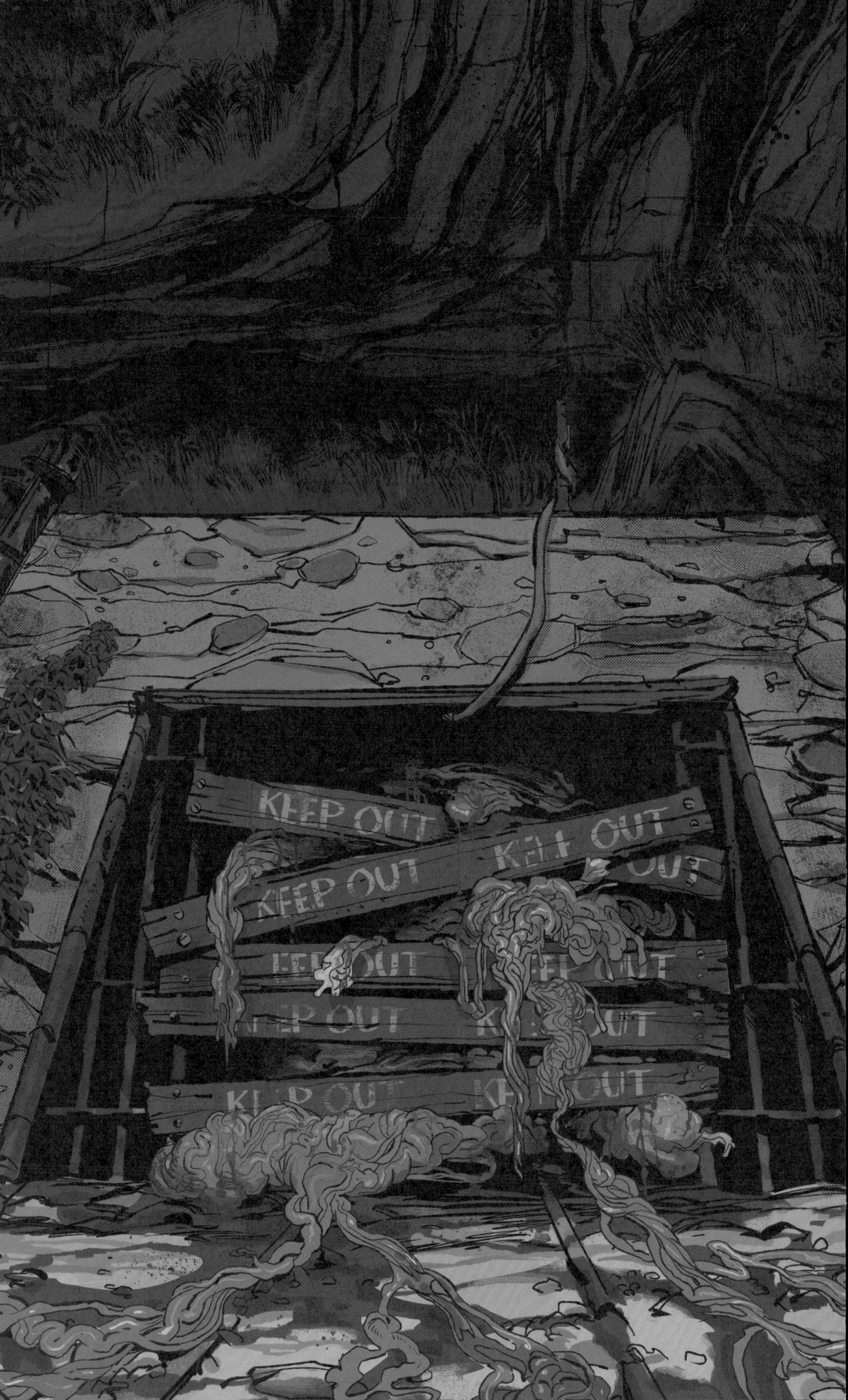
KEEP OUT
KEEP OUT

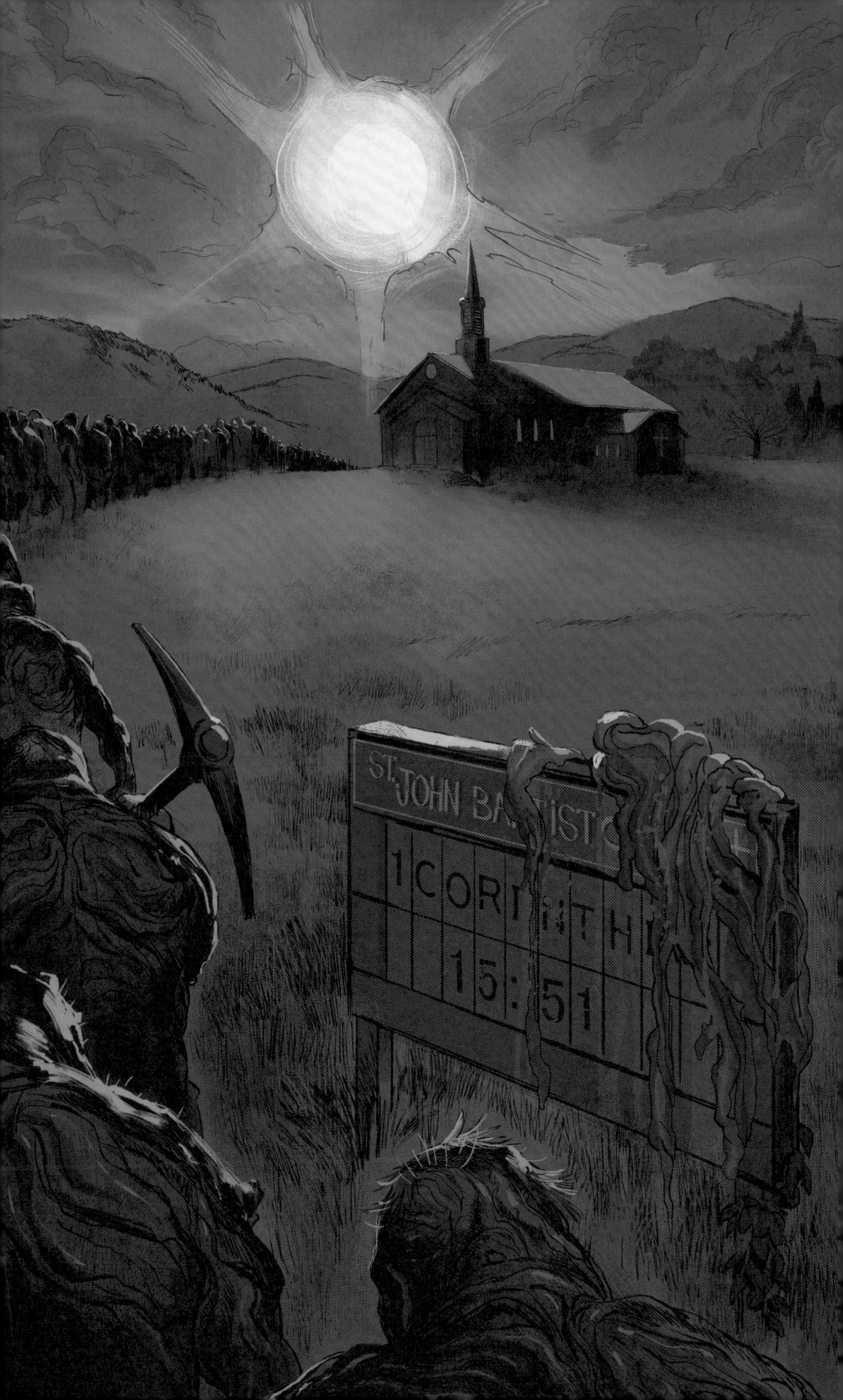
ST. JOHN
15 : 51

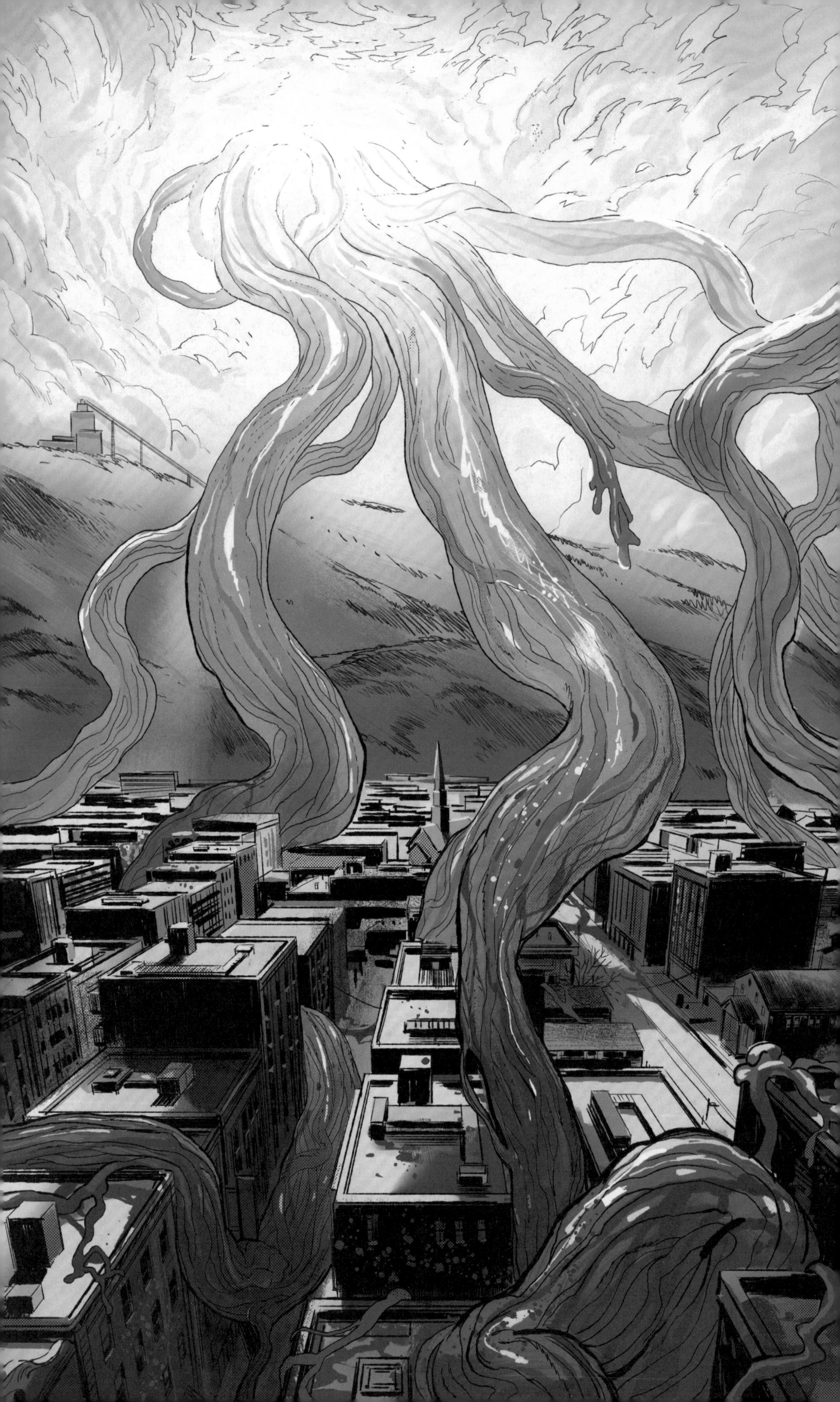

CREATORS

ALEX PAKNADEL | WRITER

Alex Paknadel is a writer and academic from London, England. His first comics work, the dark sci-fi thriller ARCADIA from Boom! Studios, met with critical acclaim and led to additional projects with a range of publishers including Marvel Entertainment, Vault Comics, Valiant Entertainment, Lion Forge, and Titan Comics. He is also a founding member of White Noise Studio alongside fellow writers Dan Watters, Ram V, and Ryan O'Sullivan.

NIL VENDRELL | ARTIST

Nil Vendrell's first foray into comics was as the artist and co-creator of SHIRTLESS BEAR-FIGHTER! His illustrations have also appeared in various webcomics and fanzines, as well as the anthology LAS VISIONES DEL FIN, published by Aleta Ediciones. He lives in Barcelona, Spain.

GIULIA BRUSCO | COLOR ART

Giulia Brusco is Italian and lives in London. She has colored comic books since 2000, working on titles such as SCALPED, DJANGO UNCHAINED, and THE GIRL WITH THE DRAGON TATTOO.

RYAN FERRIER | LETTERER

Ryan Ferrier is a Canadian comic book writer and letterer who has been published by every major North American comics company. He is known for his acclaimed original comics such as CRIMINY, KENNEL BLOCK BLUES, I CAN SELL YOU A BODY, DEATH ORB, and D4VE.

SEBASTIAN GIRNER | EDITOR

Sebastian Girner is a German-born, American-raised comic editor and writer. His editing includes such series as DEADLY CLASS, SOUTHERN BASTARDS and THE PUNISHER. He lives and works in Brooklyn with his wife.

THE CREATORS WOULD LIKE TO GIVE SPECIAL THANKS TO:

JAMES MADDOX, BERTA SASTRE, PHILLIP KENNEDY JOHNSON, RAM V, DAN WATTERS,
RYAN O'SULLIVAN, MALCOLM PAKNADEL, BARBARA NADEL, LIA KINANE, TARA FERGUSON,
JOHN HENDRICK, SENAN PAKNADEL, HOLLY AITCHISON, KEVIN KETNER, BRIAN LEVEL,
CHRIS SEBELA, ADAM P. KNAVE AND CHRISTIAN WARD

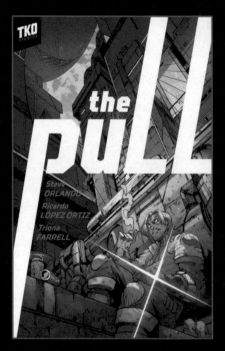
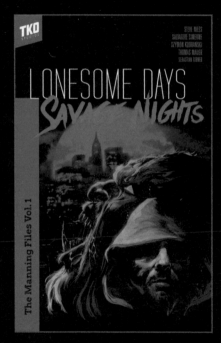
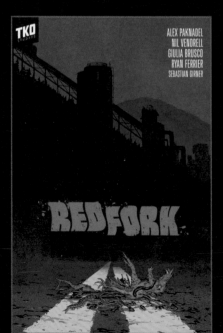